William Jones Miller

Celebration of the 200th Anniversary of the Settlement of the Town

of Bristol, Rhode Island

William Jones Miller

Celebration of the 200th Anniversary of the Settlement of the Town of Bristol, Rhode Island

ISBN/EAN: 9783744733342

Printed in Europe, USA, Canada, Australia, Japan

Cover: Foto ©ninafisch / pixelio.de

More available books at **www.hansebooks.com**

Class F 89

Book .B8 M6

CELEBRATION

OF THE

TWO-HUNDREDTH ANNIVERSARY

OF THE

SETTLEMENT OF THE TOWN OF BRISTOL,

RHODE ISLAND,

SEPTEMBER 24TH, A. D. 1880.

"A people which takes no pride in the noble achievements of remote ancestors, will never achieve anything worthy to be remembered with pride by remote descendants."—MACAULAY.

———◆———

COMPILED BY

WILLIAM J. MILLER.

PRINTED BY THE PROVIDENCE PRESS COMPANY,

PROVIDENCE, R. I.

PREFACE.

The compiler of this book was content to let it pass to the reader, without comment A preface was not contemplated. But as the last pages are passing through the press, suddenly, almost without warning, the hand of death has fallen upon Prof. J. LEWIS DIMAN. As to him—his acceptance of the post of "Historian of the Day," and his matchless address—so large a share of credit is due for the great success of our late Bi-Centennial celebration, the writer feels impelled to make note of the sad event. Few who saw and listened to Prof. Diman as he delivered the address on the 24th of September last, will forget that radiant face. His whole soul was engrossed in his theme and the occasion, and the writer knows that the day was to him a most enjoyable one.

It is hard to realize that he is dead—inexpressibly sad to think that his useful life, so full of promise for good to the world, has ended. His death will be felt as a personal bereavement by thousands not of his "kith and kin."

The following notice of his death—a portrayal of his pure life and transcendent merits—was published in the *Providence Journal* of Friday, February 4th.

BRISTOL, R. I., February 7th, 1881.

"PROF. J. LEWIS DIMAN.

"It is not often that such a thrill of surprise and sorrow is experienced in our community as was felt last evening, when the sad tidings passed from mouth to mouth that Prof. Diman was no longer numbered among the living. A few days ago, he walked amongst us, full of life and vigor, cheering us with his pleasant face, enlivening us with his genial talk, edifying us with his stores of rare and useful learning; and now, in the very bloom of life, when there seemed so much left for him to do,—which no one else amongst us could do so well as he,—the hand of death has suddenly sealed his lips.

"The shock of this bereavement has come upon us so unexpectedly, and with such overwhelming weight, as to entirely unfit us for doing anything like justice to his character. No man living in this city or State could be counted his superior. On great occasions, when we were called to revive the memories of the past, or to be informed in respect of current events, it was to Prof. Diman that we instinctively turned as the man best fitted for the work. Of late years, it has seemed as though no event in the records of Rhode Island could be duly commemorated unless he was willing to tell the story and 'adorn the tale.' He was distinguished abroad as well as at home, not only as a consummate master of history, but also as one of the profoundest philosophical thinkers of the day. His lectures in Boston and Baltimore attracted the attention and respect of the thoughtful and the learned of all classes, and brought honor not only to him, but to the State of which he was so distinguished an ornament. There was hardly any class of subjects which he was not competent to handle. He had read a great deal, and carefully digested all that he read. His resources were always at command; his thoughts never lacked utterance; his style was compact, clear as crystal, and adorned with chaste and apposite illustration. He used no superfluous words, and yet never failed to make himself intelligible, no matter how recondite the subject that he treated. The college students to whom he lectured, the private classes which he met from week to week, the smaller band of personal and intimate friends who crossed weapons with him in the social circle, will all remember his words and cherish his memory when the flowers of many a summer have bloomed and withered over his grave.

"His character was known and read of all men. He was transparent as the day, and no deceit or guile was found in him. He was *constitutionally* incapable of a mean or dishonorable or selfish act. He never appeared to be in the slightest degree conscious of his own mental greatness, and never showed the faintest indication of personal vanity—not even by self-depreciation. He could not help knowing of what he was capable, but he did not look down upon others because they were his inferiors. He was willing to learn anything which the humblest man was competent to teach him.

"Holding, as he did, very positive opinions of his own, and always ready to give his reasons for the belief that he had adopted, he was singularly tolerant of those who differed from him. He had a very broad as well as a very accurate mental vision; and if he ever seemed to be inconsistent in his views, it was because he took in a larger sweep of the horizon than most men. He was a very generous-minded as well as generous-hearted man, and looked under the surface, to find the grains of truth that might lie concealed beneath forms and formulas which he rejected. Honest error he could abide, while he despised mere sham and pretense. His sunny face was an index of the bright and genial soul that he carried in his bosom. He was, in the best sense of the words, *good company*. It was a pleasant thing to meet him on the sidewalk, as we did only the other day, and have him propose a long stroll, which, under the spell of his presence, was sure to seem very short. He was a sympathetic companion, and entered heartily into the views and experiences of those with whom he mingled.

"There were few important stations in society which he could have failed to occupy with honor. If he had given himself to statesmanship, his power would have been felt throughout the land. If he had confined himself entirely to what is called polite literature, what he wrote, 'the world would not willingly have let die.' If he had adhered exclusively to the profession for which he was bred, he would have taken rank with our most accomplished and influential preachers. 'Whatever he touched, he adorned,' and he laid his hand upon a great many rich and rare departments of knowledge.

"Prof. Diman was a true and sincere follower of his Master, Christ, not a very rigid dogmatist, not a hide-bound ecclesiastic, not a man to hurl anathemas at the heads of those who did not in all points think as he did, but he had the loving, gentle, kind and charitable spirit of Him whom he served from his early youth, and in whose arms we believe he now rests in peace. How we shall all miss him! He leaves a void that will not soon be filled. It is hard to conceive that one, in whom there was so much of life, has now so suddenly ceased to live. 'We cannot make him dead.' And he is not dead. He has only left the earthly tabernacle, in which he dwelt, and passed on to a higher and grander existence. Such men cannot die. He lives *here on earth* in the work that he has done, and in the noble impressions he has made upon the lives of those who were brought within his influence. But it is very sad to think that we shall see him no more in our daily rounds and hear his words no longer. We feel that not only has a great man fallen in Israel, but that we have lost a friend and a brother. In many a household tears are shed to-day as the tidings come to them that he has passed away. A dark shadow lies across the threshold of the dwelling, which, for many years, was made so bright and cheery by his presence, and the widow and the orphan mourn 'with a grief too deep for tears.'"

BIOGRAPHICAL SKETCH OF PROF. DIMAN.

[The following sketch, which we believe had received the approval of our lamented friend, we are permitted to use, through the courtesy of the representatives of the National Biographical Publishing Company, at whose instance it was prepared.]

PREFACE.

PROF. J. LEWIS DIMAN, D. D., second son of Byron and Abby Alden (Wight) Diman, was born in Bristol, May 1, 1831. In his early youth he enjoyed superior advantages for mental culture and discipline, which he diligently improved. He was prepared for college by the Rev. James N. Sykes, a Baptist clergyman settled in the place, and at the age of sixteen he entered Brown University. From this institution of learning he was graduated with honor in 1851, having assigned to him for Commencement the "Classical Oration." Soon afterwards he went abroad, travelling extensively on the continent, and spending several years at the universities of Halle, Heidelberg and Berlin. Returning he entered the Theological Seminary at Andover, Massachusetts, where he was graduated in 1856. In the fall of this year he was settled as pastor of the First Congregational Church in Fall River, and again in 1860, as pastor of the Harvard Church in Brookline Mass. In 1864 he was appointed Professor of History and Political Economy in Brown University, filling a vacancy occasioned by the resignation of Prof William Gammell, LL. D. Here he has distinguished himself by his devotion to his work and by his rare scholarship and attainments. In 1870 he was honored with the degree of Doctor of Divinity conferred upon him by the Board of Fellows of the University. In 1873 he was elected a corresponding member of the Massachusetts Historical Society. Mr. Diman has often been called upon to deliver sermons, addresses and lectures on important occasions, many of which have been published. Among these may be mentioned a sermon, delivered October 16, 1867, in the Chapel of Brown University, at the request of the Faculty, in commemoration of Rev. Robinson Potter Dunn, D. D., for many years Professor of Rhetoric in the University; "Historical Basis of Belief," one of the Boston Lectures, delivered in 1870; "The Alienation of the Educated Class from Politics," an oration before the Phi Beta Kappa Society, at Cambridge, Mass., delivered June 29, 1876; An Address delivered at Portsmouth, R. I , July 10, 1877, at the Centennial Celebration of the Capture of Gen. Prescott by Lieut. Col. Barton. This was afterwards published with notes, forming No 1 of Rider's Rhode Island Historical Tracts. An address delivered October 16, 1877, upon the occasion of the dedication of the monument in commemoration of the life and services of the venerated founder of the State, in Roger Williams Park. An address at the dedication of the Rogers Free Library, at Bristol, delivered January 12, 1878. Twenty lectures on the Thirty Years War, delivered in 1879, before the professors and students of Johns Hopkins University, Baltimore, Md. Twelve lectures before the Lowell Institute, Boston, delivered in the spring of 1880. He delivered the address at the two hundredth anniversary of his native town in the fall of 1880, which address has since been published with the proceedings. Mr. Diman has also furnished leading articles for the *Providence Journal, North American Review,* and other papers and periodicals. His article entitled, "Religion in America, 1776-1876," published in the January number of the *North American Review,* attracted universal attention. He edited "John Cotton's Answer to Roger Williams," in Vol. 2 of "Publications of the Narragansett Club," and also "George Fox Digg'd out of his Burrowes," constituting Vol. 5 of the same "Publications." He also furnished one of the sketches in the memorial volume entitled "Brown University in the Civil War."

Mr. Diman married May 15, 1861, Emily G. Stimson, of Providence, only surviving daughter of John J. and Abby M. (Clarke) Stimson. Four children are the fruits of this union.

BI-CENTENNIAL OF BRISTOL.

THE DATE SELECTED.

The Mount Hope lands, so called, which were incorporated into the township of Bristol, covered the southern portion of Mount Hope Neck and the peninsular of Poppasquash, and were first known to the English settlers of New England by the beautiful Indian name of Pokanoket.

The "Great Deed" of conveyance from Plymouth Colony to the four original proprietors, was made on the fourteenth day of September, 1680, "and in the thirty-second year of the Reigne of our Soveraigne Lord King Charles the Second, over England," etc.

The contracting parties were, "Josiah Winslow, Esq., Governor of his majesty's Collony of New Plymouth, in New England; Thomas Hinckley, Esq., Deputy Governor, William Bradford, Esq., Treasurer, all of the aforesaid Collony, on the one part; and John Walley, Nathaniel Oliver, Nathaniel Byfield, and Stephen Burton, all of Boston, in the Collony of the Massachusets in New England aforesaid, Merchants, on the other part." The consideration was "Eleven hundred pounds of currant money of New England." And for this sum the parties of the first part " by these presents doe fully, freely, clearly, and absolutely give, grant, bargaine, sell, aliene, enfeoffe and confirm unto the said John Walley, Nathaniel Oliver, Nathaniel Byfield and Stephen Burton, and to their heyres & assignes forever, all that tract or parcell of

Land, situate, lying and being within the aforesaid Collony of New Plymouth, commonly called and known by the name of Mount Hope Neck & Poppasquash Neck, with all the Islands lying neare or about the said Neckes, not exceeding five acres, and not already legally disposed of."

The date of the "Great Deed" (September 14, 1680,) was accepted as the beginning of the settlement of the town, and its two hundredth anniversary, September 24, 1880, (changed from the old to the new style of reckoning time), was designated as "the day we celebrate."

In the Town Clerk's office, in Bristol, is an old folio book, bound in leather, and showing marks of age, wherein is recorded a copy of the "Great Deed," from which the foregoing extracts are taken. The book also contains other deeds and conveyances, covering common, ministerial, and school lands, and the streets of the town, together with articles of agreement, and contracts between the first settlers, which are of deep interest. In it also may be found a record of the proceedings in town meeting from the first settlement to the close of the year 1718. At the end of the proceedings of the last recorded town meeting, is the following:

"Thus endeth the First Book of Records,* of the town of Bristol; Faithfully transcribed by Richard Smith, who was chosen and duly authorized for that purpose by the Freeman of said Town.

"Bristol, April 27th, A. D. 1826."

Mr. Smith adds this on the following page of the Book:—

"MEMORANDUM.

"Richard Smith, the First Recording Town Clerk for the Town of Bristol, was born in the city of London, in the year 1643. In the year 1673, came over to New England with his

---

* These Records were copied from a small book that is still in existence in the Town Clerk's office, and is doubtless the first record book of the town. It is very much worn, and fragments are missing from many pages.

little Family, and settled in Boston, and from thence with his Family to Bristol, Nov. 9th, 1680, where he erected a dwelling House at the South West corner of the eight acre square bounding West on Hope street, and South on Constitution street, in which he resided until his Death, which was in the year 1696.

"Samuel, Son of Richard, was Born June 24th, 1683. Died November 18th, 1766.

"Richard, Son of Samuel, was Born May 25th, 1720. Died February 6th, 1813.

"Richard, Son of Richard, 2d, was Born April 16th, 1753. ———.

"Samuel, Son of Richard, 3d, was Born Oct. 8th, 1787. Died June 23d, 1801.

"All the above named, excepting the ancestor (Richard Smith), was born in Bristol, within the space of five Rods square, and all of them died in the same space, excepting Richard the 3d (the transcriber of this Record Book), who is still living, this 16th Day of April, 1827, and has left a blank, to be hereafter filled up by some Friend."

Then follows this:

"Richard Smith the 3d, the transcriber of this Book, died October 17th, A. D. 1832, in the 80th year of his age. And the 'Friend' who has filled up this 'Blank' is William Throop, who, perhaps, will never perform a similar office for a more worthy Citizen.

"October 17, 1832."

Col. William Throop was appointed Town Clerk in 1832, and gave many years of faithful service in that office. In 1847 the present careful and efficient Town Clerk, Peter Gladding, Esq., succeeded him, and has served continuously in that capacity to the present time. Mr. Gladding could very appropriately add a similar endorsement to the worth of his immediate predecessor, the late William Throop.

INITIAL MOVEMENT FOR A CELEBRATION.

The first movement for a due observance of the two hundredth anniversary of the settlement of the Town, was a preliminary meeting held at the office of S. P. Colt, Esq., on the evening of March 15th, 1879.

Quite a number of citizens were present, and after organizing and exchanging views on the subject, a committee was appointed to confer with the Town Council, at their meeting on Monday, March 17th, and request them to call a meeting to consider the subject of a celebration of the day.

William J. Miller, Samuel P. Colt, Chas. A. Greene, Isaac F. Williams, Bennett J. Munro and Le Baron B. Colt, constituted the committee.

The action of the Council, as appears of record, was as follows:

"TOWN COUNCIL, Monday, March 17th, A. D. 1879.

"Upon the representation of William J. Miller, and others, asking that the Council call a meeting of citizens, to take steps to lay before the town a method of celebrating the two hundredth anniversary of the settlement of the town:— The Council voted to call such a meeting at the Town Hall, on Tuesday, March 25th, at 8 o'clock in the evening, and that said meeting be advertised in the *Bristol Phenix*.

"A report of the meeting in Town Hall is copied from the *Bristol Phenix* of March 29th, as follows:

"Last Tuesday evening a 'Citizens' Meeting' was held in Town Hall, in pursuance of a notice given by the Town Council, in the *Phenix* of last Saturday, 'for the purpose of taking into consideration the appropriate celebration of the coming 200th anniversary of the settlement of the town.' The meeting was called to order by Wm. H. Spooner, Esq., President of the Town Council, at 8 o'clock. Le Baron B. Colt, Esq., was elected Chairman, and Wm. T. C. Wardwell, Esq., Secretary.

"William J. Miller, Esq., after explaining the object of the meeting, and expressing himself as being very much interested in the matter, suggested that a committee be appointed to draft resolutions to be presented to the citizens at their next annual town meeting, held for choice of town officers and other business of the town.

"On motion of Mr. Edward S. Babbitt, it was unanimously voted as the sense of the meeting, that the 200th anniversary of the settlement of the town, which will occur in the autumn of next year (1880), be celebrated in an appropriate manner.

"It was also voted that a committee of seven be appointed to draw up a series of resolutions relative to the proposed celebration, and lay the whole matter before the town meeting, which will be held on Saturday, April 12th, requesting the town, in its corporate capacity, to take action thereon. The committee chosen consisted of Messrs. W. T. C. Wardwell, Le Baron B. Colt, Wm. J. Miller, Edward W. Brunsen, James M. Gifford, J. Russell Bullock, and Augustus O. Bourn.

"Brief and appropriate remarks were made by Messrs. Wm. J. Miller, Charles H. Spooner, Le Baron B. Colt, Edward S. Babbitt, Isaac F. Williams, W. T. C. Wardwell, Samuel P. Colt, Wm. H. Spooner, John H. D'Wolf, Augustus O. Bourn, and Rev. James P. Lane.

"There was a large attendance at the meeting, a considerable interest manifested in the proposed celebration, and the proceedings throughout were quite spirited and very harmonious."

"IN TOWN MEETING, April 12th, 1879.

"The following resolutions on the celebration of the two hundredth anniversary of the settlement of the town of Bristol, were presented by Le Baron B. Colt, Esq., which, after some pertinent remarks by him, were unanimously adopted : —

"WHEREAS, the year 1880 will mark the two hundredth anniversary of the settlement of the town, and,

"WHEREAS, the great deed of sale of the tract of land then commonly called and known by the name of Mount Hope Neck and Poppasquash Neck, from Plymouth Colony to John Walley, Nathaniel Oliver, Nathaniel Byfield and Stephen Burton, the four original proprietors of the town of Bristol, bears date September 14, 1680, O. S., corresponding to September 25, N. S., and

"WHEREAS, at a public meeting called by the Town Council, of the citizens of Bristol, in the Town Hall, on the 25th day of March last, it was unanimously resolved, that the town should celebrate, in an appropriate way, the approaching two hundredth anniversary of its foundation, and in furtherance of this object, the said meeting appointed a committee of seven, to draft resolutions and present the subject to the next annual town meeting for such action as it might deem proper to take, now, therefore,

"*Resolved*, That we, the citizens of Bristol, in Town Meeting assembled, mindful of the goodly heritage received from the fathers, and desirous of keeping in grateful remembrance the wise forecast and sterling qualities of the men who founded here a town, and laid it out in all its fair proportions, do hereby set apart the 25th day of September, A. D. 1880, to celebrate the bi-centennial of its settlement, and do hereby constitute and appoint an executive committee of forty-five, to take the whole matter into consideration; the committee to have full power to take such preliminary steps as may be found necessary and expedient, and to report such action as they have taken and such plans as they have agreed upon to the next annual Town Meeting.

"*Resolved*, That we cordially invite the co-operation of all the citizens of the town in this undertaking, that we may have a celebration worthy of the descendants of the men who founded it, and of its whole past history."

The committee of forty-five was duly elected as follows:

William H. Spooner,
William T. C. Wardwell,
Henry Goff,
Isaac F. Williams,
Charles A. Greene.
John B. Pearce,
Edward W. Brunsen,
Le Baron B. Colt,
Messadore T. Bennett,
Benjamin L. West,
Josephus Gooding,
Nehemiah Cole,
Otis Munro,
Jonathan D. Waldron,
Samuel W. Church,
Solon H. Smith,
J. Howard Manchester,
A. Sidney D'Wolf,
Charles D'W. Brownell,
James M. Gifford,
Seth Paull,
Charles H. R. Doringh,
Robert S. Andrews,
Lemuel A. Bishop,
Samuel M. Lindsey,
Lemuel W. Briggs,
Samuel S. Drury,
Benjamin R. Wilson,
Ambrose E. Burnside,
J. Russell Bullock,
Thomas F. Usher,
John Collins,
Charles F. Herreshoff,
Bennett J. Munro,
Joseph B. Burgess,
Augustus O. Bourn,
Horace M. Barns,
William Bradford,
Herbert M. Howe,
Samuel Norris,
Samuel P. Colt,
William J. Miller,
Edward S. Babbitt,
James Lawless,
William R. Taylor.

The first meeting of the "Bi-Centennial Committee of forty-five," was held at Town Hall, on Saturday evening, June 28th, 1879, and steps were taken for a permanent organization. Frequent meetings were held during the year, and several entertainments were given in Town Hall in aid of the bi-centennial fund.

At the annual town meeting held April 10th, A. D. 1880, the report of the committee upon the bi-centennial celebration was presented, read, and ordered to be recorded, as follows:

"The committee upon the bi-centennial celebration, appointed at the last annual town meeting, in compliance with the resolution empowering them to take such preliminary steps as may be found necessary and expedient, and to report such action as they may have taken, and such plans as they may have agreed upon, to the next annual town meeting, beg leave to report:

"That soon after their appointment the committee met and organized by the selection of the following officers and sub-committees:

"President—Le Baron B. Colt.

"Vice Presidents—Samuel W. Church, Jonathan D. Waldron, William R. Taylor, James Lawless, James M. Gifford.

"Treasurer—Henry Goff.

"Secretary—William H. Spooner.

"Executive Committee—Chairman, William J. Miller; Secretary, Edward S. Babbitt; members, Messadore T. Bennett, Edward W. Brunsen, Samuel P. Colt, John Collins, Charles A. Greene, Wm. H. Spooner, Solon H. Smith, William T. C. Wardwell, Isaac F. Williams.

"Committee on Correspondence—Chairman, Bennett J. Munro; members, Charles D'W. Brownell, J. Russell Bullock, Edward W. Brunsen, Edward S. Babbitt.

"The committee took early action upon the subject of an historical address and poem for the occasion, and they have invited Prof. J. Lewis Diman, of Providence, to deliver the address, and the Rt. Rev. M. A. D'W. Howe, Bishop of Central Pennsylvania, to deliver the poem. Both gentlemen have responded favorably to the invitation.

"The committee also took early action in regard to raising funds, and they have succeeded in accumulating a fund of about $270, the same being the proceeds of the various entertainments kindly volunteered for this object.

"The committee after carefully considering the subject of the due observance of the day, at the various meetings held during the year, agreed upon and recommend a celebration which shall embody substantially and in brief an historical address, an historical poem, tents upon the common, in which appropriate exercises are to be held, and dinner served to invited guests, the ringing of bells, national salutes, music, a procession, decoration and illumination of the town, and an exhibition of ancient portraits and relics connected with the history of the town.

"In order to carry out the above plans, your committee, after carefully considering the probable expense of the same, estimate that they will require from the town an appropriation of $1,500, and recommend that the same be made; and to this end the delegation in the General Assembly from the town have had an enabling act passed covering the said amount.

"Your committee take pleasure in acknowledging the interest manifested generally by the citizens of the town and State in the proposed celebration, and especially the expression of hearty good will and pledge of active co-operation on the part of the Rhode Island Historical Society.

Respectfully submitted,

LE BARON B. COLT,
For the Committee."

The following resolution was presented by Charles F. Herreshoff, Esq., and adopted:

"*Resolved,* That the sum of $1,500 be, and the same is hereby appropriated, for a due observance of the two hundredth anniversary of the settlement of this town; and that Friday, the 24th day of September next, be, and the same is, hereby designated as the day for such celebration."

After the action of the citizens in town meeting, making the liberal appropriation asked for, the committee moved forward with confidence. Sub-committees for the various objects in view were appointed, and an increased interest in the proposed celebration was manifested on the part of the citizens generally.

At a meeting of the committee on the 5th of May, vacancies caused by the death of Dr. S. S. Drury and A. Sidney D'Wolf, and the resignation and removal from town of Lemuel A. Bishop, were filled by the appointment of Peter Gladding, John Howland Pitman, and Charles H. Spooner.

It was voted that the planting of four trees upon the Common, in memory of the first four proprietors, be referred to Edward S. Babbitt, Josephus Gooding, Henry Goff, C. H. R. Doringh and S. P. Colt, with full power to carry out the same.

Sub-committees were appointed as follows:

On Instrumental Music—C. A. Greene, T. F. Usher, J. B. Burgess.

On Tents and Dinner—C. F. Herreshoff, J. M. Gifford, Henry Goff, H. M. Howe.

On Procession—I. F. Williams, W. T. C. Wardwell, Wm. H. Spooner, N. G. Herreshoff, J. B. Burgess, G. O. Eddy, C. A. Waldron.

On Vocal Music—W. T. C. Wardwell.

On Odes—Wm. J. Miller.

On Decorations—C. A. Greene, T. F. Usher, J. B. Burgess.

On Transportation—J. B. Burgess, T. F. Usher, C. H. Spooner.

On Police—E. S. Babbitt, W. H. Spooner.

On Platform and Seats in Tent—John Collins, E. S. Babbitt, W. T. C. Wardwell.

On Carriages and Reception of Invited Guests—R. S. Andrews, H. M. Howe, H. M. Barns, J. Lawless, W. J. Miller, E. W. Brunsen, W. T. C. Wardwell, J. B. Burgess, E. S. Babbitt, C. D'W. Brownell, T. F. Usher.

On Loan Exhibition—Wm. J. Miller, John Collins, C. F. Herreshoff, E. S. Babbitt, John H. D'Wolf, John H. Pitman.

Col. C. A. Greene, of the *Phenix*, was appointed a committee to provide suitable facilities for the members of the press, and to see that they were properly entertained, but being confined to his house by severe illness, Col. J. B. Burgess was designated for the purpose, and discharged his duties in the most satisfactory manner.

Charles H. Spooner was appointed a committee to ask of the trustees of the several churches in town, that they be open for the inspection of the public on the day of the celebration.

Messrs. S. H. Smith and E. S. Babbitt were appointed a committee to arrange for the proper seating of the audience in the main tent.

E. W. Brunsen was appointed to distribute badges and dinner tickets to visiting Sons and Daughters, and to arrange for sale of same, with power to appoint assistants.

E. S. Babbitt was appointed a committee for floral decorations on dining tables.

By request of the general committee, the school committee ordered the public schools closed on Thursday and Friday, the 23d and 24th, and arranged for the Byfield school building to be open to visitors on Friday and Saturday, 24th and 25th of September.

Thursday, the 23d of September, was appointed for the illumination of the town, and the citizens generally were invited to illuminate their residences on that evening.

Arrangements were made for lighting the main tent by electric lights, and for a promenade concert by the bands, as the closing exercises of the day.

Early in July a communication was received tendering the room of the B. Y. M. Christian Association in Rogers Free Library building, for the use of the general and executive committee, which was accepted with thanks, and thereafter used and made general headquarters. Before that time the committee had used the Town Hall and Council Chamber for their meetings, through the courtesy of the Town Council. The Town Council also kindly placed the Town Hall in possession of the Loan Exhibition Committee from Monday, September 20th, to Tuesday, 28th, inclusive.

It coming to the knowledge of the committee that the Providence Light Infantry Veteran Association contemplated visiting Bristol on September 24th, it was voted that the chairman of the committee be requested to communicate to said Association that the committee would be much pleased to have them join in the procession on that day, and to accept such courtesies upon the occasion as might be in the power of the committee to extend to them.

The mansion house of Mrs. Julia S. Perry, at Silver Creek, was the first, or one of the first, houses built in the town, and in the southwest parlor the first religious meeting was held. A note from Mrs. Perry was received by the committee, kindly offering to open her house for the reception of such visitors as might desire to call on the day of the celebration. Notice of this invitation was given in the *Bristol Phenix*.

The following circular was prepared and sent to every absent Son and Daughter whose name and address could be ascertained by the committee on correspondence:

BI-CENTENNIAL OF THE TOWN OF BRISTOL.

The Town of Bristol, having determined to celebrate her Two Hundredth Anniversary, has set apart Friday, the 24th day of September, 1880, for such commemoration.

One pleasant and highly interesting feature of the day will be the Reunion of the Sons and Daughters of Bristol. As one of them, you are cordially invited to be present, and unite with us in making the occasion worthy of the Town and of its history. A warm and hearty welcome will greet you.

In behalf of the Bi-Centennial Committee.

LE BARON B. COLT,
President.

Many matters of detail were referred to the Executive Committee, such as the order of exercises in the main tent, and at the dinner table, the audit of bills, all printing, the preparation of suitable badges, the selection of invited guests, etc. They were also requested to obtain the names of visiting Sons and Daughters.

A list of about one hundred names of invited guests was prepared and accepted, and a copy of the following circular sent to each:

1680   1880

BI-CENTENNIAL OF THE TOWN OF BRISTOL.

BRISTOL, R. I., September 1st, 1880.

The Town of Bristol having set apart Friday, the 24th day of September, 1880, to celebrate the Two Hundredth Anniversary of its settlement, the Committee appointed for the purpose, have the honor to invite you to be present on that day as the guest of the Town.

A favorable and early reply will oblige,

Very Respectfully Yours,

LE BARON B. COLT,
WM. J. MILLER,
EDWARD S. BABBITT,
Committee.

The Committee on Instrumental Music, early reported that they had engaged the services of the Bristol Cornet Band, and the Boston Brigade Band. The same committee also arranged for the salutes and ringing of bells.

The Committee on Vocal Music reported that through the courtesy and hearty co-operation of the School Committee, about three hundred pupils of the public schools were, under the supervision of Mrs. S. B. Spinning, practising several original odes to be sung on the day of the celebration.

Mr. Babbitt, from the Committee on Badges, reported with samples, which were adopted, and the Committee was instructed to procure the number required.

The Committee on Tents and Dinner reported that they had contracted for two tents, to be set up on the Common, near the line of State street. The main tent for the literary exercises to be 80 by 200 feet, with seats for 5,000 persons, and a platform for the seating of the committee and invited guests. The dinner tent to be 50 by 300 feet. They further reported that they had contracted with L. A. Tillinghast, the well known caterer of Providence, to furnish dinner for one thousand persons.

The Committee on Decorations reported, that they had contracted with the veteran decorator, Col. William Beals, of Boston, to decorate the public buildings of the town.

Arrangements were made with the Chief Engineer of the Fire Department, to have the several Fire Engine Houses and Pumping Station open to visitors.

All these reports were accepted and approved by the Executive and General Committees, and as the day approached, all matters were in a forward state of preparation.

The large number of strange faces to be seen on the streets of the town indicate how promptly and heartily absent sons and daughters have responded to the call to return to the old hearth stone. Hearty greetings are exchanged on every hand, and many incidents of early life and childhood sports are rehearsed. Oh! how the old days come back with all their precious memories. The intervening space of ten, twenty, thirty, forty, aye fifty years, seems but a dream now, and we are children again, and in the dear old home.

On Wednesday, September 22nd, the Loan Exhibition in Town Hall was opened to the public, and attracted great interest. To John DeWolf the credit is due for the large number of portraits and other interesting relics gathered, and the good taste displayed in their grouping and arrangement.

Thursday, September 23rd, opened bright and mild, and during the day many visiting Sons and Daughters arrived by boat and train. A more beautiful evening for the illumination could not be desired. It was so calm that a lighted taper could have been carried through the streets. The decorations and illuminations were general—almost universal —so much so, that to mention any without naming all, seems almost invidious.

The *Providence Journal* of September 24th, contained the following article on

"BRISTOL'S BI-CENTENNIAL.

"GRAND ILLUMINATION AND ELABORATE DECORATION OF THE TOWN. ENTHUSIASTIC GATHERING OF HER SONS AND DAUGHTERS.

"Ye ancient towne of Bristol is stirred to its utmost depths on the occasion of its two hundredth anniversary, and a visit to the usually staid and unobtrusive old town yesterday afternoon and evening, would have convinced a stranger within its gates that the bustle and excitement that pervaded its streets and places of business, betokened its metropolitan character and enterprise. The trains and steamboats brought loads of people, as well as vehicles of all descriptions, from the surrounding country, and it was estimated that at eventide, in addition to a majority of its six thousand inhabitants, there were upwards of two thousand strangers and natives upon the streets and in the town. The applications for badges and dinner tickets, by sons and daughters, reached three or four hundred during the day, and the latch-strings on the outside of dwelling houses were remarkably numerous. There has been a wide-spread and hearty response to the invitations extended by the committees and townsmen, and the exercises of to-day will attract many thousands.

"ILLUMINATION OF THE TOWN.

"The observance of the bi-centennial anniversary began last evening with a magnificent and extensive illumination and decoration of the town in patriotic dress, and residents vied with each other in the elaborateness and brilliancy of their displays at their residences and places of business. Col. Beals, of Boston, and J. Harry Welch, of Providence, lent their experience and good taste in the combination of colors and appropriate designs, and it was noticeable that excellent taste and discrimination in the arrangement and selection of material was shown by the townsmen. Where the display on all of the public thoroughfares was so brilliant and imposing, it would require unlimited space to particularize even the most prominent and artistic demonstrations of public spirit and pride. Hope street, which may be termed the 'Broadway' of the town, was radiant with the glow of myriads of lanterns and transparencies, while colored lights and bonfires were shown on the corners of the intersecting streets in lavish profusion. The residences of James DeWolf Perry, Philip Bourn, and Col. C. A. Greene, of the *Phenix*, shone gayly in their dress of national colors in bunting, with lanterns and transparencies prettily arrayed, and the Hydraulion Engine Company displayed an elaborate fire scene in front of their house, with lanterns and bunting, and 'Welcome,' in gold lettering. On Franklin street, from High to Hope street, long lines of lanterns, bunting and transparencies, greeted the eye. Mrs. Babbitt made a handsome display of colored lights and transparencies, and Captain Collins transformed his house and grounds into a national garden, with its rows of lanterns across the piazza, and flags of all descriptions suspended about the premises. Wm. J. Miller and J. Howard Manchester made handsome displays, and at the Rogers Library lights gleamed from every window, while shields, bunting and festoons were gracefully arranged in its front. In front of the elegant residence of Col. S. Pomroy Colt, a dense crowd was assembled, and one involuntarily paused to admire the magnificent display. A large flag floated from a pole on top of the house, and a golden eagle was poised on the roof, holding in her beak the streamers and bunting which completely enveloped the front of the house. A crystal refractor emitted prismatic lights from its station on the piazza-roof, and the pillars were entwined with tri-colored streamers. Two knights in full armor stood on either side of the portal, and a revolutionary soldier in a medallion frame stood above the State seal, with flags on both sides of the entrance. The grounds were brilliantly illuminated with lanterns, and over the postern was the inscription, 'Welcome, our Governor.' Locomotive head-lights turned their full radiance on the building, and colored fires added to the superb effect of the scene. Capt. Norris, corner of Hope and State streets, made a pretty display, and the Bristol Hotel was gayly trimmed and illuminated. The post office was dressed from roof to basement in festoons and streamers, held in the beak of a noble eagle. The residence of Edward W. Brunsen was greatly admired, the stars and stripes and scores of lanterns making the grounds and interior singularly beautiful. Capt. Lawless illuminated his handsome residence, and displayed mottoes and bunting, while the dazzling lights of locomotive head-lights made the grounds of Col. A. C. Eddy as bright as day, and set off his decorations to the best advantage. The light of colored fires was reflected on the waters of the harbor and the craft anchored therein, and produced a charming scene. Hon. Augustus O. Bourn and Le Baron B. Colt, Esq., illuminated their residences, and the latter made a splendid display of flags and bunting. W. H. Manchester's store, and the house of the Dreadnaught Hose Company, with its triple row of torches, emitted a brilliant light. At the Byfield School the decorations were beautifully arranged, a large picture being stationed over the porch, with mottoes, a figure of the goddess of liberty, streamers and bunting. The Thompson Brothers made a brilliant showing, and on the east side of the Common strings of lanterns were observed reaching its entire length. The Court House was finely decorated, the greeting, 'We greet the present and remember the absent,' being conspicuously posted over the entrance, and a profusion of tri-colored streamers and flags prettily draped. At Masonic Hall the flags and emblems of the Order were suspended across the street. The residence of the Town Clerk, Peter Gladding, was elaborately dressed and brilliantly illuminated with lanterns. It was utterly impossible to hire a conveyance in Bristol or Warren during the afternoon, and the stable keepers turned away hundreds of applicants to house their teams. A continuous stream of vehicles of all descriptions passed along the road between Providence and Bristol during the afternoon and evening, and an extra train was run from Warren to Bristol to accommodate the excursionists. It was a gala night for Bristol, and it will live long in the memories of the oldest inhabitant and rising generation, as the grandest display of public spirit and enthusiastic pride in its ancient and honorable history."

The *Providence Press* account, from their regular Bristol correspondent, describes "the scene on Hope, State and Bradfords streets, as very beautiful. Colored fires, burning barrels, and fireworks of all descriptions, with the brilliant illuminations, called forth the warmest praises from the assembled thousands on the streets. As we passed down Hope street, the New York Store, John G. Sparks, proprietor, attracted much attention from the very elaborate decoration and the magnificent display of lanterns, while the large show window contained the goddess of liberty, very artistically and elaborately dressed. This store attracted general attention from all passers. Thompson's boot and shoe store looked finely, as did the Boston Store and others. The humble cottage of the widow, with its one light placed in the window, to show her interest, though but a mite as compared with the outlay made by those near by, was appreciated by all who passed that way."

The Town Hall was decorated on the outside with flags and streamers, but the great attraction was the relics gathered within its walls.

The Post Office and Custom House building was also elaborately dressed in flags and streamers. The *Press* names other places illuminated as follows :—"King Philip Steam Fire Engine House, No. 1, Hugh Holmes' market. George H. Farrington's store, and the residences of Dr. Canfield, William Pierce, William B. Kimball, and the Misses Codman."

In addition, the *Bristol Phenix* gives the following list of residences decorated and illuminated :

"James M. Gifford, Dr. L. W. Briggs, Mrs. R. D. Smith, Mrs. Henry Wardwell, James A. Miller, George W. Easterbrooks, Otis Munro, Rev. Dr. W. V. Morrison, Col. E. M. Wardwell, Baptist parsonage, William H. Spooner, N. S. Burnham, Bennett J. Munro, Charles A. Johnson, Horace M. Barns, Isaac F. Williams, Edward S. Babbitt, Andrew R. Trotter, Henry R. Cooke, Benjamin B. Morris, John W. Munro, Frederic A. Easterbrooks, Ozro C. Barrows, George H. Farrington, Miss Sarah Cutler, Samuel B. Spinning, Robert N. Church, Major Henry Goff, Augustus N. Miller, Dr. T. S. Shipman, James D. Wardwell, Jesse Wilson, and the stores of Richard Dunbar, Samuel Corwin, Charles A. Johnson; the *Phenix* office, the stores of J. H. Young & Co., George W. Easterbrooks, Misses Thompson and Hunnewell, Benjamin M. Lincoln, Frederic A. Easterbrooks, Thomas C. Church, David A. Pierce, Louis Kunze, John Connery, John Lake, Benjamin L. West, Wm. Fred. Fish, William H. Buffington, William H. Bell, and Allen M. Newman."

The correspondents of these papers worked industriously and gave very full reports, but many places deserving of notice doubtless escaped attention.

The morning of the 24th, the eventful day which had been so long anticipated, broke bright and clear, with a mild, genial air, and throngs of people were early astir to join in the festivities.

At sunrise, a national salute of thirty-eight guns was

fired on the common, by the Bristol Train of Artillery, under the direction of Col. R. B. Franklin. Bells of the churches were rung for one hour, commencing at the time of firing the salute.

The steamer from Newport was one of the first arrivals, and landed about one hundred and fifty persons, and throngs continued to arrive by boat, train and other conveyances, until, at the time fixed for the procession to form it was estimated that there were fully six thousand strangers in the town. The Town Hall was early filled with interested visitors, and continued to attract large crowds throughout the day and evening.

THE PROCESSION.

At 10½ o'clock A. M., the procession was formed on High street, in front of the Court House, right resting on State street, in the following order:

Police skirmishers. Platoon of Providence Police.

Chief Marshal—COL. S. P. COLT.

Aids—Capt. John Collins, Mark A. DeWolf, Frederick F. Gladding, James A. Renwick, Benjamin L. West, Capt. Charles Norris, Col. T. F. Usher, James C. Church, Henry M. Gibson, J. Howard Manchester, Wilfred H. Munro, Charles Paull, Robert D. Andrews.

FIRST DIVISION.

Marshal—Col. George O. Eddy.

Aids—P. L. Garrett, Orrin Wilson, W. Fred Williams, William H. Munro.

Bristol Cornet Band, James Allyn, leader; C. H. Straight, drum major; 22 pieces.

Bristol Train of Artillery, Col. Richard B. Franklin, commander; Lieut.-Col. Henry F. Card; Capt. William B. Burnham; Lieut. Frisbie; 50 men.

National Band, Providence, W. E. White, leader; 25 pieces.

First Light Infantry Veteran Association Band, of Providence, Benjamin P. Robinson, leader; 8 pieces.

First Light Infantry Veteran Association, Providence— Col. W. W. Brown, commanding; Adjt. Dan. Remington: 75 men, in three companies—two in uniforms and one not uniformed.

First Company—Capt. Eddy; Lieuts. Greene and Bradford.

Second Company—Capt. Potter; Lieuts. Anthony and Bradford.

Third Company—Gen. William R. Walker.

Bristol Light Infantry—Capt. Michael Cahill; Lieuts. Dwyer and Brunnell; 25 men.

SECOND DIVISION.

Marshal—Col. George T. French.

Aids—Edward F. Lucas, Maj. Wm. P. Merritt, Edward Coward, A. L. Howe.

Company of gentlemen dressed in ye ancient pilgrim costume, formed in a hollow square, in the centre of which was borne the flag presented to the town by Colonel Byfield in the year 1710. Color-bearer—A. B. Corthell.

Twenty carriages containing President and members of Town Council of Bristol—C. A. Greene, A. J. Trotter, Henry Goff, Samuel M. Lindsey, Hezekiah W. Church; His Excellency, Governor Littlefield; His Honor, Lieutenant-Governor Fay, Adjutant General Barney and LeBaron B. Colt, Esq., Chairman of the Bi-Centennial Committee; Hon. Joshua M. Addeman, Secretary of State; Hon. Samuel Clark, General Treasurer; Hon. Joel M. Spencer, State Auditor; Hon. Thos. B. Stockwell, Commissioner of Public Schools; Hon. Thomas W. Bicknell, former Commissioner of Public Schools; Cols. Pierce, Littlefield, Clarke and Francis, of the Governor's personal staff; Quartermaster-General Dennis and Col. J. C. Seabury; Surgeon-General Budlong, Assistant Adjutant-General Turner, and Assistant Quartermaster-

General Nickerson; Prof. J. Lewis Diman, of Providence, orator; Rt. Rev. Bishop Howe, of Central Pennsylvania, poet; Rev. George L. Locke, chaplain; Hon. Henry B. Anthony; Hons. Nelson W. Aldrich and L. W. Ballou, Representatives in Congress; Hon. John H. Stiness, Judge of the Supreme Court of Rhode Island; Col. T. W. Higginson, Senior Aid of the Governor of Massachusetts; Rt. Rev. T. M. Clark, Bishop of the Diocese of Rhode Island and Chaplain of the First Light Infantry Veteran Association of Providence; His Honor H. K. Oliver, Mayor of Salem, Mass., a descendant of Nathaniel Oliver; Hon. Francis Brinley, of Newport, a descendant of Nathaniel Byfield; Hon. Zachariah Allen, of Providence, President of the Rhode Island Historical Society; Hon. Amos Perry, Secretary of the Rhode Island Historical Society; Rev. S. H. Webb, Chaplain First Battalion Rhode Island Militia; Ex-Governor Van Zandt; His Honor Thomas A. Doyle, Mayor of Providence; His Honor Stephen P. Slocum. Mayor of Newport; Ex-Lieutenant Governor Charles R. Cutler, President of the Town Council of Warren; Henry F. Drown, Ezra M. Martin and George Smith, of the Town Council of Warren, and Nathaniel Peck and Mark H. Wood, of the Barrington Town Council; Rev. Dr. Robinson, President of Brown University; Hon. Rowland Hazard, of South Kingstown; Prof. Jencks, of Brown University, and Rueben A. Guild, Librarian of Brown University; Hon. Rowland G. Hazard, of South Kingstown; Prof. William Gammell, of Providence; Hon. William Goddard, of Providence; Rev. Joel Mann, of New Haven, Conn.; Rev. Francis Peck, of Baltimore, Md.; Rev. Thomas F. Fales, of Waltham, Mass.; Rev. James P. Lane, of Hyde Park, Mass.; Rev. Mark Trapnell, former rector of St. Michael's Church, Bristol; Rev. Benjamin B. Babbitt, of Columbia, S. C.; Rev. C. B. Perry, associate rector of Mount Calvary Church, Baltimore; Rev. W. J. Tilley, of Middletown, Vt.; Rev. Dr. W. V. Morrison, of the Methodist Episcopal Church, Bristol; Rev.

J. H. Johnson, rector Trinity Church, Bristol; Rev. H. Crocker, pastor of the Baptist Church, Bristol; Lewis T. Fisher, Sheriff of Bristol county; H. H. Luther, Town Clerk of Warren; Peter Gladding, Town Clerk of Bristol; William R. Taylor, Deputy Town Clerk; Hon. Charles H. Hardy, of Warren, State Senator; John C. Burrington, Esq., of Barrington, Representative in the General Assembly; William H. Spooner, Esq., Representative in the General Assembly, from Bristol, and others.

Four trees, which were subsequently planted on the common, to the memory of the four original proprietors of the town, on a carriage prepared for the purpose.

THIRD DIVISION.

Marshal — Isaac F. Williams.

Aids — Charles Hosmer, W. Russell Bogert, John H. Smith, Charles A. Waldron, Preston E. Day.

Boston Cadet Band, J. Thomas Baldwin, leader; 26 pieces.

Chief Engineer of the Fire Department — J. Howard Manchester. Assistants — Charles H. Allen, George W. Simmons.

Hydraulic Engine and Hose Co., No. 1, Capt. Eugene Rounds; 25 men and their machine.

Progress Fire Company, of New Bedford, Mass., Charles S. Paisler, Foreman.

King Philip Steam Fire Engine Co. No. 1, Robert Lawder, Acting Foreman; 15 men with the machine.

Dreadnaught Hook, Ladder and Hose Co., No. 1, Charles E. Card, Captain; 25 men, with the hose carriage.

FOURTH DIVISION.

Marshal — Charles V. Perry.

Aids — N. R. Middleton, James Gooding, Lewis DeWolf, Ricardo D. B. Smith.

Bristol Bi-Centennial Drum Corps, Capt. George Warren; 8 drums.

Sons and daughters of Bristol, under charge of Col. E. M. Wardwell.

Cavalcade of citizens, in which conspicuously appeared Gen. A. E. Burnside, under command of Chandler H. Coggeshall. Aids—Wilfred H. Munro, Frank J. Gladding.

FIFTH DIVISION.

Marshal—Hon. William T. C. Wardwell.

Aids—James D. Wardwell, Jr., Edward Anthony, Jr., James M. Usher, Charles F. Chase.

TRADES' PROCESSION.

Team of Boston Store, T. T. Allan, proprietor, a fine display of goods; wagon of Adams Express Company filled with boxes, trunks, etc.; team of W. T. C. Wardwell, containing lumber of all kinds, doors, blinds, etc.; team of the Reynolds Manufacturing Company containing cotton in all processes of manufacture; Singer Sewing Machine team; M. A. Card's local express wagon, with boxes, packages, etc.; N. N. Cole's display of coal, flour, grain, hay, vegetables and all sorts of produce, with flags and national bunting; market wagon of Hugh Holmes, full of provisions; display of the Herreshoff Manufacturing Company, compound engines, boilers, etc.; paints and oils, display by William H. Spooner; grocery wagon of Thompson Brothers; large wagon of boots and shoes, from C. H. Thompson; wheelbarrow, from the market of W. Fred Fish, as showing how the business was conducted when he started in business in 1869, followed by a wagon well filled with orders as showing how the business is conducted to-day; two wagons containing dry and fancy goods, and clothing, from J. G. Sparks; wagon containing stoves, from Richard S. Gladding; wagon of F. A. Geisler, containing a blacksmith's forge, anvil, etc.; and showing the different processes in the manufacture of carriages; team of William Johnson, harness maker, with a good display of trunks, harnesses, etc.; boat on wheels, gaily trimmed with national colors and evergreen, containing several young ladies and a display of millinery trimmings, from Misses Thompson and Hunnewell; display of drugs, perfumery and fancy goods, from J. H. Young & Co.'s; stoves, pumps, etc., from J. Howard Manchester, dealer in stoves and tinware; a small house on wheels made of national bunting, with doors, windows, blinds, etc., from Marshall Prarie, contractor and builder; two large wagons, finely decorated, from the National Rubber Company, well filled with a variety of goods of their make; farm wagon filled with all sorts of farm produce, H. M. Gibson; two ice carts and a milk wagon, from J. Gooding. All the teams were more or less decked with flags and bunting in the national colors.

The procession commenced to move about $11\frac{1}{2}$ o'clock.

The line of march was as follows: High street to Franklin, Franklin to Hope, Hope to Walley, Walley to High, High to Church, Church to Wood, Wood to State, State to the tent on Common, where the exercises in the tent were held.

The tent was reached about one o'clock. Most of the prominent guests from the carriages took seats on the platform. The Town Committee of Arrangements were also seated upon the platform, forming, with the invited guests, a group of some two hundred persons. As the exercises were about to commence, the venerable and Rt. Rev. Benjamin B. Smith, Senior Bishop of the Protestant Episcopal Church, of the United States, a native of Bristol, came in and was seated upon the platform. His very presence was a benediction.

More than five thousand people filled the tent to overflowing.

The exercises were as follows:

ORDER OF EXERCISES.

"Overture to William Tell," by the Boston Cadet Band.
Prayer, by Rev. George L. Locke.

Le Baron B. Colt, Esq., President of the Bi-centennial Committee, made an address, as follows:

ADDRESS OF WELCOME.

It is my pleasant duty, on behalf of the town, to welcome you, one and all, sons and daughters of old Bristol, invited guests and friends. This is the native town of most of you, the adopted town of others, the loved and respected town of all; and here upon this, her two-hundredth birth-day, in honor of her long life, of what she has been and is to all of us, you come from far and near to join us in laying these offerings of affection at her feet.

Her history, her early and romantic past, the circumstances of her settlement by our ancestors, the story of her life during two eventful centuries, her rapid and prosperous growth at the beginning, the commercial importance she once attained, the calamities by wars, fire and tempest she has suffered, this and much more will be told you in prose and verse from the lips of her most distinguished children. It only remains, therefore, for me to welcome you to all the enjoyments of this day—to the sight once more of these goodly Mount Hope lands, these pleasant waters, this beautiful prospect, these broad streets, with their archway of noble trees, these old churches and homesteads, with the many memories they call back into life. May your stay among us be as happy as you anticipate. May you find the town as fair as when you left her, and her people as worthy of her.

The dwellers upon this territory have always regarded it with a peculiar devotion. The Wampanoags of old returned to this spot with pride and pleasure, cherished it beyond all others, made it their kingly seat, clung to it until conquest and death, and we in the same spirit of devotion have met to-day.

The Chief Executive of the State, those who represent us in the councils of the nation, the representatives of our cities, colleges and historical societies, and other distinguished gentlemen from neighboring States and from our own, have honored us with their presence upon this occasion. To all these we extend a cordial greeting. May the exercises of this day serve to deepen our attachment for the town, our reverence for its history, and make us better and more worthy citizens.

Two hundred and fifty children of the public schools, under the direction of Mrs. S. B. Spinning, then sang the following invocation ode, written for the occasion by Abby D. Munro:

INVOCATION ODE.

Oh, Thou, within whose bounteous hand,
The circling years in order stand,
A thousand years within whose sight,
Are as the watch of one lone night;

To thee our tribute now we bring.
Let every tongue thy praises sing.
While homage to thy name we pay,
For this returning festal day.

When first our fathers sought a home,
Thy blessing on their choice was shown.
Thou mad'st the wilderness they chose,
To bud and blossom as the rose.

What wonders has thy goodness wrought!
What changes has thy wisdom brought!
Who has made these blessings to abound,
And all these years with plenty crowned.

Our Father, and our father's God!
Oh, be thy glorious name adored!
Now, and through each succeeding age,
For such a goodly heritage.

The following congratulatory telegrams were received:

"Received at Bristol, R. I., 8.42 A. M. Sept. 24th, 1880.
To Bi-Centennial Committee, Bristol, Rhode Island:
With best felicitations.
                                        DIMAN.
Lisbon."

"Santa Fe, N. M., Sept. 23rd, 1880.
Received at Bristol, R. I., 8.40 A. M , Sept. 24th.
To Le B. B. Colt:
Regretting distance prevents attendance, I send greetings from the far Southwest.
L. Bradford Prince."

The first telegram was from Henry Wight Diman, Esq., United States Consul at Lisbon, Portugal. He has been in Europe eighteen years.

Mr. Prince is Chief Justice of the United States Court of New Mexico.

Prof. J. Lewis Diman, the orator of the day, delivered the following address :

HISTORICAL ADDRESS.

We have met to commemorate the founding of this ancient town. Two hundred years have fled since the hearths of our fathers were planted here. Well nigh seven generations have completed their mortal term since these broad streets were opened, since this spacious common, on which we are gathered, was set apart for public use. As we enter upon the third century of our history, we pause, for a brief space, to confess the debt which every community that has done anything worthy of remembrance owes to itself, and which no community swayed by generous sentiments, and mindful of its own best interests, can refuse to pay. There is no more becoming impulse than that which brings us hither. The most elevated instincts of our nature are enlisted in such a service. The deep and wide-spread interest which this occasion has awakened, this great multitude before me, afford convincing proof that we are not insensible to the obligations which our connection with a community like this imposes. We have gladly heeded the summons to this festival; we have trodden with willing feet these familiar paths. It is a festival in which we cannot join without emotion. It has for all of us a meaning which no ordinary festival can have. Amid the ringing of bells, and the inspiring strains of music, we can none of us forget that we have come to a spot hallowed by our most affecting memories. Here we were born: here by the fireside we heard the first accents of affection:

here in the school-room we learned our earliest lessons; here in the house of God we were taught the consoling truths that alone compensate for the losses which a day like this brings so vividly to mind. A cloud of witnesses, invisible to mortal eye, look down upon us. Everything around us invests these services with an exalted and religious sentiment. There are no ties more sacred than those of which we are now reminded. We have come to the home of our childhood; to the graves of our fathers. The words of Holy Writ leap unbidden to our lips: "If I forget Thee, may my right hand forget her cunning; if I do not remember Thee, may my tongue cleave to the roof of my mouth!"

The circumstances under which we meet may well call for our heartfelt gratulation. We have come to a spot beautiful for situation, lovely indeed at all times, but never more lovely than at this season, when lingering summer bathes the landscape in the pensive beauty that so well befits the strain of thought in which we cannot help indulging. We have come at a time when we may turn without effort from our common avocations and cares, a time of great prosperity, when our land is teeming with abundant harvests, when, after years of weary depression, commerce and industry show everywhere signs of healthy revival, when our public credit is restored, when peace reigns in all our borders. No dreg of bitterness poisons our overflowing cup. Nor should the fact that we are now engaged in one of the great periodical contests which determine the political character of our government, when throughout its length and breadth the land is stirred with the eager strife of conflicting parties, lessen in the least our interest in these services. To one who rightly apprehends the nature of our political system, and who correctly estimates the real sources of its strength, they will seem invested with additional significance. For even amid the excitement of a national election, and with the inspiring spectacle before us, of fifty millions of freemen choosing their chief magistrate under the wise and regulated restraints of constitutional law, we may well turn our gaze, for a few moments, to those ancient sources from which the broad stream of our national life has flowed; we may well remind ourselves that our local institutions form, at once, the foundation and safeguard of our federal system; that from the broad support of numberless scattered municipalities like this, whose founding we commemorate to-day, springs the splendid arch that gilds with promise the future of American civilization. Let us never forget that American liberty had its cradle in towns; that here the earliest lessons of self-government were learned. And let us rest assured that long as the traditions of these local rights are zealously cherished, American liberty will never be subverted.

Nor can I count it inopportune that our services so nearly coincide, in point of time, with the great and splendid commemoration, which, during the past week, has concentrated the gaze of the entire nation upon the chief city of New England. At first sight, indeed, it may well seem that our modest festival cannot fail to suffer from too close proximity to another so similar as to provoke comparison, and yet so much more impressive in its historical associations, and so much more elaborate in its attending circumstances. Still even this seeming disadvantage, when we reflect a moment, gives additional meaning to our celebration. There is a peculiar fitness in having one so soon succeed the other. For it serves the more forcibly to call attention to that feature in our early history which gave this town its distinctive character, and drew the broad line of distinction between this settlement and the earlier settlements upon the shores of the Narragansett. It reminds us that Bristol was the offspring of Boston. At the ripe age of fifty years the sturdy Puritan mother gave birth to this beautiful child. It was the sagacity of Boston merchants that first saw the admirable adaptation of this commodious harbor to the purposes of commerce, it was the public spirit of Boston merchants that reserved for a remote posterity the ample provisions of these streets and squares, it was the intelligence and piety of Boston merchants that planted by this shore the institutions of education and religion which their Puritan training had taught them to reverence, and which they brought with them to their new home, as their most precious heritage. Here, so far as their circumstances would permit, they sought to build another Boston; and surely as they gazed on the fair surroundings of this favored spot, as they surveyed the gentle slope of the ground, as they followed the graceful course of the silver bay, as they pictured, perchance, the possible success that might attend their enterprise, they may well have been pardoned if they sometimes exclaimed,

O matre pulchra filia pulchrior!

Two hundred years do not cover a long period when we reckon the centuries of the world's history, yet two hundred years carry us back to a time when much that now seems majestic and venerable, existed only in the womb of futurity. The faded banner that was borne in our procession to-day, precious as the gift of one of the first proprietors, is the symbol of a municipal organization that went into operation more than a century before our Federal Constitution was adopted. When this town was founded, the kingdom of Prussia had not been established, the empire of Russia had not become a European power. Charles the Second was still degrading the crown of England, the fierce contest caused by the Exclusion Bill was raging, the great revolution had not taken place which drove the Stuarts from the throne. Our town government is, therefore, older than the English constitution as it now exists, older than the Bill of Rights, older than the Act of Settlement, older than the great division of parties that ran through the reigns of Anne and the Georges, older than the England of Bolingbroke, of Walpole and of Pitt. Two hundred years of the quiet annals of a neighborhood like this do not, it is true, appeal to the imagination like two hundred years of the history of a famous State. The stage is small, and the interests seem trivial, the actors are not heroes and statesmen and kings. But it is, after all, a history that touches us more nearly than the plots of rulers, or the devastating march of armies. It is the history of the human life which we all are leading. And when we reflect what two hundred years of the history of a community like this really represent, when we consider the inestimable benefit diffused by a well ordered social system, the wholesome restraints of law, the sweets of domestic life, the elevating influence of education, the priceless blessings of devout religious instruction, the influence of good example transmitted from generation to generation, we shall feel that two hundred years of history like this are as worthy of our study as much that fills a larger and more pretentious page.

When the first houses were built upon this spot, two of which still remain to attest the solid workmanship of our fathers, there already existed four settlements on Narragansett Bay. Forty-four years earlier Roger Williams had undertaken, upon the banks of the Mooshausic, the unique and memorable experiment of founding a community upon the principle of obedience to the civil magistrates only in civil things. A little later the great antinomian controversy had driven to the island of Aquidneck another company, who, planting themselves just at the northern end, had afterwards removed to the unrivalled harbor which excited the admiration of the Florentine navigator, Verazzano, more than a century before; and almost directly opposite, upon the western shore of the bay, that singular enthusiast, Samuel Gorton, after coming into collision with the authorities both at Providence and Newport, had founded Warwick. In the year 1663 the three settlements had been united under the charter of Charles the Second.

The course of events which reserved this territory for a later occupation, and for a different jurisdiction, forms one of the most interesting chapters in the history of New England. The neck of land on which this town was built, called by the English Mount Hope, but known to the Indians as Pokanoket, was the last recognized possession of the aborigines in this portion of the country. Here was their final refuge ; here began the great struggle which resulted in their overthrow ; here was witnessed the last tragic act in the bloody strife. I shall not transgress the proper limits of my subject if I glance briefly at events which were directly connected with the founding of the town, and which explain the distinctive characteristics of its early history. It is only from a review of these events that we can understand how this community presented, at the outset, such marked contrast to the other settlements upon our bay.

Whether, as has been claimed by enthusiastic Scandinavian scholars, the Northmen ever visited these shores, is a question we need not discuss. There seems, indeed, no reason to doubt the substantial truth of the narratives which describe the adventurous voyages of Biorne, and Leif and Thorfinn ; we may accept without hesitation, the claim that they discovered Greenland, that they cruised along the coast of Labrador and Nova Scotia, that they pursued their dangerous navigation as far south as Cape Cod and Narragansett Bay. But when we seek from any of their own statements, to determine the precise localities they visited, we are involved in insuperable difficulties. The attempt from a passage of doubtful meaning respecting the length of the day at Vinland, where they wintered, to identify its latitude with Rhode Island, can hardly be accepted as conclusive. The most that we can safely say, is, that they may have been here ; that there is nothing improbable in the supposition that they may have found in this bay their winter refuge. But if they did they left no trace behind them. Their daring enterprise had no influence whatever upon subsequent events. To suppose, as some have done, that the name of the neighboring summit is the corruption of the Norse word with which they marked their resting place, and that it was preserved in the traditions of an alien race for more than six hundred years, is to carry credulity beyond the limit of common sense. We may please ourselves with the fancy that the dark barks which arrested the troubled gaze of Charlemagne, which at a later period carried terror to the coasts of France, and pushed up the Seine to the very gates of Paris, may have anchored in these waters; a halo of romance will surround these shores if we connect them with those adventurous vikings; but the course of events that claims our serious attention belongs to a far later period. Let us leave these obscure legends and pass to the region of unquestioned fact. We shall find enough here to invest this familiar region with a singular and enduring interest.

At the beginning of the authentic history of our town, we are confronted with the most venerable figure among the aborigines of New England. When the Pilgrims landed at Plymouth, they were told that the desolate region around them belonged to the great sachem, Massasoit, whose sway extended from Cape Cod to the shores of the Narragansett. With him their first treaty was concluded. In an unfinished building near Plymouth, the floor spread with a rug and cushion to give dignity to the proceedings, were conducted the simple negotiations which are memorable as the beginning of American diplomacy. The treaty was one of alliance, and not one of subjection, and the sachem was assured that "King James would esteem him as his friend and ally." In the following summer, the first passed by the Pilgrims in New England, envoys were sent by the colonists to visit the sachem at Pokanoket. The narrative of this visit, the earliest ever made by Englishmen, of which any account has been preserved, while it presents a vivid picture of the squalid surroundings of the Wampanoag chief, furnishes at the same time, abundant evidence of his hospitality and kindness. It is impossible to read it without recognizing in Massasoit a genuine courtesy. His guests came upon him unexpectedly, and "he was both grieved and ashamed that he could no better entertain them." In this visit the compact already concluded was renewed, and the relations between the two races thus established upon a permanent basis. For more than fifty years it was faithfully observed. Long as Massasoit lived no charge was made that its stipulations were either broken or evaded. He lived to see his territories melt away before the steady inroad of the whites, till at length at the close of his long reign, he found himself shut up to the narrow peninsula of Pokanoket. But he remained to the last true to the compact he had made. And when we remember on what flimsy pretexts the most Christian kings of Europe, Charles II, and Louis XIV, violated their most sacred engagements, shall we withhold some tribute of respect to this pagan chief?

With the death of the kindly and faithful Massasoit, we pass to the most tragic chapter of our story. The causes of the bloody struggle which, fifteen years later plunged New England into mourning and wrested this, their last refuge, from the Wampanoags, still remain obscure. From his first accession to power, Philip, for some reason, seems to have excited the suspicion of the Plymouth authorities. He was summoned before them, and though he earnestly protested that he knew of no plot nor conspiracy against them, he was compelled to sign an instrument by which he acknowledged himself a subject of the King of England. When more positive charges were brought against him, five years later, he repeated with great fervor his protestations of innocency and of faithfulness to the English. And when, after four years more had passed, new apprehensions were awakened, he desired to renew his covenant with his ancient friends, and freely engaged to resign to the government of New Plymouth all his English arms. As Philip was still accused of evading this agreement, he was once more summoned before the authorities and compelled to acknowledge himself not only subject to the King of England, but to the government of the Plymouth colony. It is not difficult to conceive how this increasing pressure of a foreign authority must have affected a haughty spirit. The long established relation between Massasoit and the English was now completely reversed. Massasoit had been treated as an equal; Philip was reduced to the condition of a subject. Massasoit had been regarded with confidence; Philip, whether justly or unjustly, was viewed with constant distrust. That the sachem, doubtless ignorant of the full force of the submissions he had made, and only conscious that a net was being skillfully woven about him, was wholly free from blame, no one would venture to affirm, but that the authorities of Plymouth were pushing matters with too hard a hand, was the manifest opinion of their Massachusetts brethren. These doubted whether the engagement of Philip imported more than "a friendly and neighborly correspondency."

In the cabinet of the Rhode Island Historical Society there is preserved a curious paper which purports to give the substance of a reply made by Philip to his friend, John Borden, of Portsmouth, who sought to dissuade him from engaging in the war. The statement was not committed to writing till many years after the sachem's death, and cannot claim the authority of an historical document. Yet undoubtedly it preserves the tradition respecting the causes of the war that lingered in Philip's own neighborhood, and among those who knew him best. While the language belongs to a later period, the general representation may be accepted as correct. In this reply the sachem contrasts the reception which his father had extended to the English, with the ungenerous treatment to which he had been himself subjected. Unfounded charges had been brought against him, and he had been compelled to part with his territory to make restitution for injuries that he could not prevent. Thus tract after tract was gone till only a small part remained. "I am determined," said he, "not to live till I have no country."

That the Indians, in the main, were unfairly treated, there is, indeed, no evidence. Where the Pilgrims landed the territory had been depopulated by a pestilence, and they interfered with no rights by bringing once more under cultivation a desolate and deserted tract. The subsequent acquisitions of the settlers were made by purchase, to which the natives, for the most part, gave their free consent. And in their transactions the authorities took special care to guard the Indians from imposition. Yet the policy was avowed of crowding them upon narrow peninsulas, and they saw their territory continually wasting away. And it may be questioned how far the chiefs had authority to alienate the lands of their tribe, and how far they understood the full meaning of the transfer they made. Still less could they comprehend the nature of the allegiance which they were compelled to swear to a sovereign who lived three thousand miles away. Added to this was the unconcealed suspicion and contempt with which they were regarded, and which led the whites to insist strenuously "on the distance which is to be observed betwixt Christians and barbarians."

It is an interesting fact that we find the most favorable representations of Philip's character in the region where he lived, and among those who had the best opportunity for judging him. Thus the earliest historian of Rhode Island, Callender, tells us that Philip entered reluctantly upon the war, and that he shed tears when he heard that the first blood was spilled. To the same effect is the tradition of his grateful treatment of the Leonards. Though his ordinary residence was at Mount Hope, in the summer time he frequently found his way to Taunton. Here he became acquainted with this family, and received many acts of kindness at their hands. When the war broke out, his gratitude saved Taunton from destruction. "You have made him ready to die," said one of his men to the English commander, "for you have killed or taken all his relations." It has been urged against him as a reproach, that, when his prospect darkened elsewhere, he did not join himself to the Eastern Indians; but is it not a touching trait in his character, that when wife and child had been taken from him, he turned back to die in his own home?

It is claimed by some that Philip of Pokanoket is simply a hero of romance; that fancy has arrayed with fictitious majesty a squalid savage, whose dwelling was a sty. No doubt many of the representations of his character are incorrect. It is folly to speak of him as a great warrior, a penetrating statesman, a mighty prince. Such exaggerated language does him gross injustice, for it applies to him the standards of a wholly different social state. There is no proof that he was at the head of a great conspiracy, or that he possessed the capacity of inflaming his race with a common impulse. But we are equally wide of the mark when we picture him, in the coarse epithets of Church, as "a doleful, great, naked, dirty beast." In spite of all detraction, he remains the most picturesque and striking figure in Indian history. His tragic fate lends a sad interest to yonder mount. We are standing on soil that was wrested from him; we are enjoying privileges which were purchased by his ruin; but can we pass a harsh judgment on this hero of a lost cause, who fell, in an unequal fight, by a traitor's hand, and whose corpse was insulted by an ungenerous foe?

By the overthrow of Philip, the Mount Hope lands were, for the first time, thrown open to the occupation of the English, but the question was yet to be determined in whom the title to the newly-conquered territory was vested. The manner in which this question was settled forms the most curious episode in our early history. We can hardly fancy a more striking contrast than between the wilds of Pokanoket and the sumptuous palace of Whitehall, between the stern, resolute men who were here laying the foundations of a new English empire, and the gay and dissolute throng who formed the court of Charles the Second. Our story carries us to the Privy Council chamber where the dull routine of business was at this time so often lighted up by the wit of Shaftesbury. Among those whose occupation it was to amuse the King, was a dramatic poet named John Crowne. He is said to have been first brought to the notice of the Queen through the dislike which Rochester cherished for Dryden, and to have gained the favor of the good-natured monarch by a mask which had been performed before the court. Reckoning on this favor, Crowne came forward with a petition for the Mount Hope lands. His father, who had purchased an estate in Nova Scotia, had been impoverished by the cession of that province to the French, and upon this circumstance the poet based his claim to restitution. The matter was brought before the Privy Council, who directed that, before any action should be taken, inquiries should be made respecting the title to the territory. Plymouth claimed the lands as lying within her patent, and in this view the agents of Massachusetts concurred. The two Rhode Island agents, on the other hand, maintained that the tract, up to the recent war, had belonged to the Sachem Philip, and that no corporation in New England had any title to it. Although the Plymouth authorities had sought to gain the favor of the King by sending to him the greater part of the ornaments and treasures of Philip, the Privy Council adopted the Rhode Island view. But, at the same time, they recommended that the lands be granted to Plymouth, reserving only to the Crown, by way of quit rent, seven beaver skins to be paid yearly at Windsor Castle. No other lands in the colony were held upon this tenure.

The title to the newly conquered lands having been thus confirmed to Plymouth, measures were at once taken to dispose of them. The most powerful reason which had led the Plymouth authorities to claim the territory was that it "was well-accommodated for the settlement of sea-port towns." The evident advantages which it possessed as a commercial mart could not long remain unnoticed. On the fourteenth of September, 1680, corresponding, if we allow for the difference of style, to the day selected for these services, and in consideration of the sum of three hundred pounds, the

Mount Hope lands were conveyed to four citizens of Boston, John Walley, Nathaniel Byfield, Stephen Burton and Nathaniel Oliver. By the terms of the sale, a "town for trade" was to be at once established. To promote this end, extraordinary privileges were granted, and most liberal provisions were made. The four proprietors reserved to themselves an eighth each, and proceeded to dispose of the remainder. The new settlement was exempted from all colonial taxes for five years, the privilege of sending deputies to the General Court was conceded to it, a local court was established, and it was provided that it should be the shire-town of a new county to be established. The tract was laid out on a plan of which up to this time there had been no example. In contrast with the crowded streets of Boston, it presented these broad and regular avenues, but like Boston it had a public common reserved in the centre of the town, while six hundred acres, in addition, were devoted to the general improvement. It is impossible to glance at these provisions without recognizing the fact that the first proprietors of this territory were men of liberal views and large public spirit. While engaged in an enterprise which their own private advantage had no doubt suggested, they scorned to look at it in the light of mere private and selfish interest. The generous conception which they formed of their undertaking received its reward. The best class of settlers was attracted, and in five years, where had been a wilderness, there stood the most flourishing town in the colony.

The great purpose which they had in view was intimated in almost their earliest corporate act. On September 1, 1681, the people assembled together and agreed that "the name of this town shall be Bristol." The only reason that can be assigned for such a proceeding is that at this time Bristol was, next to London, the most important seat of maritime commerce in the mother country, and in founding their new port of trade, the settlers of this town wished to borrow some of the associations of such a famous mart. We may derive a natural satisfaction from the reflection that their confidence in the experiment they had undertaken gave us even this trifling connection with a city which, though stripped in part of its commercial eminence, is still one of the most beautiful in England, the city from which Sebastian Cabot sailed on the voyage that resulted in the discovery of the American continent, the city which Edmund Burke represented in Parliament, when he vindicated, in strains of unsurpassed eloquence, the rights of the colonies. In several striking particulars, a resemblance between the towns might be traced. The distinctive character of the new enterprise, that which marked it so strongly from the earlier settlements upon the bay, is expressed in this proceeding. The founders of Bristol were not, like the settlers of Providence and Newport, exiles for conscience' sake, smarting with sense of wrong, and cherishing a bitter feeling of resentment against the community from which they had been driven; on the contrary, they were men of wealth and standing, of high consideration in the colony which they voluntarily left, for which they cherished the most affectionate attachment, and whose institutions they zealously labored to perpetuate. In coming here they were not seeking for any larger religious liberty, for that they already enjoyed in as great a measure as they deemed consistent with their own good; they were not aiming to emancipate themselves from any restraints of law. They came here under due authority, to establish a town for trade, and they sought, from the outset, to surround themselves with all the sanctions of social order.

Every community is stamped with the impress of its founders. Who, we naturally ask, were the men to whom Bristol owes its origin? The four original proprietors, with one exception, were actual settlers, and became earnestly identified with the interests of the town. Mr. Oliver sold his share to Nathan Hayman, another leading merchant of Boston, who soon after died. The names of the remaining three are written in enduring characters on our early annals. Of Stephen Burton less is known than of the others, but he is said to have been bred at Oxford, and as recording officer of the county, he filled a responsible position until his death in 1692. John Walley, whose name stands first on the Grand Deed, was the son of an English clergyman, and held high rank in the Massachusetts Colony. While devoting himself with success to mercantile pursuits, he was called at various times to discharge important public duties. He was a member of the Council, a Judge of the Superior Court, and had command of the land forces in the expedition of Sir William Phipps. These great trusts were executed with an ability and fidelity which gained him universal respect.. During his residence in Bristol, he stood always among the foremost in promoting every public interest. His substantial dwelling still remains among us. Near the close of his life he returned to Boston, where he died in 1712. But the most prominent and influential of the original proprietors yet remains to be mentioned. Nathaniel Byfield was also the son of an English clergyman, a member of the famous Westminster Assembly. His mother was sister of the upright and courageous Bishop Juxon, who attended Charles the I. upon the scaffold. He landed at Boston only six years before the purchase of the Mount Hope lands. Coming to this town with the first settlers, he remained here for nearly half a century, choosing for his home the beautiful peninsula on the opposite side of the harbor, the greater part of which belonged to his estate. Like Walley he returned to Boston in his old age, and died there in 1733. His remains rest in the old Granary Burial Ground. When Bristol was incorporated, it was a part of Plymouth Colony, but after the union of Plymouth with Massachusetts in 1690, an ampler field was opened to its citizens. Colonel Byfield was several times elected Speaker of the House of Representatives; for many years he was a member of the Provincial Council; for a long period he presided in the County Court;

from no less than three English sovereigns he received a commission as Judge in Admiralty. In the notice called forth by his death, he is described as a man of great courage, vigor and activity; of plain and instructive conversation, and of unquestionable faithfulness and honesty. Nothing is more to his credit than the fact that during the Witchcraft delusion, which remains such a dark spot upon the fame of Massachusetts, he had the courage to oppose and denounce it. He was a man of strong convictions; he was engaged in bitter controversies; and he did not escape the aspersions which were as freely lavished in that day as in ours. But when his long and useful life was ended, his character and public services called forth unqualified eulogium. In this community his memory has always been gratefully cherished. To no one has Bristol been so much indebted. To him, more than to any other, we owe these broad and beautiful streets; to him we are indebted for this common on which we stand; to his foresight and generosity was due the early provision for schools, which has been such a material aid in the cause of public education. Fitted by his eminent abilities for the highest positions in the colony, he was never unmindful of his obligations to the community in which he lived. And with great appropriateness, when the High School was erected, a few years ago, the town decided that it should bear the name of Byfield. No nobler memorial can be erected to the dead than a memorial like this which is a perpetual blessing to the living, and no more worthy example can be held up to the generations of children who shall receive their training there, than the example of one who in the pursuit of his private interests never neglected the public good. Well may we be proud to enroll such names as Walley and Byfield among our founders!

I have called attention to the fact that the settlement of Bristol was essentially a commercial enterprise. At first sight, no doubt, this feature in its history seems to detract from the significance of the undertaking. Especially in comparison with the neighboring towns, it seems to lack those characteristics which awaken the most enthusiastic interest. We cannot claim that on this soil, so dear to all of us, any novel truth was evolved, or any great principles defended. The fame which justly belongs to Providence and to Aquidneck, does not belong to us. Our early records do not bear the names of any martyrs for conscience, of any pioneers in the vindication of spiritual truth. We have no Roger Williams upon whose statue we can gaze with reverence, we have no Anne Hutchinson, whose clear perception of first principles may extort our admiration, and whose pathetic fate, after so many years have passed, must excite our warmest sympathy. We are forced to confess the absence, in our local annals, of those elements which lend to history its highest and most absorbing charm. But there is another side to all this which we must not overlook. In the complex system under which the human race is working out its destiny, it seems to be the rule that an advantage in one direction is always purchased by the sacrifice of some corresponding advantage in another. There are two great principles that control the movements of society, the principle of progress, and the principle of order. If we reckon it a blessing to enjoy an unchecked liberty, if we count it a privilege to dwell in a community where there is no restraint upon the expression of opinion, where every one is free to follow his own course, and to attain the largest measure of individual development and of individual action, we must, on the other hand, admit that there is some advantage in an orderly society, some benefit to be derived from connection with a community where the common interests are not disregarded, where mutual obligations receive full recognition, and where the claims of positive truth are not forgotten in the assertion of the rights of private judgment.

It is impossible not to contemplate with admiration the early history of the State of which, for near a century and a half, we have been a loyal part ; not to gaze with reverence at the little community which, in an adverse age, had it in its heart "to hold forth a lively experiment that a most flourishing civil State may stand and best be maintained with a full liberty of religious concernments;" and which in an age when toleration was hardly known, boldly affirmed that not toleration merely, but complete religious freedom, was the right of every human being; but it is impossible to read the history of Rhode Island and not to recognize the fact that those who drank of this great cup of liberty were compelled to pay a heavy price. When they threw their doors wide open to the distressed in conscience of every name, when they held out so boldly the alluring bait of exemption from all external restraints, they drew together elements so incongruous, so inharmonious, so discordant, that even the invincible patience of Roger Williams at length recoiled from "such an infinite liberty of conscience." The extremely democratic basis upon which the body politic was rested, while it reduced the functions of government to the very narrowest limits, at the same time left the control of affairs in the hands of the least intelligent portion of the population. While it cannot be said that the first settlers were insensible to the importance of education, still education never received any generous public support. The complete separation effected between church and state, by remitting the support of religious institutions to a community divided, beyond all previous example, in religious sentiment, deprived them of the inestimable benefit of an educated clergy. In the town which Williams founded, and to which he gave a name expressive of his reliance upon divine help, no place of public worship existed until the beginning of the following century. Freedom, of every kind, prevailed in unexampled measure, but an enlarged public spirit, an intelligent appreciation of the higher interests of the social body, a recognition of what was due from the individual to the community of which he formed a part, were not then traits of Rhode Island character.

The Puritan colonies of Plymouth and Massachusetts, but more especially the latter, stood in striking contrast with all this. Firmly knit in religious faith, making no pretence whatever of toleration, often harsh in their treatment of dissenters, they were eminent for public spirit, and showed the characteristics of homogeneous and highly organized communities. Led by their peculiar theory to invest the State with the largest powers, and ally it with all the supreme concerns of life, they regarded no political duties as more sacred and more imperative than those connected with the promotion of education and the maintenance of pure religion. The public support accorded to religious institutions secured for every town the services of a well educated minister. On the other hand, this close alliance of church and state gave additional import to civil obligations. Public functions were held in high esteem, magistrates were regarded with reverence, and even the ordinary duties of the citizen were discharged in a religious spirit. Equally in civil and religious things the Puritan viewed himself as living unto God.

Coming, as they did, from a Puritan colony, the founders of Bristol did not seek in their new home to throw off the Puritan traditions in which they had been trained. They walked with undeviating steps in the faith to which they had been accustomed. They came to establish a town for trade, but they did not for a moment forget the higher conditions on which the welfare of every community depends, and without which material prosperity can only prove, in the end, a curse. Though engaged in a commercial enterprise, all their proceedings evinced a noble and conscientious recognition of the fact that society is bound by obligations which transcend all private and selfish interests. I have already alluded to the liberal provision, made at the settlement of the town, for the promotion of education. Almost their first care was to secure the services of "an able schoolmaster." And by a subsequent vote, by which a small additional fee was exacted from children who studied Latin, it appears that the course of study was not confined to common branches, but embraced the classics. But still more characteristic was their concern for the support of religion. When the town was laid out, lands were set apart for the support of the ministry, and in the articles of agreement between the original proprietors and the settlers, it was expressly stipulated that each should pay his proportion for erecting a meeting-house, and a home for the minister. At the very first town meeting, before their own dwellings had been closed against the winter wind, they voted to carry the latter part of this agreement into effect. For a short time they worshipped in a private house, a house whose sturdy frame, solid and unyielding as the creed of its builders, still defies decay. Soon as arrangements could be completed, they proceeded to erect a meeting-house. The massive timbers were cut from the common about us. It stood on the site of yonder Court House, and in it, for a hundred years, our fathers assembled to worship God. Around it were the graves of the first settlers, the most hallowed associations gathered about it, and we can but marvel at the stupidity which sacrificed that sacred and commanding site. According to well authenticated tradition, the building was square in shape, having two rows of windows, with a roof rising to the centre, and surmounted by a cupola and bell. The interior was surrounded by a double row of galleries, and the floor was covered, as time went on, with square pews, through the rounds of whose oaken doors the children sought relief from the tedium of the protracted services. I know it is the habit of some to express contempt for the old-fashioned New England meeting-house. But if the principle laid down by the highest authorities on architecture is right, that all genuine and noble building has its origin in actual needs, and finds the measure of its excellence in its adaptation to the use intended; if the Grecian temple, the Gothic minster, the feudal castle, derive their charm from their conformity to this fundamental law, then our Puritan fathers built wisely and well. They built according to their means, and with reference to their wants. Their plain meeting-houses harmonized with their simple worship. To the eye of taste they are far more venerable, and far more interesting, than the more ambitious structures with which they have so often been supplanted.

The men who made such liberal provision for the support of public worship, were not likely to be indifferent to the ministrations under which they sat. Exalting the pulpit to such supreme rank, they cherished a not less exalted ideal of religious teaching. Accustomed to accord the minister the first place in the community, they exacted, in return, the highest qualification. After one unsuccessful experiment, they secured for their first settled pastor, a renowned scholar, who brought to the infant settlement the ripest discipline of the old world. Son of a wealthy London citizen, he received his early training at the famous St. Paul's school, which John Colet, the friend of Erasmus, founded; the school in which Milton acquired the rudiments of his matchless scholarship. Proceeding at the early age of fifteen, to Oxford, he won a distinguished rank, and was rewarded with a fellowship at Wadham College. A conscientious non-conformist, he came to this country in 1686. It was said of him by one well qualified to judge, "that hardly ever a more universally learned person trod the American strand." It is true that he remained here but a short time, but we may safely infer something respecting the character and intelligence of a community which, even for a short time, could command and appreciate the ministrations of such a man as Samuel Lee.

Here let us pause. I have narrated the circumstances that led to the founding of this town, I have sketched an outline of its distinguishing features. I repeat that no such halo surrounds our early history as that which illumines the beginnings of the neighboring settlements. We have no claim to the distinction which Providence and Newport boast. But we may justly claim praise of a different kind. We may claim that here was planted a town which illustrated the advantages of social order; which was enriched, beyond ordinary measure, with the best conditions of social progress; which entered on its career with high and generous appreciation of social obligations. It had no rude beginnings. It is not too much to say that few rural neighborhoods in the mother country could boast the educational and religious privileges which they enjoyed who followed the wise lead of Walley and Byfield to these untrodden wilds.

Two hundred years have passed since the work which I have described was done. The dream in which our fathers indulged, when they borrowed for their little settlement the name of the famous English mart, has not been realized; in the main object they had in view the course of events has not corresponded with their expectations. The transfer of the town from Massachusetts to Rhode Island, which took place two generations later, lessened its importance; the hard struggle with the mother country bore heavily upon it; and not even the extraordinary enterprise of its merchants, during the half century that followed, could withstand the inevitable tendency of trade which collected foreign commerce into a few great centres. Bristol shared the fate of so many famous New England seaports. The harbor is deserted which was once crowded with vessels from every clime; the wharves are rotting where, within my own memory, were piled the costly products of the tropics, the Mediterranean, and the Baltic. The jargon of strange races is heard no more in our streets; the bustling port is tranformed into a summer watering place. Yet I cannot doubt that the best work of the founders remains. The mark they made on the character of the town, the impulse they gave to its higher interests, the deep lines they cut upon its moral foundations,—these have not passed away. There is not one of us here, to-day, who is not better for the work they did. We trace their beneficent influence in the conservative character which has always been the just boast of this community, in the regard for social order which has made it always prompt and unswerving in its support of authority and law. We trace it in the generous support of public institutions, of which there are so many striking proofs around us; in the churches, where, under different forms, the God whom they worshipped, is adored; in the noble school, which, bearing the name of Byfield, shows that his spirit is not extinct; and in the most recent ornament of our town, the beautiful Library, the gift of one who still survives, as an embodiment of the gentler and more winning virtues of the olden time, virtues which find small place on the page of history, but which form so large a part of all that gives value, and happiness, and blessing to human life.

Much that the fathers believed, we question; much that they deemed essential, we have put aside. But let us rest assured that it remains as true in our day as in theirs, that religion and intelligence are the foundations of a well-ordered and prosperous community. The example they have given us is an example which we cannot afford to forget. It is the example of an enlightened public spirit, the lesson that we are members one of another, that our individual concerns are wrapped up in the general welfare, that we best promote our private interests when we seek the common good. This, as I read New England history, was the great and admirable feature of Puritan character; this it was that made them strong, and prosperous, and honored. Let this be the lesson which we carry from these services, that in a community like this every member must do his part; that no matter how small its size, no matter how local and limited the interests involved, we have no right to hold ourselves aloof from its concerns. The possession of large means, of superior culture, only adds to the obligation. This, I repeat, is the great lesson the fathers teach. May we so ponder it that when another two centuries have passed, when seven generations more have been laid in their silent graves, we ourselves may be as gratefully remembered as we, to-day, have remembered them!

The following ode, written by Miss A. J. Coggeshall, was sung by the school children. *Tune*—Keller's American Hymn:

BI-CENTENNIAL ODE.

Hail to thee, Bristol! Our time-honored town:
Fair in thy robes of rejoicing arrayed;
Twice o'er our shores has a century rolled,
Since by firm hands thy foundations were laid;
Proudly we greet thee, our beautiful home.

Rich are our valleys in song and romance;
We roam the hills by the Norsemen roamed o'er;
Stand by the rock with their rude symbols carved,
Long ages past when they moored near our shore;
Sons of the North land! The mystical North.

Regal in rich robes of crimson and gold,
Mount Hope stands silent beside the still bay;
Stately as when in the days long ago
Sons of the forest held unquestioned sway;
Home of King Philip! We cherish thy fame.

On thy lone summit the chieftain once stood;
Th' proud Indian chieftain undaunted and brave;
His realm th' dim forest that skirted thy side,
No spot in thy broad lands could grant him a grave;
Noble King Philip! We moan thy sad fate.

Here stood th' lodge of renowned Massasoit,
Staunch friend of th' Pilgrims, unchanging and true;
On famed Pokanoket his council-fires blazed,—
Th' home of Wamsutta and proud Weetamoe,—
Th' bold, haughty princess; how daring in war!

Blue Narragansett! whose bright waters gleam
Round lovely Aquidneck's and Poppasqua's side,
No more where thy countless sails whiten th' wave,
Th' bark of the red man will silently glide;
Fairest of waters! Our isle-dotted bay!

Closely our heart strings around thee entwine;
We love thy broad streets and o'ershadowing trees,
Thy dark ivied churches, thy mansions so fair,
Thy harbor whose blue waves dance in the breeze;
Sweet Peace attend thee, our sea-girdled town!

Home of our fathers! While centuries last,
God whom they trusted, from danger defend!
Glad Plenty crown thee with rich golden sheaves,
And th' bow of His promise in love o'er thee bend!
Hail to thee Bristol! Our time honored town.

Rt. Rev. MARK A. DeW. HOWE, D. D., Bishop of the Diocese of Central Pennsylvania, poet of the day, delivered the following poem:

HISTORICAL POEM.

When life was fresh, and pulse beat full and strong,
Free fancies came, and wove themselves in song:
But age has checked the currents of the heart,
And care constrained its day-dreams to depart.
The chords unstrung which once attuned my lyre;
The hand its skill has lost;—the soul its fire;—
The broken shell lies voiceless on the shore;—
The fickle muses heed my suit no more;
And yet I strive by simple force of will,
With quavering voice to chant in numbers still.
For 'tis a gala day, joy rules the hour,
Young men and maids from happy homes outpour:
Their hastening feet trip light upon the green,
And music lends enchantment to the scene.
From distant marts and climes beyond the main,
The wandering exiles childhood's haunts regain.
In glad Thanksgiving, round th' ancestral board,
The living generations sit, restored.
They come to greet the mother of us all,
Whose bonds of love our willing hearts enthrall;
Whose years by centuries may now be told,
While spot nor wrinkle shows that she is old.
More fruit in age, her vigor still brings forth,
And spreads her teeming offspring South and North.
To-day, each filial heart its tribute brings,
And at her feet the roseate garland flings,
And witness,—stiffened age attempts to glean
Its withered chaplet;—fields no longer green,
Supply autumnal flowers in colors gay,
Fragrant no more, like blossoms of the May.

Sauntering along this ancient town,
    Its tasteful homes, its busy streets,
Its cross-crowned turrets shadowing down,
    Its sea-board girt with white-sailed fleets,

We dream not of their bold emprise
    Who here, two centuries agone,
Saw, forest-clad, with prescient eyes,
    The choicest spot for homes' hearth-stone.

Four stalwart men, alike prepared
    To quell the foe, or till the ground,
(Heroic dames their fortunes shared)
    Amid these wilds a refuge found.

They felled the wood, the log-house piled,
    They burned the bramble from the sod,
And sense of loneliness beguiled,
    With research in the Book of God.

The stealthy wolves from jungles swoop,
    And howl about their cots at night;
Or, wakened by the Indian's whoop,
    They see the torch's lurid light.

The snow four times the vales had filled,
    Four summer suns dissolved the frost,
Since the great Metacom was killed,
    His braves dispersed, his fastness lost.

The treach'rous savage, fierce with hate,
    Sought vengeance for his people's wrong:
Skulking where once with pride elate
    He strode the sun lit heath along,

Watching to light the vengeful fires,
    To steal the wife, to slay the child!
Such were the foes our gallant sires
    Encountered in the forest wild.

Where we, their sons, luxuriate,
    In homes with peace and plenty stored,
They wrestled with beleaguering fate,
    Armed with the plowshare and the sword.

Alas! for that evanished race
That once pursued the eager chase
    Along these hills and dales;
Or o'er the tide with light canoe
Clave the white-crested billows through,
    Now spangled thick with sails.

Born to this princely heritage,
They sojourned here from age to age;
    Who knoweth whence they sprung?
Though errant as the winds they roam,
Their hunting-grounds to them were home,
    To these dear haunts they clung.

Relics of their heroic sires—
Withheld from the funereal fires
    Which wrap far India's dead—
As waiting warriors calmly rest
In all their savage armor drest,
    With trophies rich bestead.

And dear to them that honored dust,
As where, in Christian hope and trust,
    We lay our dead to sleep.
Sacred—until the white man came
To obliterate their tribal name,
    Their souls in grief to steep.

When, tempest-tost, the pilgrim stood
On the cold margent of the flood,
    The Indian grasped his hand;
Bade him to rove the seas no more,
But bring his treasures to the shore
    And share the rugged land.

But soon before the favoring breeze
Came other laden argosies
    Astir with Saxon bands;
Invaders on the shore grew bold,
As wave on wave successive rolled,
    O'erspreads the shelving sands.

Victims of violated troth,
The Indian chiefs with vengeance wroth.
    Uprose to stay the flood.
Where'er the intruder chose his way,
The savage hordes in ambush lay,
    And deluged him in blood.

But ah! the pebbles on the shore
Cannot repel the sea's uproar,
　　Though countless as the stars;
The feathered shaft, the uncertain bow,
Are powerless 'gainst a steel-clad foe
　　In panoply of Mars.

Vanquished in fight, yet undismayed,
In a yet deeper everglade,
　　The sachem found retreat;
There plumed again his savage horde,
And from his lair in wrath outpoured
　　The unguarded host to meet.

At length the Chief, by foes sore-pressed,
Here, at his mountain-home sought rest,
　　In counsel with his braves.
Before,—the bog with brambles grown,
Defies approach like wall of stone,
　　Behind—the ocean laves.

In order, round his rocky throne,
High-canopied with vine-clad stone,
　　The solemn conclave meet;
The spring from out whose limpid edge
They quaff in nature's wine their pledge,
　　Flows placid at his feet.

Alone upon the mountain's head,
Where woods, and plains and seas outspread
　　In beauteous prospect lie,
The sentry stands with search intent
Graven on every lineament
　　And flashing from his eye.

He sees the hostile scouts afar,—
The heralds of advancing war,
　　Stretching from shore to shore,
The serpent's coil in deadly ring,
The doomed chiefs encompassing,
　　To crush them evermore.

Instant adown the dizzy steep,
More swift than startled reindeer's leap,
　　The faithful sentry sped;
His hurrying step the chieftains heard,
Nor paused to catch the warning word,—
　　To the deep thicket fled.

In the black mire immersed they lay,
Eluding then the fierce foray,
    Each in his grim retreat.
But the keen huntsman knew his game,
(Descendants bear his honored name
    In this, his chosen seat.)

He lingered through the live-long night
Till, passed away their wild affright,
    They lit the wigwam fire:—
Brought forth their scanty stores forlorn
All in the twilight of the morn,
    To sate their hunger dire.

Then tracked them to the tangled fen,
As beasts are baited in their den,
    And set his marksmen round.
And one, in that fierce hunt took part,
With vengeful hand and trait'rous heart,
    A Wampanoag hound.

His recreant arm the death-shot sped,
Brought to the dust that royal head,
    The peerless Metacom.
The last and foremost of his race!
Where erst *he* sought a resting-place,
    Our fathers found a home.

Doubtless it was the will of Heaven,
That o'er the coasts where once was given
    Welcome to pilgrim band,
Their sons, as forest leaves are strewn,
Should spread; assuming as their own
    Dominion of the land.

They brought intelligence and skill
The seas to span, the earth to till,
    To wave the magic rod—
Transforming quick the desert wild
To home, for Heaven's elected child,
    A Paradise of God.

Yet lives there one with heart so sere
That from his stony eyes, no tear
    On Indian graves may fall?
No pity for an outcast race
Upon whose camping-ground, through grace,
    We hold our Festival?

With foothold on th' Atlantic strand,
The Briton strove, on every hand,
    New conquests to secure.
The Indian tribes were backward borne,
Still struggling with their fate forlorn,
    Still fated to endure!

O'er stream and mountain-top afar,
Pursued by unrelenting war,
    They took their westward way;
Still following the setting sun,
The remnant of the race march on
    To the oblivious sea.

Swiftly the tide of time has run
Since from this coast to Oregon,
    The red men ruled the land!
Say if two centuries more will leave
One living representative
    Before our sons to stand?

Here in dim days of yore—
Six centuries before
Saxons sailed these waters o'er;
    Norsemen found haven!
Tread we historic ground,
Where, on the shores around,
Records of them are found
    On the rock graven.

From the bleak Norway coast,
Soon in grey twilight lost,
On the seas tempest tost,
    Launched the bold seamen!
Fear in each bosom slept;
Forth from the strand they swept,
While, on the shore, there wept
    Children and women.

Neath the cold Polar star,
Mount they the waves afar,
As on triumphal car,
    Rides the proud hero.

Down from the crystal seas,
Sweeps the chill northern breeze,
Frosts on the voyager seize,
    Cold—cold below zero!

Still on their westward way,
Lit by pale astral ray,
O'er the wild waste they stray
    Groping for Greenland.
Veered by the polar wind,
Down these coasts forest-lined,
Here clustering grapes they find,—
    Name the shore Vinland.

Skirting this shining bay,
Vines spread their rich array,
'Neath them, his roundalay
    Sang the gay sailor.
Over the biting frost—
O'er the seas tempest-tost,
O'er the stern rock-bound coast,
    Sang the prevailer.

Who, 'neath the circling sun,
Hath their bold voyage outdone,
Brave hundred fifty-one—
    Thorfin their Viking?
He with that Corsair crew
O'er the far waters blue
Gudrid, the princess, drew,
    Maid of his liking.

Under his own roof-tree,
Sped the time cheerily,
In the dark forest, she—
    Heart's troth unbroken—
On her breast, undefiled,
Bare the lone Norseman child—
Flower of the desert wild—
    Love's precious token.

Thrice had the pallid sun
Stooped o'er the southern zone,
Thrice from his height shed down
    Summer's soft burning—
When, tired of Skraelling strife,
Weary of exile life,
Norsemen, 'mid perils rife,
    Launch forth returning.

Yet, o'er the Arctic main,
Ships came and went again,
Crossing in proud disdain,
    Seas that dissever
Our Vinland's balmy clime
From Iceland's mantling rime;
But, since that primal time,
On this coast maritime,
    Norsemen dwelt never.

So has it fared, from age to age:
    Race has supplanted race;
New names are writ on history's page,
    The new the old replace.

Into the cities Canaan stored,
    The ruthless Hebrews came;
The Turk now holds them by the sword
    In false Mahomet's name.

Etruscan soil, Imperial Rome
    With power and wealth o'erspread;
The Goths despoiled the lofty dome,
    The crown from Cæsar's head.

Saxons and Normans trod, in turn,
    Britannia's sea-girt shore;
The Druids gone, their altars burn
    With mystic fires no more.

Under the crust of present life
    A buried past lies hid,
As 'neath fair fields with verdure rife,
    The cities of the dead.

We dream that we have reached the goal
    For man's achievement set,
And scout the thought that a long roll
    Of nations follows yet.

May there not rise some nobler stock
    To stand where we have stood,
To leave memorials on the rock,
    Of still transcendant good?

To touch the harmonies that wait
 In nature's depth, concealed,
Till science shall reverberate
 Religion's truth revealed;

To know no law save that of love,—
 The law that rules in Heaven;
To glow in sunlight from above,
 Through Christ's effulgence given?

To stand in pristine form restored
 God-like in soul and mien;
At set of sun to meet the Lord,
 As friends meet on the green?

The heroes of the golden age
 No pen may now portray;
We may not read th' unwritten page—
 I chant an humbler lay.

Dear shrine of my heart, bright realm of my childhood!
 Where thro' the long vista my memory strays—
The shells on the beach, the flowers in the wildwood,
 The boat on the billow, bring youth's halcyon days.

Unknown to the nations that 'yond the broad ocean
 In peace or in conflict long ages had passed,
Till, bent on adventure, with saint-like devotion,
 This fair land the Norsemen discovered, at last.

Here flowed the free rivers; the primeval forest
 O'er valleys and mountains its banner unfurled,
Till voyagers, who sought from their wand'ring no rest,
 Ope'd the gates of a continent wide to the world.

Since in these waters that compass our dwelling,
 The first sail was furled, the first anchor let fall,
Rebuke not the pride in our bosoms now swelling,
 That we live on the shores most historic of all.

No sprite of the Indian, no wraith of the Norsemen,
 Confronts us in darkness or vexes our sleep;
We trust in the God whose chariots and horsemen
 Encompass'd the prophet on Dothan's dark steep.

By the arm of the Lord we rest in these borders,
    Pioneers of religion, advancement and right;
The dominion is ours, while, true to our orders,
    We fulfil our errand and " walk in the light."

See signs of his presence where erst the bold Briton
    Drave out the rude savage and planted his home;
The dwellings, the churches, the Common we meet on,
    The raiment we wear, and the fields that we roam

King Philip again on the crest of his mountain,
    Surveying the realm he commanded of yore,
Might see the broad bay—might drink from his fountain—
    All else he once looked on would greet him no more.

To poets of old the rare instinct was given
    To forecast the future, portray it in song.
To your rhymster, alas! less favored of Heaven,
    Just the shades of the past and the present belong.

What glories may crown this fair spot by the sea,
    When the dial of time shows a century more,
I wist not, I care not, since never to me,
    Can it boast of a lustre it wore not before.

Could the men, and the beasts, and trees of the wood,
    Once spell-bound by Orpheus, be held by the Poet,
No scene should be changed, no new-fangler intrude,
    He would crystallize Bristol just as we know it.

No rock should be smitten, no landmark removed,
    The gray moss on the walls, green sedge on the shore,
All, all should remain in the guise we have loved,
    Mementoes of Eden, preserved evermore.

Generations that crowd on our footsteps, all hail!
    We vacate the homestead, our leasehold expires;
If our counsels may guide, or our prayers may prevail,
    You'll on the old hearths keep alive the old fires.

Montaup looketh down on a landscape serene;
    'Tis a garden the Master entrusts to your care.
Your art may embellish, yet not supervene
    This perfection of nature in earth, sea and air.

The stream from Helicon runs low:
The winged horse is jaded now:
The Sisters nine have tripped away,
And left me halting and astray:
Folding his wings on life's far shore,
The Cygnet dies, and sings no more!

1. The patent under which Bristol was held was given to four men, John Walley, Nathaniel Oliver, Nathaniel Byfield, and Stephen Burton. These were joined in the course of the year 1680 by twelve other men.

2. Massasoit, the chief Sachem of the Wampanoags, whose range extended from Plymouth to Narragansett Bay, was, from the first, very friendly to the English immigrants, and maintained peace with them all his days. At his death he was succeeded by his eldest son, "Wamsutta," to whom the Colonists gave the name "Alexander." In a few months after his accession, rumors reached the English that he was plotting with the Narragansetts, a large tribe, or nation, on the west of the bay. An armed escort was sent with a summons calling him to appear before the Plymouth authorities. He went, unresisting. In Hubbard's history of Indian wars, it is reported that as he returned to his people, his spirit was so chafed with the indignities to which he had been subjected, that he fell into a fever, of which he died before reaching his destination. The suspicion obtained among his people that he had been poisoned by the whites. Under such circumstances his younger brother, "Metacom," commonly known as King Philip, became the Sachem of his tribe. For a while he bore himself peaceably towards his foreign neighbors. But a sense of wrongs, real or imaginary, was all the while rankling in his breast. And at length a fierce war of extermination was commenced, in which Philip enlisted other tribes besides his own. After repeated disasters, he fell back with a few of his braves, to Mount Hope, his natural fortress, that he might take counsel with them in regard to future operations. His purpose of hostility to the whites and their encroachments, is said to have been so determined, that, when one of his counsellors advocated concession and peace, Philip slew him on the spot. Meanwhile Capt. Benjamin Church, who had already large experience in Indian warfare, had knowledge of his retreat, and, with a chosen band, drew near to attempt his capture. He might have failed in his effort, had not a brother of the man whom Philip slew for differing from him, bent on revenge, allied himself with Captain Church, and piloted him and his company to the Sachem's hiding place. This occurred on the 12th of August, 1676, four years before the settlement of Bristol. King Philip was killed in the edge of the swamp into which he was fleeing. His seat and spring on the other side of the Mount is familiar to most persons who have visited the locality.

Philip's death was the end of the great war, but his dispersed followers lurked around the white settlements ready for any kind of mischief, for which they might find opportunity, and keeping the Colonists in continual alarm.

3. In the archives of Copenhagen is a manuscript book called "Codex Flatœensis," a skin book which was finished in 1387. A carefully printed copy of it is to be found in the Library of the University of Wisconsin. In this is contained a detailed account of the voyages of the Norsemen,—their settlement in Iceland, their conquest of Norway, their discovery of Greenland and of Labrador, Newfoundland, Nova Scotia, and in the year 1000 of Vinland, under Leif, son of Eric the Red. The authenticity of these histories is recognized by Von Humboldt and Malte Brun. In 1007, Thorfinn and Gudrid, his newly married wife, set off to colonize Vinland, a region which had been so named by Lief Erickson, because he had found grapes along its shores. The expedition consisted of 151 men, and 7 women. They made their settlement, it is believed, on the shore of Mount Hope Bay. The description of the coast and the way of approach, indicate that this was the

spot; and the impression is confirmed by a singular hieroglyphic inscription on a rock at the head waters of Mount Hope Bay. It is known as the "Dighton Rock," and Scandinavian scholars have interpreted the inscription as signifying, "Thorfinn with 151 Norse seafaring men took possession of this land." At the lower corner of the inscription is a figure of a woman and a child, with the letter (S) near at hand, answering to the historic fact that Gudrid, while in Vinland, gave birth to a son, whose name was "Snorre."

After three years continuance on these shores, they were so much worried by the natives, whom they called "Skraellings," that the whole party abandoned their settlements, and returned to Norway.

See "Historical Sketch of the discovery of North America by the Norsemen in the tenth century, by R. B. Anderson, A. M., University of Wisconsin."

An inscription in characters, apparently of the same period and race, is found on a rock on the shore just north of Mount Hope.

The Boston Cadet Band then gave some selections from "Nebuchadnezzar."

This was followed by singing by the school children, of several verses of "Our Century Hymn," written for the occasion, by John H. Wardwell, Esq., of New York, a native of Bristol. The music was also arranged for the ode.

OUR CENTURY HYMN.

We celebrate our natal day,
    Two hundred years have flown,
While God our King has led the way,
    Whose guardian care we own.
Through many years of gloom and night,
    We come to this fair morn!
And peace and love with emblems bright,
    Our banners now adorn.

We gather here on this glad day,
    One Family in love;
While we our willing homage pay,
    To Him who reigns above
And standing on our native soil,
    Breathing our native air;
We recognize our parents' toil
    And their unwearied care,
Which gave us health and courage, too,
    To fight life's battles o'er;
And taught us children how to do
    What they had done before;
And never in our cause to yield
    The right! what'er the cost;
Although on bloody battle-field,
    For this our lives are lost.

Freed by their acts, from fear of kings,
    And on their native sod;
They gave us what our birthright brings,
    Freedom to worship God.

Thus pilgrims from a foreign shore,
  From mountain, or from plain,
Find welcome and an open door,
  To all our broad domain.
And never more through future years,
  May fratricidal strife,
With war's alarms, break on our ears,
  To rob us of our life.
But art and science joined in hand,
  Winged like celestial dove;
Spread their rich fruits o'er all our land,
  Combined with truth and love.

God of our fathers! hear our song
  We lift on high to Thee this day;
Be Thou our God! our life prolong
  While we our grateful homage pay
To Him, who rules the World by love,
  And by omnipotent command
The nations live! while from above
  He guides them with His gracious hand.

The last stanzas, commencing, "God of our fathers," was sung in the tune of "Old Hundred," the vast audience rising and joining in the song, the Band leading.

THE BENEDICTION,

pronounced by Rev. W. V. Morrison, D. D., pastor of the Methodist Episcopal Church, closed the exercises in the tent.

THE DINNER.

After the close of the literary exercises, about 3 p. m., dinner was served in an adjoining tent, plates having been laid for one thousand persons.

Le Baron B. Colt, Esq., President of the Committee, called the assembly to order, and the divine blessing was invoked by Bishop Clark.

The company were then invited to partake of the viands spread before them, of which the following is the

MENU.

FISH.

Salmon, Mayonaise Dressing.

MEATS.

Turkey, Beef, Tongue, Ham.

SALADS.

Lobster Salad, Chicken Salad.

CAKE.

Currant, Citron, Pound, Sponge, Jelly Roll.

ICES.

Vanilla, Strawberry, Lemon,
Coffee, Chocolate, Italian,
Pine Apple Sherbet,
Orange Sherbet, Lemon Sherbet.

FRUIT.

Bananas, Pears, Grapes.

DRINKS.

Coffee, Tea, Lemonade.

POST PRANDIAL EXERCISES.

At about 4 o'clock, dinner being over, President Colt called to order, and introduced Senator Burnside as the toastmaster of the occasion, who, on rising, said:

REMARKS OF SENATOR BURNSIDE.

Mr. President and Ladies and Gentlemen:—It has been rightly said that I have a great affection for Bristol. More than thirty years ago I first placed foot upon its soil. Soon after that I became a resident, and I have, notwithstanding the vicissitudes of my life since then, considered this as my home, at all times. I have passed all the time here that I could, and when I have been away I have longed to return to you. I feel very much gratified at having been called upon to preside as toastmaster at this meeting. I consider it very complimentary to me, and I am very proud of the honor done me. I shall proceed at once with my duties.

The first regular toast is:

The State of Rhode Island. I have the honor to call upon one of Rhode Island's distinguished citizens, now its Chief Magistrate, to respond to this toast. I take pleasure in introducing to you His Excellency Governor Littlefield.

SPEECH OF GOVERNOR LITTLEFIELD.

Mr. Toastmaster, Ladies and Gentlemen:—In behalf of the State, I extend to the town of Bristol cordial greetings on this, its two hundredth anniversary. Though venerable in years, it is by its adoption, one hundred and thirty-three years ago, into our family of towns, one of the youngest sisters in the goodly company. But in its beauty of situation and lay-out, in its record in the past and in the enterprise and intelligence of its citizens, it may well claim to be the peer of any town in the State. We can well understand and appreciate the regret of our friends of the old Bay State (turning to Colonel T. W. Higginson, of Gov. Long's staff), that a territory so attractive should have been severed from their Commonwealth; but it may be a gratification to them to see how well it has thrived under our care. The founders of the town of Bristol displayed a foresight and enterprise which has not been surpassed in the early history of any of our towns. One very gratifying result we see in the spacious thoroughfares, laid out with such convenient regularity and shaded with stately and beautiful trees. With the commercial prosperity of Bristol in former times we are all familiar. Its enterprising merchants sent their ships to the four quarters of the globe, and its wharves, laden with products of distant climes, were the scenes of varied and stirring industry. Its commercial importance has, owing to changes beyond its control, been superseded by the claims of other and, perhaps, less meritorious ports; but the beautiful harbor, in which great navies might ride at anchor, remains awaiting, let us hope, at no distant day, a return of that prosperity which it witnessed in the past. Among the many pleasant characteristics of your town, I may be permitted to note a few in which it holds an exceptional position. Within its borders it has the only mountain of the State, the place so identified with the career and fame of the brave Philip of Pokanoket. Though the town is no longer a place of meeting of the General Assembly, yet here alone are the electors of the President and Vice President authorized to meet, as soon they will again do, to cast the vote of this State for those important officers. And in one industry, at least, the enterprise and capital of your citizens have developed a business whose products are found and used throughout the land. The prominent features in the history of the town have been so ably presented by the accomplished orator of the day, and will be set forth in so much detail by the able gentlemen who will in the course of the celebration address you, that little remains for me except to congratulate you on the success of this occasion, and to wish for the town so ancient in time, but so youthful and vigorous in appearance, a continuance of the prosperity which has attended it in the past; and to hope that future generations will maintain that high standard of patriotism, that sturdy devotion to virtue, morality and religion, which their fathers have displayed, and on which rests to so great a degree the success of any community.

SENATOR BURNSIDE. The second regular toast is:

The State of Massachusetts.

A letter from His Excellency, John D. Long, Governor of that State, will now be read.

[The letter was in answer to the letter of invitation written by one of the Committee, in which he referred to the early connection of Bristol with the State of Massachusetts.]

Governor Long's reply, read by Mr. Miller, was as follows:

COMMONWEALTH OF MASSACHUSETTS,
EXECUTIVE DEPARTMENT,
BOSTON, Sept. 11, 1880.

Wm. J. Miller, Esq., Bristol, R. I.:

I am in receipt of your kind invitation to be present at the celebration of the two hundredth anniversary of the settlement of the town of Bristol. I am engaged the same day at Marlborough, in this Commonwealth, and am therefore unable to accept. If possible, one of my staff will be present, who will convey the congratulations of Massachusetts to this one of her daughters, who has gone out from the parental roof and taken up her abode in a neighboring State. If we must part with one of our towns, it relieves our regret that by its prosperity and good character it reflects so much credit upon us.

With best wishes for the occasion, I am,

Very respectfully, yours,

J. D. LONG.

General Burnside then added: Although the Governor of Massachusetts is not able to be with us to-day himself, he has sent a representative here, a member of his staff,—a gentleman distinguished in literature, distinguished for gallantry in the field, and above all distinguished for his great patriotic love of country. I take great pleasure in introducing to you Col. T. W. Higginson.

SPEECH OF COLONEL T. W. HIGGINSON.

Mr. President and Fellow Citizens:—I have the honor to appear here, as you have been told, as in a manner the representative of "the elder generation,"—the generation of Massachusetts, whose child, according to your Chairman, the town of Bristol is, and whose grandchildren, consequently, you all are—and you cannot help yourselves. (A voice: "We don't want to.") And if the daughter, as General Burnside has said, has married and left the paternal home, we can at least have the satisfaction of thinking in the old homestead that she has already done credit to the paternal stock by adding very largely to the family. Massachusetts sends you greeting, cordially and most heartily. You are very unfortunate in the fact that Gov. Long is not here himself to present that greeting. Nobody here has reason to be glad that he is not here except myself, and I am very glad, partly because it gives me the opportunity of being here, and partly, perhaps, because when I have the good fortune to go to the same place with the Governor, I sometimes have to make a speech after him,—and if you had ever tried it, you would know how hard a thing that is. If Gov. Long were here himself to address you, and if I, or anybody else were to speak after him, you would remember, perhaps, that account in the Irish newspaper of a celebrated duel, where, it said, "two shots were fired at the unfortunate gentleman; the first shot killed him; the second shot, however, was not fatal." That is the case with any shot or any speech that comes after our Governor. (Laughter and applause.) He has at this time so much of that sort of sharp shooting to do —so many towns are at this time having their anniversaries, and so many counties their cattle shows, that I am afraid if there ever was a time when he did not covet a single square inch outside of Massachusetts, that time is now. His State is quite large enough for him to have to speechify in, as it is. The time has long passed, I trust, when any such spirit of coveting exists. And I know this morning, speaking as a somewhat new-fledged citizen of Massachusetts, and a somewhat recent exportation out of Rhode Island, I found myself not absolutely coveting for Massachusetts anything which is now the possession of Rhode Island, unless it be the eloquence, the grace, and admirable candor of the orator of the day.

After all, ladies and gentlemen, this is one-half a Massachusetts occasion. At the time of that great Indian war, which was undoubtedly the greatest era in New England before the revolution—at the time of the death of King Philip (which took place by a singular coincidence in 1676), this was Massachusetts soil. Philip himself, if I remember rightly, began and ended the great scenes of his war within the limits of what is now the town of Bristol. But at any rate, it was Massachusetts then, and it was so eminently Massachusetts that I believe one of those four founders—that quartette of heroes who were celebrated this morning—I believe that Judge Byfield himself was somewhat criticised in Rhode Island for being too aggressive on the subject of the boundary line, and trying to get for Massachusetts more than belonged to her. After you had annexed to Rhode Island, I believe there was no complaint of anybody's being aggressive. It was all right then. The heroes of that day were heroes of the two States conjointly; and Colonel Church himself, undoubtedly the greatest military character in the New England Colonies, after Miles Standish, and down to the time of the revolution—Colonel Church himself divided his life with singular impartiality between these two Colonies, first colonizing Little Compton, then coming here to live when Bristol was a part of Massachusetts, then going to Fall River to live; and finally concluding that Little Compton was a good place to die in, he went back and died and was buried there. Thus closely during that period were the two commonwealths united. Thus closely may they always be united. Never, after that noble oration of to-day—so delicately discriminating what each of the early settlements contributed to the common civilization of New England—never after that oration may the old jealousies revive again. And lest they should revive, ladies and gentlemen, let me at least do justice to the character of Massachusetts, and of my chief, by not being tempted to talk to you too long. We have a saying up there, among the Governor's staff (I don't know how it is in the State of Rhode Island), that the real meaning of the word aid-de-camp is that each should be prepared to decamp as soon as possible when there is any fighting or talking to go on—and that is what I propose to do.

SENATOR BURNSIDE. The third regular toast is:

The Town of Bristol.

This will be responded to by one of Bristol's most eminent citizens, a man well posted in all her history, as he is, indeed, in all history. He needs no introduction. I will simply present to you Hon. William J. Miller.

SPEECH OF WILLIAM J. MILLER.

Ladies and Gentlemen:—In this presence you will pardon me if I feel a diffidence in responding to this sentiment. I think, perhaps, that Bristol to-day needs no one to speak for her,—that she speaks for herself in the gay attire that she has assumed; that she speaks for herself in her sons and daughters who have returned to greet her on this her natal day;

that she speaks for herself in the eminent guests who are here with us. But it seems to me very proper that for the moment that is allotted me to respond to this toast I shall glance at her early history. I naturally go back to the time when the earliest settlers came here—when they became familiar with these "Mount Hope lands," this "Pokanoket," this home of the red men—of Massasoit, the great sachem of the tribe, of whose good faith they had learned; and of his son, King Philip, whose vengeance they had felt. I want to talk to you of this "Mount Hope neck," heavily wooded, as it then was, so heavily wooded that they had to cut down sturdy oaks to make a place for the first meeting-house that was erected here, which stood, as you have been told this morning, where our Court House now stands. That building stood just one hundred years, and when it was taken down the timber was sound, and some of the same timber was put into that second house of worship; and that second church has been used for nearly one hundred years, and is now our Town Hall, where we have gathered the relics of the past, and that timber is as sound as when it was put in; and we may imagine that those oak trees had a good growth when the Pilgrim Fathers first landed in Plymouth. With these links connecting the present with the past, it seems but a span, and that we have only to put forth an arm, in order to reach and clasp hands with the fathers and mothers who landed from the May Flower.

When the four proprietors laid out this town for "a port of trade," they invited in their friends. I want to read to you the names of a few of those men. Richard Smith, the first Town Clerk of Bristol, who came here at the very beginning of the settlement of the town. On the 9th of November, 1680, Richard Smith came here, and from that date to the present, there has been no time in its history when there has not been a resident Richard Smith in Bristol, a descendant of the first Richard. His descendants are as thick, almost, as the leaves of autumn. Then there were

Benjamin Church, Isaac Waldron, Nathaniel Reynolds, William Ingraham, Nathaniel Paine, John Finney, Jabez Gorham, Hugh Woodbury, Jabez Howland, John Cary, George Waldron, William Hoar, Nathaniel Bosworth, John Gladding, Samuel Woodbury, Uzal Wardwell, Benjamin and Edward Bosworth, John Wilson, William Throop, and many others; every one of those I have named having descendants to represent them here to-day at this two hundredth anniversary celebration. Some of us can claim descent from half a score of them. These were the men who settled Bristol. "Their lines have gone out into all the earth," and their descendants are a great multitude.

For almost a hundred years, Bristol prospered and increased in population and wealth. Then came the war of the revolution, and she was baptized in fire. In the first year of the war the town was bombarded by a British fleet, and, in May, 1777, British troops marched through the town and burnt many dwellings. Every family that could, left, and her streets became desolate. After the war, most of her children returned, and the waste places were restored. Our growth from the beginning has been a slow, conservative, New England growth, up to the present time. To-day, "we raise our Ebenezer—hitherto, God has helped us." Never before in our history have there been so many happy, virtuous homes within our borders. Never before was wealth so nearly equally distributed. Never before were her people so well fed and clothed. Never before in her history have they enjoyed all the privileges of civilization as they do to-day. And I only ask, that in the future, as in the past, we may—guided by the motto on our town seal—be virtuous and industrious, and so humbly claim the protection of Divine Providence.

I will close by reading an ode written by a daughter of Bristol, now one of the teachers in our public schools, Miss A. J. Coggeshall:

BRISTOL, 1680—1880.

Our native town! whose homes within,
    Old friends are gladly meeting,
We ring thy happy birthday in,
    With joyous bells of greeting.

Many to thy loved homesteads come,
    To live their boyhood over,
And once again in thought, to roam
    The wide fields sweet with clover.

September brings his golden sheaves,
    And fruits for his bestowing,—
Within his crimson crown of leaves,
    The purple grapes are glowing.

Steadfast and bright upon our hills,
    The golden rod is shining;
The aster by our laughing rills,
    His dainty wreaths is twining.

The golden sheaves of time are ours;
    We hold in holy keeping,
The sacred gifts of mind and powers,
    Of those who low are sleeping.

The holy dead! to them we owe
    The freedom of their earning;
Honor to their blest names; the glow
    Of Heaven is round them burning!

We hail the day with mirth and song:
    But 'mid this feast of gladness,
My thoughts revert to scenes that long
    Have passed—dread scenes of sadness.

Old times return; I see once more
    The grand old forest, rounding
In wavy curves from shore to shore,
    With woodland echoes sounding.

Adown its pathless depths I hear
    Plaintive-voiced Autumn singing;
O'er vale and hill, afar and near,
    His gold-edged mantle flinging.

BI-CENTENNIAL OF BRISTOL. 79

On Mount Hope's wooded side I see
    The council fire's red gleaming;
O'er wild war-dance and revelry,
    Their lurid lights are streaming.

Once more King Philip's famous reign,
    Makes English hearts to tremble;
On Pokanoket once again,
    His painted braves assemble.

I see his rocky covert near,—
    His haunt for wily scheming;
While at its foot the waters clear
    Of Philip's spring are gleaming.

I hear the fearful war-whoop rend
    The night with sounds appalling;
While, where no timely hands defend,
    The red man's wrath is falling.

I see the dauntless forest king,
    From Mount Hope's summit glancing,
Where sun-lit isles their shadows fling,
    And gladsome waves are dancing.

O waters blue! no fairer bay
    Smiles 'neath the light of heaven;
No rosier waters stretch away,
    Beneath the skies of even.

Whether above thy western tide,
    More bright than dream or story,
The hands of Sunset open wide
The golden gates of glory; —

Or by the moonlight silvered o'er,
    Thy waves of light are sleeping:
While the hushed town along thy shore
    Her silent watch is keeping.

Fair Bristol! keep thy glad watch still,
    By Narragansett's waters,
And welcome with a right good will,
    Returning sons and daughters.

God grant that through the coming years,
    Over thy harbor streaming,
Their eyes may see through smiles, or tears,
    The lights of "Sweet Home" gleaming.

SENATOR BURNSIDE. The next regular toast is:

The Day We Celebrate.

This toast is to be responded to by my colleague in the United States Senate, who needs no introduction to you.

SPEECH OF HON. HENRY B. ANTHONY.

Mr. Toastmaster:—The day we celebrate is a proud day for Bristol, a great day for Rhode Island. On this day, the old town opens wide her doors, and invites her scattered children to come home to the parental mansion. She calls them from the fields of labor, from the workshops of toil, from the marts of trade, from the halls of study. From every part of the country and of the world, wherever they have wandered, she calls them and folds them in her maternal arms. This is a memorial period in our history. The Republic has just completed the first century of its existence, and the glad event has been celebrated with joyous congratulations, commencing with an international exhibition of the arts and industry of the world, in which our own country vindicated republican institutions, by an exposition that compared favorably with that of the older countries, and in some departments, notably in inventions and processes in the useful arts, taking the first place. The centennial anniversaries of great events that followed the immortal declaration which proclaimed our existence as a nation, have also been commemorated with due and patriotic pomp, and the valor and patriotism, the wisdom and virtues of our fathers, who flourished a hundred years ago, have been duly held up to the grateful admiration and the emulation of the present and the rising generations.

It would be strange, indeed, if the ancient town of Bristol, whose corporate existence antedates, by near a century, the independence of the country, should not join in this general jubilee of commemoration. Her history is rich in memorable events, her traditions, of romantic interest, stretch back to the colonial and to the Indian period. Among her citizens have been men of the highest distinction in commerce, in politics, in jurisprudence, and in statesmanship, and men who have made liberal benefactions to religion, to learning, and to charity. She has contributed her full share of the renown which the State has added to the renown of the nation. She has taken her position in the advance line of civilization, and has marched steadily on, keeping even pace with its advancing steps. She has a right to survey the past with an honest pride; to congratulate herself on the condition of the present, and the prospects of the future. Her citizens have taken up the matter with their usual spirit and enterprise, and with the thoroughness that distinguishes every thing which they undertake. They have marked the day by a commemoration, which will render it doubly memorable in her annals. The history of her origin, her foundation and her progress, and of the virtues of her earlier citizens, has been recited by one of the most eminent of her living sons, and her praises have been rendered by the muse of another. I can add nothing to the eloquent words and the diligent research of the first, who, having made the history of all nations his study, has brought his power of generalization and of the selection of striking detail especially to the illustration of that of his native town; and it is given to few, certainly not to me, to "build the lofty rhyme." There is something more than sentiment; there is a real value in commemorations of this kind. We cannot understand the present, nor provide for the future, without studying the lessons of the past. One of the greatest thinkers in Rhode Island, and many men eminent for thought in various departments of human study, have flourished in our borders: a man who lived just across the narrow water that divides the State, said: "Would to God that men would learn something from history! But it has been well observed that we ever place the lantern at the stern, and not at the prow. It sheds its light only on the tumultuous billows of the past. We there see the wreck of nations that have committed themselves to anarchy, tossing and heaving on the stormy surge. Yet on we go, exulting in our superiority over our predecessors, heedless of the rocks beneath the bow, until the billows on which we are borne sink beneath us and dash us into fragments." I apprehend that this graceful, elegant passage is not strictly accurate in fact; for we are told that history constantly repeats itself. The light that illumines the past also sheds its reflected rays upon the future, and gives its warning and its encouragement, by example.

Two hundred years ago! What mighty changes have taken place on the face of the globe since that time. France was then the leading power of Europe. Louis XIV., with his army of two hundred thousand men, and his fleet of one hundred men-of-war, was dreaming of the continental supremacy which was accomplished by his successor, the great Napoleon; Charles II., the purchased vassal of Louis, was holding high and dissolute revel at Whitehall; Russia was emerging from barbarism under Peter; the Turks,—if I have not got the date with entire accuracy, I deprecate the criticism of my learned friend, the orator of the day—but it was at about that time, that the Turks were thundering at the gates of Vienna, and John Sobieski was hastening to the relief of the Cross, sorely beleagued by the Crescent. The interior of the American continent was quite unexplored. A narrow line of adventurous colonization fringed the Atlantic coast; but all beyond was a pathless wilderness. The vast prairies that are now the granary of the world, that feed the millions of both hemispheres, where rise the palaces of luxury, the centres of commerce, the seats of learning, were the pastures of the buffalo, which shared them with the savage beasts and the scarcely less savage aborigines. The great rivers and lakes that now bear the commerce of an empire, were disturbed only by the sound of the paddle that drove the Indian's light canoe. Of the changes mighter than those of geographical discovery and mutations of power, the changes wrought by science and art, I do not venture to speak. To touch ever so lightly on these would open a discussion which would exhaust your patience, and far exceed the limits of time allotted to me.

Shall those who will stand here two hundred years hence, and review the proceedings of this day, have such a record of progress to look back upon? Will the race advance as it has advanced in the two centuries gone? or will civilization turn back and lose itself in darkness? No; the wonderful discoveries that have been made, in modern times, in the laws of nature and their application to the wants and uses and elevation of mankind, forbid the idea. The wildest flight of the imagination cannot reach the height that will be attained in the conditions of humanity in the next two hundred years. Things that do not now enter into the dreams of enthusiasm will have become accomplished facts. From the vantage ground of the present, the future will start to higher aspirations and to nobler accomplishments.

Let us so improve our advantages that the generations that come after us shall hold our example in the reverence that we hold those who have gone before us; that they may look upon a country, not only teeming with population and enriched by labor and art, but richer in public virtue and in united patriotism.

SENATOR BURNSIDE. The next regular toast is:

William Bradford.

This will be responded to by a distinguished citizen of Rhode Island, who has always been a great favorite in Bristol, and is identified with the town in a marked way through his ancestors. I have the pleasure to introduce to you ex-Governor Van Zandt.

SPEECH OF EX-GOVERNOR VAN ZANDT.

Mr. Toastmaster and Ladies and Gentlemen:—I have been for some time wondering exactly where an ex-Governor belongs; and since this is the first occasion of this sort that I have attended since I laid aside the emblems of office in favor of my excellent friend, who now fills the executive chair, I was affected with some curiosity to know whether or not, having been through all the offices in the State, I was now expected to begin anew and go all over them again. And I can only account, sir, for my being called upon at this somewhat early period in our festivities, by the fact that my name is linked with that of the great and the good man in whose honor this sentiment is proposed. But before I proceed to scatter, in my poor way, a few flowers over his grave, you will permit me to allude, generally, to the festivities of this occasion. It seems to me that for the last six or seven years, the air of the great republic, from the North to the South, and from the East to the West, has been filled with the sweet fragrance of its blossoming century-plants. In every State, in every town, and in almost every village, the hundredth or the two hundredth anniversary of some great event—or some event at any rate great to the people who celebrate it, has rolled around, and this morning the whole flower opened and the whole air was fragrant with its perfume. And this is the second time, my friends, that your dear old aloe has blossomed in your lovely old town; and I come here to keep the anniversary with you.

I am, as my friend has said, nearly identified with everybody in Bristol. If the toastmaster would allow it, I think I should take the liberty, even now, before I leave, of putting my arm around Bristol neck. (Laughter.) As I rode through your streets, embowered in greenness and rich with rainbow decorations that were hung out all along, I saw the smoke curling up from the grand old house on Mount Hope that stands just by the side of the place where my great-grandfather builded and lived. I passed the mansion that his hand had erected in your streets. I paused, in my heart, even if the procession did not stay its steps, in front of the house that my grandfather erected, and where my mother was born; and is it strange that I came here now, if not the son of Bristol, her grandson and her great-grandson—or perhaps I had better say that if not her son, I am her most constant lover?

And you propose a sentiment to the memory of William Bradford. So rapidly does time move on, and so fast do events tread, one upon the heels of another, that we are too apt to forget the great men in the early days of the republic. But who was William Bradford? He came from old Plymouth, in Massachusetts, a lineal descendant of the Plymouth Governor Bradford, who landed with the Pilgrims. He was for eighteen years, Mr. President, the Speaker of the House of Representatives in our State. He was a member of the Continental Congress. He was a Senator in Congress, and he was for three years Lieutenant Governor of this State.

And since this is the day of memories, you will pardon me for being a little personal; and painting for you, just for one moment, in my poor way, a picture of my childhood. I remember sitting by my grandmother—and she was blind, but now she sees—and hearing her tell, when she was nearly ninety years old, of the old days of Bristol, when it was bombarded by the British fleet, and many of the people fled from the town, or the then village, up to Mount Hope for refuge and for safety; of how Washington visited this fair town and passed a week at the Mount with Governor Bradford; of how she sat at the table with him and heard him talk; of how the two, clad in that beautiful, old-fashioned attire of black velvet—dressed very much alike—with ruffles around their wrists and at their bosoms, and with powdered hair, promenaded the piazza and talked together hour after hour. And so as she went on, and I drank in her sweet words like a bee resting on a flower, I could see the whole picture before me, and it was more vital and real to me, undoubtedly, than if I had seen it myself. She told me of the good words that Washington spoke. She showed me letters yellow with age—and some of them I now have—that he wrote William Bradford after he left here. She showed me a lock of his hair, and a lock of that of her father, William Bradford, of your own town. She suffered me to read curious letters of life in Philadelphia, when Gov. Bradford was a member of the Senate, and at the time he was in the Continental Congress—describing most graphically the political and the social life of that early period of the Republic. And so, drinking in words like those, when I was a child, remembering them ever since, I have come to love Bristol for what she then was. And since I have been in public life, I have received so many favors and honors at her hands that my affection has become a real and a personal one, for the kindness and the honor which the town of Bristol and her citizens have done me.

SENATOR BURNSIDE. Our excellent friend, Bishop Howe, will now present to you a curious manuscript book, and will read a poem by Richard Smith, his ancestor, written in 1680.

Bishop Howe then made a few remarks, introducing the literary curiosity referred to, which excited much interest. He also read a paper prepared by the venerable Bishop Smith, presiding Bishop of the Protestant Episcopal Church of the United States, who was present at the morning exercises, but was unable to attend at the dinner.

MANUSCRIPT OF BISHOP SMITH.

Friends and Fellow Townsmen:—Fearing, from my extreme old age—more than eighty-six—that I shall not be able to deliver, in person, what I am about to write, I entrust it to the care of my beloved nephew, better known to you as Bishop Howe, to read it on your festival day.

(A.) First, you will naturally desire to know what records and traditions have been brought down to our times of those of our ancestors, who were amongst the first settlers of the town of Bristol, Richard Smith, and Deacon Nathaniel Bosworth. This, being personal, may not be worthy of being read, but might perhaps be thought deserving a place in your printed record.

(B.) A larger and less questionable place may be allowed for the memorable attack upon the town, and the burning of no inconsiderable part of it, by the British troops in 1777.

(C.) The question before us of much larger and more enduring interest is, the testimony which the founder of the State, Roger Williams, bore to the great principle of perfect freedom of conscience in all religious matters.

To return to our first item, the Smith and Bosworth families amongst the first settlers. Bishop Howe will show you a little manuscript volume, given to me by the last Richard, of the original stock. It mainly consists of brief outlines of Puritan sermons, listened to by the stone mason, Richard Smith, for several years, about 1672. The double eff's, instead of the single, the odd shaped ees, and the many abbreviations, make the reading of it rather difficult. Several pages show that a little poetic blood flowed through his veins, perpetuated and highly improved amongst several of his descendants, down to this very time. On one page he commemorates a favorite son, Benjamin. On another, there is a distich. Of course, these are not at all to be compared with the higher flights of one of his contemporaries, a certain John Milton, but they shine rather conspicuously along side of another, one John Bunyan, and are very devout, which is far better : —

"Close then, my soul, Oh close with Christ, and be
"Secure from evil for eternity."

There is a tradition in the family, that the first child born in Bristol would have been his, had he not been obliged to send his wife over to Rhode Island, in order that she might have the necessary medical attendance.

There is another tradition, concerning our other ancestor, which I fear the records disprove, that Deacon Nathaniel Bosworth was one of the six first proprietors of the original six thousand acres. At any rate, in point of social position he belonged to the same class with the first proprietors. In proof of which we find amongst his children, or grand-children, the Rev. Bellamy Bosworth, a Puritan Divine, as his name shows, but of no marked zeal or fiery eloquence, as is proved by his never having had a settlement. But this anecdote shows that he was not lightly esteemed by his brethren, for, it is related, that having to go to New York, he started on horseback with a pistareen (twenty cents) in his pocket, and timing his stops at night to the distances of the Connecticut clergy, he returned safely, with the same coin on hand. For, in those days, the clergy had free passage over the many ferries and the few bridges.

My dear mother has often told me of her visits to his study, adorned, where a cornice should be, by a row of old wigs; he mounted a new one every year.

(B.) My father, Stephen Smith, and my uncle, Samuel Bosworth, were in the service of their country at the time of General Sullivan's expedition, when a corps under Lafayette was stationed on Fort Hill; the former a Commissary, the latter as his Secretary. I am not informed at what period, whether before or after this, a fleet of war vessels entered Bristol harbor, and, as a punishment for not complying with a requisition for cattle and other stores, commenced sweeping the narrow neck, at the north end of the town, with grape shot, completely preventing ingress or egress by that route, and occasionally discharging shells and balls over the town. I have often heard my uncle describe the events of that time; such, at least, as he himself witnessed, or heard discussed on the streets, at the time or afterwards. One cannon ball passing over my father's house, went through

Governor Bradford's town house, which stood somewhat above it. His old colored servant, witnessing it, immediately took up his stool and placed it before the hole, grumbling as he went, "no two balls ever go through the same hole." It is matter of conjecture whether the rush of another ball close by the head of the Rev. John Burt, the minister of the Congregational Church, was the cause of his death, but it is a fact that he was (after the bombardment) found dead, in a lot, back of his house.

A small detachment of troops, Hessians, marched through the town, burning the Episcopal Church, and several houses, and amongst them that of my father, on the very spot, where, after it was rebuilt, less than twenty years later, I was born.

A colored man, sexton of the Episcopal Church, for safety, had run off. Returning, he was told that the Church had been burnt. "Oh, no!" said he, "that cannot be. They would never burn *our* Church; besides, I am sure it is not true, for I have the key in my pocket!"

(C.) We come now to the graver and most important part of our record, not so much for the benefit of Bristol, or Rhode Island alone, as for that of all the nations upon earth, to the end of time—what Roger Williams, the founder of our State, did, for the cause of free thought and free worship, in a free State.

He fled from the severe intolerance of the National Church of England, only to encounter the rough intolerance of the Established Congregational Church in Massachusetts. He hoped to find the perfect freedom of conscience he longed for among the Baptists. For its sake he became an exile, and in time the founder and father of our small free State.

Towards the close of his eventful life, either from dissatisfaction with their organization, or their want of it, or for lack of more perfect concord or sympathy with his brethren, he seems to have withdrawn himself somewhat from them, preferring the title of a SEEKER.

All this time the fire burned within him of an intense desire for something better than toleration, however generous and free. He did not write, but he intensely felt the words I am about to quote of a distinguished author, whose name I have entirely forgotten : "Toleration, what is it? The very word is a badge of bye-gone slavery ! What does it mean? Why, that *I*, your supreme ruler and master, have a sovereign right to compel you to believe, in all religious matters, as I believe, and to worship God, as I worship Him ; but, out of mere condescension and pity, I allow you to believe and to worship as you like !"

The response was very slow to come even from Massachusetts and Connecticut, which is hard to believe, now, when there is not a State in the Union of whose very constitution it does not form a part.

If my memory serves me aright, the original Charter of Rhode Island was so very liberal in all these respects, that, whilst all the other States were adopting new constitutions, Rhode Island remained quite satisfied to live under her old charter, granted in (1663) until (1843), when the present constitution was adopted.

Soon after my ordination, in the fall of 1818, I had occasion to pass through a portion of Connecticut. I found many people greatly excited over the downfall, as it was expressed, of the Standing Order (Congregationalism), brought about (in a way that rather shocked me) by the united vote of all other denominations, and all the misbelievers and unbelievers in the State. And yet I could not but rejoice, for it was the triumph of free thought and free worship. A marked incident is thought to have contributed in no small degree to bringing it about. An intelligent and substantial Baptist farmer, it is said, for twenty successive years, bought a new Bible, which was regularly handed over to pay the enforced assessment for the established minister's salary.

Taking all the nations upon earth, there are but few who have accepted this grand idea. One of the first iron-bound governments which accepted it was Sweden. The few Baptist missionaries who have been laboring there with singular wisdom, patience, and faithfulness, have recently received permission to exist from a Protestant government. Even Russia has relaxed its severity, by acknowledging the existence of a body of pious Separatists.

Most wonderful of all, Italy, of all the European States, has come nearest to solving the problem of a Free Church in a Free State. There is entire and strict equality, both in a civil and religious sense. In France, civil freedom is well secured, but toleration, instead of equality, for the present, rules the hour.

In the more enlightened States, Germany and England, and especially in England, toleration has become and is becoming so very expansive, as hardly to be covered by that almost obsolete term.

Oh! for the coming day, when the Christian's Charter of Freedom, an open Bible in the hands of an enlightened people, shall make glad all the waste places of the earth.

It seems to be the gracious purpose of our Heavenly Father that America shall bear no secondary part in hastening the coming of that day, and God forbid that dear Rhode Island, small as she is, should be behind the very chief of all her sisters, in efforts to perfect the diadem with which Christ, at no distant day, let us hope, shall be crowned King of Nations, as well as King of Saints!!!

SENATOR BURNSIDE. The next regular toast is:

Brown University.

We are fortunate in having with us to-day, the President of this time-honored institution. I have the honor to present to you the Rev. Dr. E. G. Robinson.

SPEECH OF PRESIDENT ROBINSON.

Mr. President and Ladies and Gentlemen:—There is, perhaps, a fitness in the recognition of Brown University here to-day. The light of that institution first fell upon this State from the immediately neighboring town of Warren. That light of course fell upon the streets and homes of Bristol. The light was both of a restraining and of a stimulating influence. It was restraining. There is an incident in the history of Bristol to which the orator of the day did not allude. Soon after the founding of this town, it protected itself against evil doers by the erection of stocks and a whipping post. During the five years of the continuance of Brown University—then " Rhode Island College "—in Warren, the stocks fell into disuse, and the whipping post decayed and disappeared. Immediately after the removal of Brown University to Providence, which took place in the year 1770, the Town Meeting in 1771, ordered John Howland to re-erect stocks and a whipping-post. It was evident that the restraining influence of Brown University had been removed. Its influence has been felt among the distinguished men of this part of the State for the last century. The most distinguished sons of Bristol were graduates of Brown University. Its clergy and its gentlemen of other professions I need not enumerate. To Brown University is due not a little of the credit of the elegance, the eloquence, the philosophical spirit of that admirable oration to which you listened to-day. To Brown University is due the imagination, the rhythm, the rhyme of the admirable poem to which we listened. I need enumerate no others. Brown University is closely allied to Bristol. Bristol has to-day shown its appreciation of that institution.

Pardon me for a word personal. I have a personal interest in this celebration of the town of Bristol. The first of my own American ancestors that I know anything of was a resident of the neighboring town of Rehoboth. He was stimulated, with others, by the example of those Boston merchants who purchased this land, wrung from King Philip. They purchased what was called "The Rehoboth North Purchase," out of which were divided the town of Attleboro', in which I was first permitted to see the light, and the town of Cumberland, which belongs to the State of Rhode Island. But for the example of those Boston merchants, I should very likely have first seen light on the fair hills of Pappoosesquaw, or some other part of this town. I feel in some sense related to the descendants of the first settlers of Bristol.

But, gentlemen, I have thought to-day several times: What did Nathaniel Byfield anticipate as he looked down the centuries? Had he the remotest thought of what we to-day see, of what this town has accomplished and is to-day accomplishing? We have excelled the brighest promise of their futurity.

> "Good which they dared not hope for we have seen;
> A State whose generous will through earth is dealt;
> A State, which balancing herself between
> License and slavish order, dares be free,"—

all attributable to the principles of those from whom we descended.

I have felt, as I have to-day turned my thoughts backward and forward, how we ought to prize the *convictions* of the Puritans. It is easy to criticize them. It is easy to speak of their acrid spirit, of their controversies. I tell you, friends, it is something to have convictions. It is something to be proud of, to be descended from men who *believed*, and because they believed, dared to *do*. And all belief, and all daring, is troublesome—troublesome to those who hold the convictions; they quarrel with one another, do you say? But out of their quarrels came strength, and beauty, and order. We have entered into their heritage. And I have thought it is well for us to remember, on such a day as this, that in our spirit of calm judgment, of criticism, of deprecation of the animosities of the past, we may fail to remember that there are truths to-day endangered, as there were truths endandered in the times of the Puritans, and it is well for us to ask, What are the perils? What are the convictions—there are some views, some thoughts, some principles, political, personal, and even religious, which it is worth while to think of and suffer for, and if need be, to emigrate and die for. We are in danger of forgetting them. The founders of this town believed, among their first principles, in education. Their first provision was for the school-master and the minister—the meeting-house and the school-house—primary education, education for the child, education for the youth, education for the young man. The school, the high school, and the college are indissolubly allied. To encourage one, is to encourage the other.

Let me beg you, therefore, cherish the primary school, cherish the high school, cherish your college. Brown University is the college of Rhode Island, and it relies upon the sympathy, the support, and the friendship of the sons of Rhode Island. As an immediate neighbor of Rhode Island by birth, I feel that in a certain sense I am a Rhode Islander. Standing in my old homestead, as I almost bare one foot in Massachusetts and one in Rhode Island, and I stretch out the hand, rejoicing that I was born in Massachusetts, and equally rejoicing that I was born so near to the State of Rhode Island. So that all that belongs to the distinguished history of Rhode Island and Massachusetts—admirably blended in this town of Massachusetts origin and of Rhode Island history—we alike may cherish all that is good and praiseworthy in education and in religious teaching.

SENATOR BURNSIDE. The next toast is:

"*The Providence Light Infantry Veteran Association:*—We honor them for the interest they manifest in historic matters. Their participation in our celebration to-day, is cause for gratulation."

This toast will be responded to by a distinguished divine, who has been a great favorite in Bristol ever since he came to Rhode Island. I present to you Rt. Rev. Bishop Clark.

SPEECH OF BISHOP CLARK.

Mr. Toastmaster and Ladies and Gentlemen:—It is natural that our Veteran Association should manifest an interest in historic matters. We ourselves are beginning to be historical, and yet we hope the time is far distant, when it will be said of us,

"Superfluous lag the veterans on the stage."

We are glad that we were not so far advanced in years, as to prevent us from participating in this delightful celebration. We have marched with you through your pleasant streets, and seen how the old town of Bristol still continues to glow with the life and joy of youth. You have inherited a goodly legacy from your fathers.

I have been asked on this occasion just "to say a word." That I consider equivalent to a request that I shall not make a *speech*. I am very glad it is so. It seems to me somewhat of an impertinence for anybody who has not had the good fortune to be born and bred in Bristol to make any appearance on this occasion. After such indications of transcendent talent and complete culture as have been presented to us to-day, both by the orator and the poet, and by others who have spoken, it seems becoming in all outsiders to keep silence.

There is one thing about Bristol which is not so peculiar to this place. It belongs to all these decayed seaboard towns, in one of which I had the good fortune to be born and bred—the old town of Newburyport, Massachusetts, which was a kind of fac-simile of Bristol. It is a peculiarity of these places that all their children seem to cherish a very special attachment to their birth-place. Wherever they go —and they have the faculty of going almost everywhere— their motto seems to be always: "My heart untravelled, still turns,"—well, to Bristol, or Newburyport, or wherever the place may be. And so, to all Bristol people, Bristol is the centre of all things, the centre of their affections, the centre of the land, the centre of the world, and in some sense the centre of the universe.

Now this is a feeling worth cherishing; for a man who does not care about the place where he was born, cannot be good for much. To be sure if it had been our fortune to be born in the centre of one of the great flat prairies of the West, where there is nothing of mountain or valley, or forest, or brook, or stream, to vary the landscape, it might be difficult to get up any attachment to our birth-place. But with such surroundings as you have here, there is no such difficulty. And even the old mouldering peculiarities of the place—the quiet streets, the ancient, weird sail-lofts down on the wharf, and the little relics that remain of a past commercial prosperity, have their peculiar charm, and they hold us as with an iron grasp. We never get away from the influences and associations of our native town.

I rejoice to have been here to-day. I rejoice in the fact that so many of the sons and daughters of Bristol have come home to their old mother to do her honor. And if any of us are so fortunate as to live to meet our successors here on the next centennial, I hope that we shall cherish the memory of those who have addressed us to-day, and who have left an impression upon our minds which is indellible.

SENATOR BURNSIDE. The next regular toast is:

The Rhode Island Historical Society.

This will be responded to by one of Rhode Island's distinguished and venerable citizens, President of the Historical Society, Hon. Zachariah Allen, of Providence.

BI-CENTENNIAL OF BRISTOL.   97

SPEECH OF HON. ZACHARIAH ALLEN.

Mr. President and Ladies and Gentlemen:—The members of the Rhode Island Historical Society join, with others, in cordially congratulating the good people of Bristol on the two hundredth anniversary of the planting of their pleasant town. They all unite also in praising the hospitality they have received, and in complimenting the distinguished citizen who has enlightened them by presenting some of the historical details, to the study of which he has been devoted professionally during his entire life. Still his allusion, in the course of his remarks, to the good old Massasoit, has opened a field which deserves further investigation concerning the merits of that noble chief, and concerning the friendship which existed for many years between him and the founder of the State of Rhode Island. Having investigated this subject for some time past, I have become convinced that had it not been for the befriending of Roger Williams by Massasoit, and his hospitable reception of him when he was expelled from Massachusetts and fled into the wilderness, he would have been sent away from Boston on board the vessel then waiting in the harbor, and transported back to England, precisely as the two brothers Brown had been transported back to England, for their opinions in matters of religion. He had, however, some place to flee to, sure friends to receive him during those cold, bitter days of winter; otherwise he must have been carried across the water, and could not have been the founder of the State of Rhode Island. I look upon it, therefore, as owing especially to the friendship of Massasoit, that Rhode Island now exists. There would not have been any Rhode Island had it not been for that friendship; for the Massachusetts people would have absorbed this State as they soon afterwards absorbed the other little colonies, and amalgamated them into one. There would have been no establishment here of religious liberty, or of a constitutional basis of a free State. I hope that the discussion of this theme, which has been opened by the historian to-day, may be further pursued, and that due justice and credit may be awarded to Massasoit in this regard.

The following poem is from the pen of a son of Bristol "by adoption," his wife being a native:

POEM ON THE BI-CENTENNIAL CELEBRATION.

BY E. W. ROBBINS, A. M.

Two hundred years have come and gone—
  Of sunshine and of shade.
Since on this memorable spot,
  In faith and prayer were laid
The first foundations of this town,
  Distinguished in our State,
Whose annals at the old hearth-stone,
  To-day we celebrate!

'Tis well at this convivial board
  We should their deeds recall—
Immortal founders of the race,
  In our home festival—
WALLEY, and BYFIELD[1], OLIVER,
  And BURTON, with their peers,
(Whose names these trees[2] perpetuate)
  Of the two hundred years—

Descendants of the Pilgrim sires,
  (Sprung from no common stock),
Who trod the May Flower's wintry deck,
  And hallowed Plymouth Rock—

---

1. The Byfield School—so called in honor of Hon. Nathaniel Byfield, this early benefactor to the town—is his latest, and, perhaps, best monument. The late Rev. Dr. SHEPARD, pastor of the Congregational Church, whose portrait hangs side by side with that of Judge Byfield, in the above building, was no less devoted to the cause of education.

2. Referring to the planting of four memorial trees on the Common, in honor of the four founders of the town.

Howland[1] and Bradford[2]—him renowned
   Alike with sword and pen,
Of Plymouth Colony the chief—
   A princely man of men.

Nor in this brief review forgot,
   (Perchance left in the lurch)
The brave Miles Standish of his time,—
   Heroic Captain Church,[3]
Who eminent in *Church* and State,
   An added laurel wore,—
Who slew the Wampanoag's pride,
   And its dread Sagamore!

Two hundred years have come and gone—
   And Bristol sits to-day,
Nor yet like Venice—discrowned Queen,
   By her bright, beauteous bay,
Still musing on her splendors past,
   Which this gay sight recalls,—
On her rich freighted Argosies,
   And her Armada walls,—

(Save, where invaded by the foe,
   In scene of ruthless strife,
The flaming fire-brand[4] was applied
   To desolate her life;)
In factory and dock-yard, now,
   Once more the stranger greets
The hum of active industry
   Resounding in her streets.

---

1. John Howland, (a lineal descendant of whom, Mrs. Rebecca Smith, has lately deceased at the great age of nearly 99 years). From him are derived the Howlands of Newport and Bristol.

2. Hon. Wm. Bradford, second Governor of Plymouth Colony, was both a military leader and an historian. His son, Wm. Bradford, was Deputy Governor of the same Colony. Governor Wm. Bradford, of Rhode Island, was his lineal descendant; also, Major Wm. Bradford. These still are represented by their descendants, living in Bristol.

3. Capt. Benjamin Church, a son of Richard Church, was born in Plymouth, Mass., and married Alice Southworth, the granddaughter of the distinguished wife of the first Governor Bradford. He was at the head of the party by whom King Philip was slain in the swamp at the foot of Mount Hope.

4. Bristol was invaded by the combined forces of the British and Hessians, May 25, 1777, resulting in the burning of a part of the town, and the taking of some prisoners. Before this, in 1775, a British squadron fired on the town.

Nor yet unfitting in this place
Their praises just, to speak,
The proof of whose munificence
We have not far to seek—
You graceful structures late proclaim,
Which to our view appear—
Religion, Education, both
Have found their patrons[1] here!

Then, to hand down to future times
The glories of this day,
Let the historian[2] weave his web—
The poet[2] sing his lay—
As rises near yon eminence,
With its green, beckoning slope,
One backward glance to—*Memory*—
The future trust to—HOPE![3]

KENSINGTON, Berlin, Conn., September, 1880.

1. The Memorial Chapel of the Congregational Church, and the Rogers' Free Library, will long perpetuate—the former, the memory of the munificent donors, Miss Charlotte DeWolf, and Mrs. Maria DeWolf Rogers, whose modesty is equalled only by their benevolence—the latter is the gift of Mrs. Rogers, in memory of her deceased husband, Mr. Robert Rogers.

2. The historian, and poet, of this occasion.

3. Mount Hope. To those not "to the manner born," it will be enough to say, that it is a picturesque and romantic height in Bristol, R. I., and noted as being the residence of Philip, the Chief Sachem of the Wampanoags.

SENATOR BURNSIDE. The next regular toast is:

The Honored Dead.

This toast will be responded to by the Hon. J. Russell Bullock.

SPEECH OF JUDGE BULLOCK.

Mr. Toastmaster, Ladies and Gentlemen:—In responding to this sentiment, it will not be expected that I should speak of the many men, now gone, who in their day and generation filled important official stations among us, and exercised a controlling influence both in the councils of the town and of the state. There was Simeon Potter, and Governor Bradford, and after them Judge Bourn, and James D'Wolf; all stalwart men, eminent in their various callings, and the impress of whose lives remain among us, even unto this day.

I shall come down to a later generation, and speak of one whom I knew, and who, descending from an early settler of Bristol, was himself born here, passed here the three-score and ten years allotted to life, and was here gathered to his fathers; and who, so far as I know, has been the only native of Bristol ever chosen to the office of Governor of the State. I refer to BYRON DIMAN.

After receiving the usual academic education of his day, Governor Diman entered the counting-room of the late James D'Wolf as a clerk, and remained there many years, and until the death of that eminent merchant. During the latter part of Mr. D'Wolf's life, Governor Diman became his confidential adviser, and was entrusted by his employer with large and responsible business duties. After his death, Governor Diman was intimately associated with the acting executors of Mr. D'Wolf's will, in the care, management, and settlement of his large estate. This embraced extensive and complex landed, commercial, and manufacturing interests, in different States, and in a foreign country.

This service to the family of his late friend and early patron, no one else could render as he could; but he rendered it cheerfully, and in some measure without a compensation adequate to its value, and often under circumstances of embarrassment and disadvantage to himself; for there was no *streak* of avarice in his composition.

In person, Governor Diman was tall, well proportioned, erect in mien, and of a commanding presence.

In character, he was what I call a *large-hearted* man, hospitable, a good neighbor, public spirited, generous, charitable to the poor of every sect, loving his friends, and *not* hating his enemies.

In politics, Governor Diman was a Henry Clay Whig, and a Puritan of the Plymouth Rock school in his religion. He early imbibed these principles, and whatever change of name these principles underwent through the mutations of time and parties, he still adhered to them, or what he believed to be the representative of them, to the close of his life. Strong and sincere as he was in these his beliefs, he was ever tolerant of the opinions of others.

Governor Diman was the most *observing* man I ever knew. When business called him, as it often did, away from his home, he saw everything, and appreciated and remembered everything that he saw. His power in this respect was remarkable. And this knowledge so acquired did not lay *loose* in his mind. He analyzed it and weighed it, and applied it to use in life. In conversation he would often draw from this store-house, much to the amusement and instruction of his friends.

For many years it was my good fortune to sustain intimate personal, political and professional relations with Byron Diman. I never knew him to harbor an unworthy motive, or be guilty of an ignoble act to others.

He served his town and state in many public trusts. He was often elected to represent Bristol in the House of Representatives, several times in the State Senate, for three successive years he was chosen Lieutenant-Governor, and in 1846 was chosen Governor. His official duties he discharged with uniform ability and fidelity. His official honors he wore with becoming modesty.

The traditions and early history of his town, Governor Diman was quite familiar with, and he loved to dwell upon them. He took a deep interest in whatever promoted its well being and prosperity.

In our past annals may be found men more successful as merchants, more distinguished as legislators, more eminent and highly gifted as public speakers; but no grave in that ancient cemetery near by us, or in those on yonder hills, holds the mortal remains of a more devoted son of Bristol, or of a truer Rhode Islander, than the grave of Byron Diman.

The "feast of reason" at the table ended all too soon, leaving much unsaid that would, otherwise, have been spoken. There were many honored guests present, other than those who had spoken, to whom it would have been a delight to listen, had time permitted. Notably of this number we take pleasure in naming the venerable Rev. JOEL MANN, of New Haven, Conn., who, albeit in his *ninety-second* year, was able to make the journey from New Haven to Bristol unattended. He rode in the procession, and was present at the table. Mr. Mann came to Bristol in 1815, and for twelve years was associated with the late Rev. HENRY WIGHT, D. D., grandfather of the historian of the day, in the pastoral charge of the Congregational Church. He resigned in 1827, and removed from Bristol; yet, during the more than half a century that has since elapsed, he has kept up his interest in the town and its people, and made frequent visits here.

But the "low declining sun" admonished that the "flow of soul" must cease, and our distinguished Toastmaster was reluctantly compelled to close the exercises in the tent, in order that the "Tree Planting" might be proceeded with on the Common.

MEMORIAL TREES.

The planting of four MEMORIAL TREES, to the memory of the original proprietors of the town, came immediately after the exercises in the dining tent.

The committee having charge of this matter, had in early spring placed this number of trees in large casks, and after they had formed a part of the public procession of the day, were then each put in their intended places.

The one north from the centre of the Common was first planted.

Mr. Babbitt, the chairman of the committee, in introducing the subject, spoke as follows :

REMARKS OF EDWARD S. BABBITT.

Fellow Citizens, Sons and Daughters of Bristol, and Visiting Friends:—We have come to the concluding and most important part of our celebration. What we have listened to with so much profit and pleasure will soon be forgotten, and, if desired, must be sought from between the covers of a book; and the remembrance of the feast from which we have just risen will soon be lost with our departure. But the result of that which we now propose to do will continue on for ages to come. While the wide-spreading branches of these trees catch the heat and moisture of heaven, and their deep-reaching roots draw from the earth their strength to put on each year their livery of green, they will ever be honoring the memory of those who formerly owned the very ground from which they draw their life. Let us hope that all who follow us, as they see these evidences of our appreciation of the work done by the original proprietors of the town, will be inspired to keep green in their memory the names of those whose wide views and generous impulses gave us this ample Common, our wide, tree-lined avenues, and stamped upon the town that which now renders it so inviting to all who visit it. By this act of ours, we say all honor to the memory of BYFIELD, WALLEY, BURTON and OLIVER. Let their names have a living existence in these trees.

THE NATHANIEL OLIVER TREE.

The tree now planted is to keep alive the name of Nathaniel Oliver, and his successor, Nathan Hayman. We are most fortunate in having with us to-day a direct descendant of Nathaniel Oliver, and separated from him by only three removes, Gen. Henry K. Oliver, now Mayor of Salem, Mass.

REMARKS OF GEN. OLIVER.

After brief introductory remarks, expressive of his gratification at participating in the ceremonies of the day, Mayor Oliver said: In the year 1632, there came from England to Boston (and, for satisfactory reasons, it is believed from the old city of Bristol, whence, perhaps, the suggestion of the name of your town), an emigrant Puritan bearing the name of Thomas Oliver. He was a "chimegeon" (surgeon) by profession, and brought with him his wife Anne, and seven children, they coming in the ship Lyon, with the family of Governor Winthrop, the Governor having himself preceded them, and landing at Salem in 1630. Thomas Oliver appears to have been greatly respected and beloved in the young town, and I find that by a vote of the people in 1646, it was declared that no horses should be kept on Boston Common among the seventy cows allowed to pasture there, "except that the horse of good Elder Thomas Oliver may continue there." He was Ruling Elder of the First Church of Boston, "distinguished as an apt scholar, occasionally preaching, and highly esteemed for his gentleness of temper, generous heart, pure life, and liberal public service." Very many of his descendants have been graduates of our colleges, and many distinguished in professional, mercantile, and public life. Of forty-five Olivers who are alumni of Harvard and Dartmouth, up to the present date, thirty-six are known to be his descendants, and there are very many more from intermarrying families, bearing, of course, other names ; among them being Brattles, Hutchinsons, Lyndes, Bradstreets, Wendells, Prescotts, Vintons, and Appletons.

Of the seven children of Thomas Oliver, one of them, Nathaniel, was, in 1633, most unfortunately, most sadly, and suddenly killed by the fall of a tree, which he, then a lad of fifteen years of age, was felling, whilst his father was at work near by. The sadness of that event, and the tenderness of heart which ensued, caused the name of Nathaniel to be perpetuated for the coming generations, and it has been continued down to the present day.

The Puritan Thomas had a son Peter, a Boston merchant, who, by his wife Sarah Newdigate, had a son, Nathaniel Oliver, whom I will call your Nathaniel Oliver. Born in Boston, in 1652, he there married (in 1677) Elizabeth, daughter of Thomas and Elizabeth (Tyng) Brattle. This Nathaniel, by his wife Elizabeth (Brattle), had, in 1684, a son Nathaniel, who, graduating in 1701, at Harvard, became a Boston merchant, marrying, in 1709, Martha Hobbs, a rich heiress, by whom he had a son Nathaniel, in 1713,— who, graduating at Harvard in 1733, became a lawyer in Boston, where he married, in 1741, Mercy, daughter of Hon. Jacob Wendell, their son, Nathaniel, born in 1744, dying in 1750. Another son, Rev. Daniel Oliver, born in 1753, and graduated at Dartmouth in 1785, had, also, by his wife, Elizabeth Kemble, a son Nathaniel K. G., born in 1790, a graduate of Harvard in 1809, brother of the present speaker. He was a lawyer and teacher, dying in 1832, and leaving a son, by his wife Anne T. Hunt, named also Nathaniel (Cordis), born in 1830, and dying unmarried in 1863. There thus appears a sequence of eight Nathaniel Olivers, and there were others in other branches of the family. Your Nathaniel Oliver was a Boston merchant, and a most sagacious, most successful, most thoughtful, most highly accomplished and enterprising gentleman. He achieved a fortune, which for those days was considered simply enormous, namely, a sum something near £5,000 sterling, the purchasing power of which at this day would be upwards of $200,000. In connection with the gentlemen whose names have been repeated to you very often to-day, he joined in the projection of this town. Seeing its very great beauty now for the first time— seeing the beauty of its streets, the intellectual beaming of the faces of its men and the beauty of its women, I regret that he did not come here to live, that I, his great-great grandson, might have been born here within your limits, and perhaps, an owner of some of his fair possessions. It is a remarkable thing and a very sad thing to their remote generations, that great-great grandfathers never think much of their great-great grandchildren. And it seems to me that ought not to be so; for why should not a reasonable man of ordinary aspirations desire to own two or three acres down here in the middle of your town, for instance—which might have come to my share if my great-great grandfather had only thought of me? My friend, Col. Higginson, in a speech which he delivered a while ago in behalf of Gov. Long, on the two-hundredth anniversary of the landing of Winthrop, said that he wished his ancestor had let him have Salem Neck, and I really wish that I had some such share of my great-great grandfather's property here; but he sold it to Nathan Hayman, as I understand it; so that I was entirely cut off, and it don't strike me as just the fair thing. Cannot you correct the blunder? (Laughter.) By the way he was about twenty-eight years of age when he entered into this enterprise, but I learn that although selling out, he never lost his interest in the town of Bristol. He kept it alive all his days, and he presented to you in those early years a bell which, as you were then a small people and had not the benefit of a tall steeple, was swung up in some tree which my records tell me was on the northwest corner of State and High streets, within sight and sound, I believe, of this place. It was swung in a tree—and that suggests to me some incidents in the history of my own town of Salem, where in 1662 certain bells of another kind, sometimes called beldames, were hanged upon trees. It is pretty well known that our good old town is renowned for the persecution of persons alleged to have been wizards and witches, who were accused, tried, condemned, and hanged. And not only did they hang the he-witches, but they hung she-witches, including one Mrs. Bridget (Oliver) Bishop, one of our tribe; and it is on record that they squeezed to death a certain Goodman Giles Corey, by enclosing him between mother earth and a stone-laden plank, as though it were possible to exterminate witchcraft by neck-roping, or by killing weight. Why, my friends, the witchery of Salem women has been transmitted all along its subsequent history, and prevails in full force to this day, and there is no respectable young man who reaches the age of twenty years, without being "bewitched" as I was sixty years ago. I know it is so, and bear personal testimony to the fact. Now the later and latter witches, distinguished for intellect and for beauty, and practical common sense, have never objected to the process of squeezing, if performed with a reasonable degree of pressure, the squeezers gently tempering the force to the squeezees, and not overdoing the thing.

Well, your Nathaniel Oliver also appeared in behalf of your town at the General Court of Massachusetts, and remained during all his life (dying in 1707) a fast friend of the town of Bristol. Moreover he was a man of energetic pluck. There was no cowardice in him—no shrinking from principles. He was of just that class which the President of Brown University so admirably portrayed at to-day's dinner, and when that tyrant Andros got to be very obnoxious, Nathaniel Oliver, with his brother-in-law, Col. John Eyre, and eleven others (thirteen in all) drew up a protest and demanded a surrender by Andros of all power that he held under the Crown. Sir Edmund had to take refuge within the fort at Boston. Nathaniel Oliver, with his brother-in-law, bore the summons for his surrender, presented it to him, and he succumbed. He yielded, and resigned the Governorship of Massachusetts. Now I like to think of an ancestor who would do a thing of that sort without fear or favor. If you feel any gratitude toward him, I feel a great pride in him. Let me say to you, if you have any pleasure in it, that the family of Oliver in the eastern part of Massachusetts has been connected by relationship and historic association with all the ancient families of that commonwealth.

Nathan Hayman, to whom Nathaniel Oliver sold out, came here, lived here, and died here, leaving no issue, as far as I can learn. He lies buried about six feet from the east wall of the Eastern Cemetery, and buried there, his grave-stone, I understand, was found and turned to account as a useful point by which to verify the location of the avenues and streets of your beautiful town.

So, then, in memory of your and my Nathaniel Oliver, and in memory of Nathan Hayman, I dedicate this tree and plant it. May the dews and waters of heaven, the warmth of a genial sun, and the blessing of a divine Providence, cause the tree to take root and grow, and live to shelter those of your descendants who may take refuge beneath its boughs.

At the conclusion of the address and whilst the earth was being placed about the roots of the tree, a selection of music was rendered by the Boston Cadet Band.

THE STEPHEN BURTON TREE.

The tree east of the centre of the Common was next planted. The chairman introduced the speaker as follows :

We have been unable to find any descendant from Stephen Burton to dedicate this tree to his memory, but would introduce to you our townsman, Wilfred H. Munro, who has kindly consented to speak to us in his behalf.

ADDRESS OF WILFRED H. MUNRO.

Mr. Chairman, Ladies and Gentlemen:—As the name of Stephen Burton is pronounced, there rises before my eyes the figure of a tall and slender man, whose appearance is in marked contrast with that of his two more prominent associates. He does not show the intense vitality and the imperious will which every action of Byfield proclaims; neither does he possess the great executive ability which is manifest in the easy bearing of Walley. His brow is seamed with the lines of anxious thought ; his face is pale and thin ; his bent head and stooping shoulders indicate the scholar rather than the man of business, while his restless eye and sallow cheek hint at the existence of some trouble which he is vainly seeking to avoid.

The rays of the setting sun warn me that I must attempt only the briefest possible sketch of the career of Mr. Burton. He was the most scholarly man of the four proprietors, and is said to have been educated at the University of Oxford. Beyond this we know almost nothing of his life in England and in this country, until his name appears as one of the purchasers of the Mount Hope lands. He was the first recording officer of the county of Bristol. In his office of Clerk of the Peace, he exercised the functions which are now divided among several different officers. He was at the same time Clerk of the Court of Common Pleas, Register of Probate, and Register of Deeds. The care with which he performed the duties of his position is indicated in his clear and beautiful handwriting, and the fact that he was five times chosen to represent the town at the General Court of Massachusetts, shows how highly he was esteemed by his fellow townsmen. Quiet and retiring in disposition, he seems to have had no share in the disputes in which his associates were often involved. Against the mental disorder which was preying upon him, he struggled manfully until the last year of his life, but being at last unnerved by its constant attacks, neglected his business and became only the wreck of his former self. Death came mercifully to his relief before his reason gave way under the terrible strain. He died on the 22d or July, 1693, the only one of the four original proprietors who ended his days in Bristol. Byfield, Walley and Oliver all died in Boston. His house stood upon Burton street, until it was burned by the British troops in 1777.

The elm which is here planted to his memory fitly typifies his character. Symmetrical is its form, and fair appears its promise, but ere long its limbs will begin to droop as did the spirit of him whom it commemorates, under the weight of the trouble which at last wore his life away. It will not command our admiration and respect, as will the massive strength of the Byfield oak, but its slender limbs will ever appeal touchingly to us for sympathy, even as the gentle nature of Burton appealed to the kindly feelings of our ancestors two hundred years ago.

The John Walley Tree.

The tree south of the centre of the Common came next in turn. As in the former case, the committee was unable to obtain the services of any descendant of John Walley for this interesting duty, being disappointed in their hopes that Hon. Wendell Phillips, or Henshaw B. Walley, of Boston, as such, would be present; but sickness prevented, and the duty of the occasion was discharged by William J. Miller, of Bristol, R. I., as follows:

ADDRESS OF WILLIAM J. MILLER.

Mr. Chairman, Ladies and Gentlemen:—The proprietor in whose honor we plant this tree is JOHN WALLEY. Mr. Walley was an earnest co-worker with Byfield and his associates in the settlement of the town, and took a leading part in the affairs of both church and State. His father was Rev. Thomas Walley, of London, at one time rector of St. Mary's, Whitechapel, and who, with seven other divines, arrived at Boston, from London, in the "Society," Capt. Pierce, on the 24th of May, 1663. He died March 24th, 1678, aged 61 years.

John came to this country before his father, and settled in Boston. He removed from Boston to Bristol in 1680. The substantial structure that he built, and in which he resided, is still standing on the north side of State street, and is known as the Walley House. While a resident of Boston he was successfully engaged in mercantile pursuits. He was for a time Judge of the Superior Court of Massachusetts, and a member of the Governor's Council. In 1690, ten years after he had become a resident of Bristol, he commanded the land forces in the expedition of Sir William Phipps against Canada, and published a journal of the same. In the latter part of his life he returned to Boston from Bristol, and died there on the 11th of January, 1712, aged 68 years.

His biographer says: "The high trusts imposed by his country were discharged with ability and fidelity. To his wisdom as a councillor and his impartiality as a judge, he added an uncommon sweetness and candor of spirit, and the various virtues of the Christian. His faith was justified by his integrity, his works of piety and charity."

THE NATHANIEL BYFIELD TREE.

The tree west of the centre of the Common was next in turn, and in this case the committee was as fortunate as in the first planted. They had secured the services of Hon. Francis Brinley, of Newport, five removes from Nathaniel Byfield, who, in the following address, dedicated the tree to his ancestor:

ADDRESS OF HON. FRANCIS BRINLEY.

When in the gladsome days of youth I used to contemplate with honest pride the old family portrait of Judge Byfield, it never flitted across my mind that I should be invited to participate in ceremonies designed to commemorate the settlement of this ancient town, of which he was one of the original founders. Yet such is the curious mutation of human events, that here I stand environed by the sunny landscape, and the sparkling waters, whose combined charms, two hundred years ago, attracted his observant eye, and induced him to make this picturesque spot his chosen home. Here I am almost in sight of the place where stood his modest mansion, and of the secluded grave in which he reverently laid the loved and the lost.

I am aware of the necessity of reducing to shape compact what I have to say in regard to Nathaniel Byfield. I will endeavor to comply with the proprieties of the occasion, and content myself with but little more than an enumeration of some of his distinguishing characteristics, and of his public honors.

He was born in England in the year 1653. His father was the Rev. Richard Byfield, the laborious, faithful pastor of Long Dutton in Surrey, and one of the divines of the famous "Westminster Assembly." His mother was of the noted family of the Juxons. He was the youngest of twenty-one children, and one of the sixteen who, on bright and calm Sabbath mornings, followed their pious parents to the house of public worship. How irresistably spring to mind the lines of Coleridge:

> "O, sweeter than the marriage feast,
> 'Tis sweeter far to me,
> To walk beside thee to the kirk
> With a goodly company;
> To walk together to the kirk
> And all together pray.
> While each to his Great Father bends—
> Old men, and babes, and loving friends,
> And youths and maidens gay."

I have not been able to detect even a glimmering of the motives which prompted him to leave the delights of the domestic hearth for the hardships of a residence in this western world. Probably it was the early manifestation of that activity and spirit of enterprise which were so strikingly exhibited in his subsequent career. He arrived in Boston in the year 1674. About a year thereafter he married Deborah Clarke, an estimable gentlewoman of Boston, with whom he lived most happily for over forty years. She died much lamented in 1717.

Judge Byfield was married twice, his second wife being (to use a phrase applied to her) "the honorable and devout daughter" of Governor Leverett.

By his first wife there were five, his only children, three of whom died when young; the other two lived to be married, the younger one to Lieut.-Gov. Tailer, and the other to Edward Lyde, Esq., of Boston. A daughter of Mr. and Mrs. Lyde married Col. Francis Brinley, of Roxbury, my great-grandfather.

Not long after the termination of King Philip's war, the General Court of Massachusetts appointed a committee to sell the Mount Hope lands, and on the 14th of September, 1680, they were conveyed to John Walley, Nathaniel Byfield, Stephen Barton, and Nathaniel Oliver, all of Boston.

Byfield removed to this place the year of its incorporation as the town of Bristol. Here he lived until the year 1724, when, by reason of his advanced age, he concluded to return to Boston, his first home, where he died on the 6th of June, 1733, in the 80th year of his age.

He was a devout Christian. The love of religion, which was impressed upon him in youth by his exemplary parents, was never effaced. It guided him through his long life, and will account for the respect and confidence which his very presence inspired.

Before the tapering spires of churches invaded the blue sky of Bristol, the doors of his house were always open to those who wished to worship God in sincerity and truth. When a Congregational Society was duly organized here, he presented to it a communion service, which is yet preserved for the sacred use for which it was intended.

On the return of Judge Byfield to Boston, he joined the Society of which the Rev. Charles Chauncy and the Rev. Thomas Foxcroft were the joint pastors. The former preached a sermon on the death of Judge Byfield, which was printed in 1733, together with a valuable prefix by Mr. Foxcroft. Both of these clergymen testify to the profound religious character and the diffusive benevolence of Judge Byfield, who made it a rule for forty years, annually to give away, or pay, as he preferred to say, a certain portion of his income for charitable purposes.

Byfield, like the eminent author of the Decline and Fall of the Roman Empire, showed by his example that he considered a citizen soldiery the cheapest and safest defence of natural freedom. Gibbon, in his autobiography, states with apparent satisfaction, that the information he obtained as a member of a militia company enabled him to comprehend, appreciate, and describe the complex organizations of the vast armies of Imperial Rome. It is most probable that the habits of order, regularity and exactitude which Byfield acquired in the ranks, or as an officer up to the rank of Colonel, were carried by him to the performances of all official duties, and to the management of his private affairs. So wisely did he conduct the latter, that he accumulated a handsome estate, for those days, which he liberally used. It may be said of him, as Gibbon states of Antoninus Pius, "he enjoyed with moderation the conveniences of his fortune, and the innocent pleasures of society."

Colonel Byfield, as an additional proof of his high estimate of the citizen soldiery, presented to the first military company of Bristol a costly stand of colors, to this day carefully preserved with the archives of the town.

He was an ardent, active and efficient politician of conservative principles. But he was not so rigid and exclusive as to prevent him from accepting a new idea, or fresh suggestion, merely because it did not present itself in an antique garb. He was conservative, but reasonably progressive. For several years he represented Bristol in the General Court, and was elected Speaker of the House of Representatives. He enjoyed a similar honor when a Representative from Boston. He was a patriotic and experienced statesman.

It should always be passed to his credit that he deprecated the witchcraft delusion, and denounced those who were active in the trial and conviction of the unfortunate accused.

His judicial career was most remarkable. For thirty-eight years he sat as Chief of the Court of Sessions of the Peace and Common Pleas for the county of Bristol, as he did two years for the county of Suffolk. From 1702 to 1710 he was Judge of Probate for the county of Bristol. He received five several commissions as Judge of the Vice Admiralty, from three sovereigns of England—from King William, from Queen Anne, and from King George II. So that for years he was Judge of Probate, Judge of the Court of Common Pleas, and of the Admiralty at the same day.

In those days the community was not overwhelmed by that cataclysm of Law Reports which now so cruelly affects both the bench and the bar. Hence very little is preserved of his judicial opinions. I chance, however, to possess one of them in his own clear hand-writing, attested by his signature, which, for perspicuity of style and legal acumen, would not discredit any jurist.

Not one of his decrees was overruled by appeal to the home tribunals.

Finally, in my judgment, one of the most valuable of his varied excellences was his early and energetic labors as an advocate of public schools, or popular education. He believed, and acted on the conviction, that if the youth of a community were shrouded in intellectual darkness, the result would be as detrimental to the common weal as the destruction of the spring would be fatal to the year. In grateful recognition of his important services on this interesting subject, a parish, or precinct, in the county of Essex, in Massachusetts, was named for him. "The Byfield Academy," there established, is still a valuable seminary of learning. A similar memorial to his merit is the tasteful Byfield schoolhouse of Bristol.

His generous anxiety for the prosperity of this town was not limited to the laying out of spacious, commodious, and ornamental streets, or the giving of ample grounds for the public convenience or necessities, but was illustrated by his liberal donation of lands for educational purposes, the benefits of which stand confessed to this hour.

I cannot do better than to repeat the lines which were inscribed on his tombstone in the Granary burying ground, Boston, and which were composed by the Rev. Matthew Byles. They are an epitome of his life, and a rare specimen of elegiac composition:

> " Byfield, beneath, in peaceful slumber lies;
> Byfield, the good, the active and the wise;
> His manly form contained an equal mind,
> Faithful to God and generous to mankind.
> High in his country's honors long he stood,

> Succour'd distress and gave the hungry food.
> In justice steady, in devotion warm,
> A loyal subject and a patriot firm,
> Through every stage his dauntless soul was tried—
> Great while he lived, but greater when he died."

May the trees we plant here to-day, as a sylvan tribute to the memory of the founders of Bristol, sink their roots deep into its soil, and as they advance to the maturity of luxuriant foliage, may their whispering branches become inspired like the sacred oak of Dodona, and oracularly predict the perpetuity of the principles and institutions of the fathers, and the permanence of this, "The Beautiful Gate" of the glorious State of Rhode Island.

The chairman concluded the ceremony by explaining that the first three trees planted were native elms, and the last an oak grown from an acorn that fell from a tree planted by Nathaniel Byfield, under whose shade he had passed many an hour as he sat at his own door and looked across the water to our side of the harbor.

At the close, and while the final act of planting was being done, the evening salute and ringing of the town bells began. No more appropriate act could have been suggested; for with the loud voiced cannon and glad sound of bells, we committed to the God of nature our offerings to the memory of the original proprietors of the town, that in their growth we may ever have a reminder of those who first planted this beautiful town.

CLOSING OBSERVANCES.

Scarcely had the guns of the Bristol Artillery "thundered forth their reverberating benediction," ere the Common was deserted. Gov. Littlefield and staff were escorted to the mansion of Col. S. Pomroy Colt, and other distinguished guests took carriages for the depot, to take the Providence train.

The Light Infantry Veterans, with the National Band, after having spent the day at the pleasant seaside residence of Col. A. C. Eddy, "whose generous hospitality and assiduous attentions to their inner comfort stamped him as a princely entertainer and glorious comrade," (says the correspondent of the *Providence Journal*, and to which, all who have enjoyed the hospitality of Col. Eddy, and his estimable lady, will most heartily subscribe), marched to the depot, and embarked for home.

In the evening, many of the residences of citizens were again illuminated, fire-works were displayed, and large crowds filled the streets of the town. Soon after eight o'clock the mammoth tent on the Common, which was brilliantly lighted with "Electric Lights," was thronged with people, to hear the grand concerts of the Boston Cadet and Bristol Bands.

The programme of selections by the organizations, who played alternately to the great gratification of the appreciative audience, was as follows:

BOSTON CADET BAND.

1. Overture—Stradella..Flotaw.
2. Potpourri of Favorite Airs..................................Henry.
3. Tuba Solo—Graf ....Arthur Graf.
4. Selections from Nabuco..Verdi.
5. Concert Waltzes—Wiener Kinder ....By Strauss.
6. Grand Selections from Il Trovatore.........................Verdi.
7. Piccolo Solo, audante with schezo movement—De Carlo..August Daun.

BRISTOL CORNET BAND.

1. Collingwood Quickstep ....Pettee.
2. Schottische—Dancing in the Barn ....J. B. Claus.
3. Waltzes—Sounds from the North........................Zikoff.
4. Overture—Luspiel..Keler Beler.
5. Galop—Phonograph...Fox.
6. Selection—Linda...Donnizetti.
7. Qickstep—To the Front ....Newton.

During the evening elegant receptions to Gov. Littlefield and staff, and distinguished guests, were held at the residences of Cols. S. Pomroy and Le Baron B. Colt, "and Col. A. C. Eddy, and those gentlemen vied with each other in the elaborateness of their collations, and generous welcome to their guests."

We may be pardoned if we add the following closing comments of the *Journal* on our celebration:

"It is a fact that, notwithstanding the presence of nearly twelve thousand people in the town during the day, but a single case of drunkenness was reported, and no unseemly disturbances or serious accidents occurred, which certainly speaks volumes for the residents, as well as the strangers attending the celebration. The 10.15 P. M. train for Providence left the depot with fourteen heavily-loaded cars, many standing on the platforms, but all were safely carried to their destination. And so ended the memorable observance of Bristol's natal day, and Old Bristol has earned a reputation for public spirit and lavish hospitality which the lapse of years can never efface from the memories of her non-resident sons and daughters, and those who visited the beautiful and historic town for the first time."

The following ode, from the pen of Mrs. T. DeW. Colt, was written to be sung by the school children on the day of the celebration, but was received by the committee too late for the purpose:

FOR THE BI-CENTENNIAL.

A grand old sturdy race,
   Were our forefathers dear,
In council firm, in battle bold,
   Unmoved by doubt or fear.

Inured to pain and toil,
   Where duty calls they go;
Their strong right arm could rend an oak,
   Or fell an Indian foe.

Their houses rude and bare,
   Soft luxury disown,
No modern elegance was their's,
   Not e'en a TELEPHONE.

Strong in defence of right,
   Tho' sometimes hard and cold,
Our fathers bravely fought the fight
   In the dark days of old.

And to their children left
   A heritage secure,
Founded on reason, faith and love,
   And morals sweet and pure.

Then let each voice to-day,
   In song triumphant rise
To the Great Father, who bestows
   All blessings that we prize.

Our lives from danger free,
  Our bodies warmed and fed,
Our minds enriched by knowledge from
  The living and the dead.

But let us now beware
  The "serpent" of our time;
Disguised in fairest form, he throws
  On us his filthy shine.

Through pleasure, power and ease,
  He lures us from the road,
The only safe and narrow path
  That leads straight up to God.

Then let us not forget
  The truths our fathers owned,
But hold them with a firmer grip,
  Till Satan be dethroned.

Tear down the idol Self,
  Forswear "the calf of gold,"
Wrong not our neighbor by a word,
  But win with love untold.

For lux'ry is no sin,
  So that the heart be pure,
And every land that God reveres
  For ages may endure.

Then let us keep a guard
  Stationed at "helm and prow,"
That children's children may us bless
  Two hundred years from now.

LINDEN PLACE, September 8th, 1880.

BADGES.

The Badges furnished by the Committee, and worn on the day of the celebration, were of seven different patterns. They were 6¼ by 2½ inches in size, on ribbon of satin finish face, and *gros grain* back, and bound across the top with gold bullion, one-half inch wide. In describing them we designate them by numbers as follows:

No. 1. The Badge of the Town Committee. This badge was Cardinal Red in color. The corners of the lower end were turned under to form a point, from which was pendant a gold tassel. The printing on the badge, in gold letter, was:

COMMITTEE.

1680.   1880.

BI-CENTENNIAL,

September 24,

1880.

No. 2. The Badge of Visiting Sons and Daughters. This badge was "old gold" in color. The lower end was cut to form points at the outer corners. The printing, in black, was:

SONS AND DAUGHTERS
OF
BRISTOL, R. I.

1680.   1880.

WELCOME HOME.
September 24, 1880.

No. 3. The Badge of Invited Guests. This badge was white, and the lower end cut to form points at the outer corners. The printing, in black, was:

INVITED GUESTS.

1680.   1880.

BI-CENTENNIAL,
BRISTOL, R. I.,
September 24, 1880.

No. 4. The Badge of the Committee on Relics. This badge was lilac in color. The lower end was trimmed with gold fringe, two inches deep. The printing, in black, was:

COMMITTEE.
LOAN EXHIBITION.

1680.   1880.

BI-CENTENNIAL.

September 24, 1880.

No. 5. The Badge of the Marshals. This badge was white. The lower end trimmed with gold fringe, two inches deep. The printing, in black, was:

DEPUTY MARSHAL.

1680.   1880.

BI-CENTENNIAL.

September 24, 1880.

No. 6. The Badge of the School Children. This badge was of light pink, and the lower end cut to form points at the outer corners. The printing, in black, was:

BI-CENTENNIAL

CHORUS.

CHILDREN OF THE

PUBLIC SCHOOLS.

1680.   1880.

BRISTOL, R. I.,

September 24, 1880.

No. 7. The Badge of the Drum Corps. This badge was of light blue, and the lower end cut to form points at the outer corners. The printing, in black, was:

DRUM CORPS.

1680.   1880.

(TOWN SEAL—OBLONG.)

BI-CENTENNIAL,

September 24, 1880.

This was a company of eight boys, who formed an organization, and gave much time during the summer months preceding the celebration, to practice—Mr. George Alger kindly volunteering to teach them. They provided themselves with drums and uniforms. The uniform was a black cap, with gold bullion band, and vizor; jacket of scarlet flannel, with white flannel trimmings, and brass buttons; and dark pants. Their names are George William Warren, leader, aged 12 years; John Henry Bartlett Mott, aged 16 years; Frederick Smith Waldron, 14; William Nelson Miller, 14; William Henry Remington, 14; Charles Gardner Sisson, 14; Arthur Emmons Card, 12; Charles Luther Miller, 12. They acquitted themselves with credit, and were a pleasant feature of the procession.

LOAN EXHIBITION.

The relics of the past—an illustrated history of the town—were on exhibition in Town Hall. This building was formerly the Congregational Meeting-house. It was built in 1784, and dedicated on the 5th of January, 1785, the day of the ordination of the Rev. HENRY WIGHT, as pastor. Its location was *in* Bradford street, a little east from the line of Hope street, with its front to the west. It was used as a house of worship until the fall of 1856, when the new stone edifice of the Congregational Church was finished. The first meeting-house was built in 1684, on the Common, the site of the present Court House, and stood one hundred years. Some of the oak timbers which were originally hewn from trees growing upon the Common, were put into the second meeting-house. This second house has stood almost one hundred years, and those oak timbers are sound to this day. It was given to the town in 1857, and in the summer of that year was moved *out of the street* to its present site on the north side of Bradford street. The next year it was fitted up for a Town Hall, and has been used as such to the present time.

In this building, so identified with the town almost from the very beginning of its settlement, was appropriately gathered the relics of bygone times. The citizens of the town in this, as in all other features of the celebration, manifested a commendable interest, and generously responded to the wishes of the committee, by loaning their treasures—many of them replete with precious and sacred memories—for the exhibition. As has before been stated, to John DeWolf is the public mainly indebted for the large and interesting collection, and the good taste displayed in their grouping.

The following is a list of the articles on exhibition:

PORTRAITS IN OIL.

Gov. Byron Diman, loaned by Mrs. E. A. Diman; painted in 1844.
Mrs. Abby Alden Diman, wife of Gov. B. Diman, l. by Mrs. Clara D. DeWolf.
Gov. Francis M. Dimond, l. by Mrs. Samuel Norris.
Mrs. Elizabeth Dimond, " " " " "
Royal Dimond, " " " " "
Lt.-Gov. Nath'l Bullock, taken at the age of 80 years, l. by Hon. J. R. Bullock.
Geo. Howe, l. by Mrs. Hope Blake.
John Howe, l. by M. A. DeW. Howe.
Maj. Jacob Babbitt, Sr., l. by Mrs. Abbey E. Babbitt.
" Jacob Babbitt, Jr., " " " " " "
Benj. B. Bosworth, " " " " " "
Mrs. B. B. Bosworth, " " " " " "
Rev. Henry Wight, D. D., l. by Mrs. Susan Gladding.
Mrs. Henry Wight, wife of Rev. Dr. Wight, with her granddaughter, G. A. Alden, l. by Mrs. Clara D. DeWolf.
Rev. C. H. Alden, l. by Miss A. Fanny Alden.
Mrs. C. H. Alden, " " " " " "
Rev. Thos. Shepard, D. D., from Byfield Hall. This portrait was painted by Miss Jane Stuart, daughter of Gilbert Stuart, the celebrated portrait painter.
" James McSparran, 1718, l. by P. Skinner.
Mrs. James McSparran, " " " " "
Rt. Rev. Alexander Viets Griswold, l. by Miss Mary Heath.
Rev. John Bristed, l. by M. A. DeW. Howe.
" Wm. Rogers, Chaplain in Revolutionary Army, and the first graduate of Brown University.
Hersey Bradford, l. by Miss Mary Baylies.
Geo. H. Peck, l. by V. G. Peck.
Capt. John Gladding, l. by Mrs. Susie Richmond.
Mrs. John Gladding, l. by Mrs. Lizzie Gladding.
Capt. Wm. H. Gladding, l. by Mrs. Lizzie Gladding.
Mrs. Wm. H. Gladding, " " " " "

Ambrose Waldron, l. by Billings Waldron.
Hannah Waldron, " " " "
Parents of the oldest male inhabitant to-day. Dying they left 9 sons, 2 daughters, and 67 grandchildren.
Mason W. Pierce, l. by F. G. Bowen.
Mrs. Mason W. Pierce, and her son, Henry Parker Pierce, l. by F. G. Bowen.
James P. Pierce, l. by F. G. Bowen.
Capt. Cory Williston, l. by F. G. Bowen.
Wm. Pearse, 2nd, born 116 years ago, l. by Mrs. W. A. Richmond.
Wm. Pierce, l. by Geo. H. Peck.
Mrs. Lemuel C. Richmond, Senior, and her son Isaac, l. by Mrs. Wm. A. Richmond.
Capt. Martin Bennett, l. by Mrs. Robert Peck.
Eliza T., wife of Martin Bennett, l. by Mrs. Robert Peck.
Benjamin Tilley, l. by Benj. Tilley.
Mrs. Benjamin Tilley, l. by Benj. Tilley.
Col. Samuel Wardwell. This portrait is interesting from being taken in the old uniform of the Bristol Artillery, organized soon after the War of the Revolution, and maintained as an independent organization ever since. L. by W. T. C. Wardwell.
Capt. John Wardwell, l. by Mrs. Mary E. Munro.
Mrs. John Wardwell, " " " " " "
Capt. John Smith, l. by Mrs. H. B. Smith.
Mrs. Anne Pratt Smith, l. by Mrs. H. B. Smith.
Capt. James Miller, l. by Augustus N. Miller.
Le Favour Howland, l. by Mrs. Phœbe H. Vickery.
Mrs. Le F. Howland and Child, l. by Mrs. Phœbe H. Vickery.
Samuel Sparks, l. by Albert Sparks.
Col. Samuel Wardwell, l. by Chas. H. H. Wardwell.
Mrs. Samuel Wardwell, Sr., l. by Chas. H. H. Wardwell.
Deacon Wm. B. Spooner, l. by Mrs. John Watson.
John Gardner, l. by Geo. W. Easterbrooks.
Mrs. J. Gardner, l. by Geo. W. Easterbrooks.
John R. Gardner, l. by Mrs. Clarissa Gardner.
   This portrait is three-quarters length, and life-size. It is very finely painted, and remarkably life-like.
Golden Dearth, l. by Mrs. J. Gooding.
Mrs. Samuel Smith, l. by Mrs. J. Gooding.
Mrs. Josiah Gooding, painted by C. Giovanni Thompson, in his best style in 1832; l. by James Madison Gooding.
Mrs. Ann Fletcher, l. by Mrs. N. Warren.
Miss Bosworth, l. by Walter H. Munro.
Jeremiah Ingraham, l. by Mrs. Eliza DeWolf.
Mrs. Ingraham, " " " " "

Capt. Leonard G. Bradford, l. by Mrs. Harriet Coggeshall.
Mrs. Sarah Bradford, l. by Mrs. Harriet Coggeshall.
Capt. Daniel Gladding, taken about 1805, l. by Wm. O. Gladding.
Mrs. Sarah Gladding, " " " " " " " "
Ambrose Waldron, l. by Mrs. Wm. H. West.
Mrs. Hannah Waldron, l. by Mrs. Wm. H. West.
Crawford Easterbrooks, Jr., l. by C. L. Easterbrooks.
Josiah Smith, l. by Miss M. E. Bourne.
Allen Bourne, " " " " " "
Benj. F. Bourn, l. by Mrs. J. DeW. Perry.
Mrs. Benj. F. Bourn, l by Mrs. J. DeW. Perry.
Mrs. Priscilla Allyn, daughter of Royal Paine.
"Capt. Tom Jones," Commander of Privateers during war of 1812, l. by Capt Geo. H. Munro.
Capt. Allen Munro, son of William and Hannah, died on a voyage from the coast of Africa; l. by A. M. Newman.
Nathan Bardin, painted about 1800, l. by Nathan B. Fenner.
Mrs. N. Bardin, l. by Mrs. Nathan B. Heath.
Nath'l Coggeshall, l. by Mrs. Harriet Coggeshall.
Mrs. N. Coggeshall, l. by Mrs. Harriet Coggeshall.
"Tom Jones," l. by Jas. D. Wardwell.
Mrs. Tom Jones, l. by Jas. D. Wardwell.

"Tom Jones" commanded the renowned privateer "Yankee," which made so many captures during the last war with England.

Abigail DeWolf, wife of Mark Antony DeWolf, Sr., ancestress of all the DeWolf family in Bristol, R. I., l. by Mrs. Eliza DeWolf.
Charles DeWolf, Sr., l. by Mrs. Theodora DeWolf Colt.

Painted by Jarvis, and considered by some judges the finest painting in the collection. Remarkable for the naturalness of the flesh tints, and life-like appearance.

Gen. Geo. DeWolf, l. by Mrs. T. DeW. Colt.
Mrs. Geo. DeWolf, " " " " " "
Hon. James DeWolf, l. by H. M. Howe.
Wm. Henry DeWolf, l. by Mrs. Wm. B. DeWolf.
Francis Le Baron DeWolf, l. by Mrs. Wm. B. DeWolf.
James DeWolf, Jr., " " " " " "
Catharine DeWolf, " " " " " "
Hon. William DeWolf, l. by Mrs. M. DeW. Rogers.
Mrs. William DeWolf, l. by Mrs. Rogers and Miss C. DeWolf.
Wm. DeWolf, Jr., " " " " " " " "
Abby DeWolf Davis, " " " " " " " "
Charlotte DeWolf, " " " " " " " "
Maria DeWolf, l. by Mrs. M. Rogers and Miss C. DeWolf.
Henry DeWolf, l. by Fitz Henry DeWolf.
Mrs. Henry DeWolf, l. by Fitz Henry DeWolf.
Prof. John DeWolf, l. by Brown University.

Mrs. Elizabeth J. DeWolf, wife of Prof. DeWolf, l. by Winthrop DeWolf.
Charlotte DeWolf, l. by Miss C. DeWolf.
Rob't Rogers, painted by Head, l. by Mrs. M DeW. Rogers.
Mrs. Rob't Rogers, painted by Healy, l. by Mrs. M. DeWolf Rogers.
Nathaniel Byfield, from Byfield Hall. This portrait is a copy from an original portrait in the possession of Hon. Francis Brinley, of Newport. The copy was made by Miss Jane Stuart, and is remarkable for its truthfulness.
Gen. Andrew Jackson, (visited Bristol in 1833), l. by S. Pomeroy Colt.

When Gen. Jackson visited Bristol, in June, 1833, he had just entered upon his second term as President of the United States. He was accompanied by Martin Van Buren, Vice President of the United States; Lewis Cass, Secretary of War; Levi Woodbury, Secretary of the Navy; Major Donalson, and Col. Earle, of the President's suite. He landed from steamboat Boston, Capt. Wm. Comstock, from Newport, at Long Wharf, foot of Church street, and walked, with his hat in his hand, through a shower of rain, up Church street and along Hope street, to the Bristol Hotel on State street. Capt. James DeWolf was conspicuous in his efforts to hold an umbrella over "Old Hickory's" head, to keep the rain off. At the hotel, a few citizens had an opportunity to be introduced to the President, and shake his hand. The distinguished party almost immediately re-embarked on the steamer for Providence, where they arrived at 10 o'clock, A. M.

—— **Davis,** ancestor of Church and Wardwell families, brought from England in 1680, and then over fifty years old. Wonderfully painted and well preserved. Considered by many the finest painting and most interesting relic in the collection. L. by Mrs. H. E. Coggeshall, Fall River.
Geo. Washington.
Martha Washington.

These remarkable portraits were painted by the elder Peale, of Philadelphia, for Washington, and by him were presented to John Brown, of Providence. They represent this illustrious couple at a much younger age than most of their portraits. Washington is taken in the uniform of a Colonel in the Virginia militia, and these pictures were probably taken about the time of Braddock's defeat. L by the Misses Herreshoff

Her Gracious Majesty Queen Caroline, wife of George II., King of England. This curious old portrait was brought from England, with several others, by Rev. John Usher, the first minister of St. Michael's Church, in 1720. It was torn from its frame and much injured by the Americans during the Revolutionary War. It is now in the original frame of carved oak. L. by Mrs. M. Luther Simmons.
Com. C. H. Perry, l. by Mrs. James DeW. Perry.
Geo. H. Reynolds, l. by Mrs. John Burgess, Jr.

Capt. James Usher, l. by Mrs. John Burgess, Jr.
Mrs. James Usher, " " " " " "
Benj. Franklin. This portrait was painted from life, and is very much thought of by artists. It is taken with fur cap and spectacles. It was formerly owned by the late Prof. A. D. Bache. L. by Mrs. H. W. Bache.

MINIATURES ON IVORY.

Gen. James M. Varnum, painted in 1770, l. by Miss Betsey Bourn.
Mrs. James M. Varnum, " " 1770, l by Mrs. J. DeW. Perry.
Mary Ann DeWolf Sumner, daughter of Hon. James DeWolf, painted by Miss Ann Hall, l. by Mrs. J. DeW. Perry.
Bishop Griswold, l. by John Allyn.
Hon. Wm. DeWolf, painted by Malbone, l. by Mrs. Rogers and Miss C. DeWolf.
Capt. John DeWolf, l. by Mrs. Clara D. DeWolf.
Mrs. John Norris, with her father and mother in shadow, taken in 1817, l. by C. H. Norris.
Capt. Daniel N. Morice,
Madame Theresa Morice, and a beautifully painted miniature of an aunt of Capt. Morice, name unknown; all three l. by Mrs. Edward S. Babbitt.
Golden Dearth, l. by Willie Bradford.
Capt. Fletcher, l. by T. W. Easterbrooks.
Capt. John Norris, painted in 1825, l. by Capt. C. H. Norris.
Mrs. John Norris, painted in 1825, l. by Capt. C. H. Norris.
Wm. Coggeshall, l. by Mrs. H. E. Coggeshall.
Mrs. Wm. Coggeshall, l. by Mrs H. E. Coggeshall.
Mrs. Prudence Richmond, l. by Mrs. Rebecca Simmons.
Mrs. Sarah W. Shepard, l. by Miss Shepard.
Gen. George DeWolf, l. by Mrs. T. DeW. Colt.
Henry Goodwin, " " " " " "
Mrs. Le B. Goodwin, " " " " " "
Mariana DeWolf, " " " " " "
Judge Joseph Russell, by Fraser, one of the finest miniatures in the United States, l by N. R. Middleton. Joseph Russell was a son of Rev. Jonathan Russell, the minister of Barnstable, Mass., and the grandson of Rev. John Russell, who for more than fifteen years concealed in his house at Hadley, Mass., Generals Whaley and Goffe, two of Cromwell's Judges who condemned Charles I. to the block.

Silhouette of Mrs. Sally Sandford, l. by Miss Lizzie Simmons.
" Mrs. Hannah Norris, l. by Mrs. Morgan.
" John Howland, cut sixty years ago.
" Hon. Benj. Bourn, l. by Mrs. J. DeW. Perry.

Silhouette of Nelson Miller, l. by William J. Miller.
This profile was cut more than fifty years ago, and is a striking likeness. Mr. Miller was a Revolutionary soldier and pensioner, having been in the service six of the seven years of the war. Fifty or more years ago, the writer remembers to have heard his grandfather relate an incident that transpired at Valley Forge, while the American army was encamped there in the winter of 1777-78. As he has never seen it in print, he ventures to give it here. It was the scene when Washington made known to the army the "Conway Cabal." His description of the event, although so many years have elapsed since the writer heard it from his lips, is still vivid in his memory. It was, he said, on a mild, pleasant Sunday morning, (probably in the latter part of February, or early in March, 1778). The entire army was mustered, and Washington, surrounded by his officers, addressed the army, and told them of the conspiracy to supersede him. He then, with deep feeling, vindicated his motives and course of action, and closed with a most earnest appeal to the army—officers and men—to remain true to the great cause in which they had all suffered and sacrificed so much. When the writer heard him relate the incident, it was more than half a century after the event; and yet he well remembers, child as he then was, how visibly the old man was affected, as he described it. He said it was one of the most impressive scenes that he ever witnessed, and one that he should never forget,—officers and men wept like children. His position in the line was near where Washington sat upon his horse, and he heard distinctly every word he spoke.

Two Miniatures, Capt. Daniel Gladding and Wife, l. by William H. Gladding.

John Bullock, one hundred years old when taken, l. by Miss Mary Bullock.

PICTURES.

Oil Painting of Venus and Cupids.
" " **Diana at the Bath.** In this, Acteon is represented undergoing transformation into a stag, with Diana and her attendant nymphs, dogs, game, etc. These pictures were brought from England by Rev. John Usher in 1720. L. by the Misses Usher.

Abraham Sacrificing Isaac, a very old painting, unfortunately indistinct and much injured; l. by Mrs. Thomas J Usher.

Painting of Ship "Joshua Mauran," l. by Capt. Isaac Liscomb.

Privateer "McDonough," painted by Jonathan Alger, l. by George Alger.

A Flemish Entertainment, A Moderate Gale, A Brisk Gale, A Calm, four Engravings, all over 100 years old, l. by C. F. Herreshoff.

Apotheosis of Washington, l. by C. F. Herreshoff.

Gen. Jackson, l. by T. L. Fisher.

George Washington, l. by George Smith.
Five Old Prints, " " " "
John Darling, framed and illustrated Eulogy, written by Gov. Charles Collins, l. by Capt. I. Liscomb.
Lorenzo Dow and Peggy Dow, l. by James A. Miller.
Privateers, "Sea Pieces," etc., four curious old pictures of, l. by Mrs. Gideon Sherman.
Departure of Prodigal Son, a print of 1735, l. by Mrs. R. S Andrews.
Prodigal Son, two old pictures, l. by Mrs Rebecca Simmons.
Triumph of Liberty, an engraving, l. by Capt. George Coggeshall.
Engravings, 200 and 150 years old, l. by Mrs. W. A. Richmond.
Old Talbee House. Drawing of house built by Col. Benj. Church in Bristol in 1690, l. by the Misses Shepard.

Interesting copies of the coats of arms borne by the early settlers were shown. The following were copies taken before the separation from the mother countries: **Usher, Dimond, Leonard and Ingraham Families.**

OLD SILVER.

Five Silver Spoons, all over 100 years old, l. by Mrs. Clara D. DeWolf.
Cream Jug and Sugar Bowl, formerly owned by Bishop Griswold, l. by Mrs. R. S. Andrews.
Tankard, marked H. L., was brought from Plymouth by Hannah Loring, who married Jonathan Peck about 1731, l. by George J. Adams.
Two Silver Chaffing Dishes, l. by Mrs. Wm. B. D'Wolf.
Cup, " " " " " "
Porringer, used for soup on board the ship "General Washington," l. by C. F. Herreshoff.
Plate, l. by C. F. Herreshoff.
Two old Silver-Handled Forks, l. by C. F. Herreshoff.
Silver Ladle, with a coin of the reign of Queen Anne, 1711, set into the bottom, l. by Mrs. C. F. Herreshoff, Jr.
Silver Chain and Pendant, formerly belonging to the grand-daughter of Col. Benj. Church, l. by Miss Mary F. Norris.
Silver Paten, formerly belonging to Rev. John Usher, l. by the Misses Usher.
Curious Small Silver Spoon, l. by Miss Rebecca Turner.
Eight Tea-Spoons, old fashioned marks and chasing, l. by Ezra B. Chadwick.
Silver Pitcher. This interesting relic was brought from France by Gabriel Bernon, a French Huguenot, who fled from France upon the revocation of the edict of Nantes, and came to this country and brought this with a few other valuables. In 1738 it came to his granddaughter, Esther Powell, and has been in the possession of an Esther Powell

ever since, being now owned by the ninth of that name. It was requested for exhibition at the Centennial Exhibition held in Philadelphia, but the then owners felt constrained to refuse. L. by Mrs. Esther Powell Snow.

Silver Ewer and Basin, formerly used by Charles DeWolf, Sr., l. by Mrs. T. DeW. Colt.

Wine Tester.

Old Communion Service from Congregational Church.
2 cups, the gift of Nathaniel Byfield in 1693.
1 cup,   "   "   "   Rev. John Sparhawk in 1718.
1 cup, the donor unknown, given in 1723.
2 cups, the gift of Hon. Nathl. Blagrove, in 1745.

Communion Service from St. Michael's Church.
2 large flagons, the gift of Nath'l Kay in 1734.
2 double-handled cups, the gift of Nathl. Kay in 1734.
1 large chalice,   "   "   "   "   "   "   "
1 large basin, the gift of Isaac Royal in 1747.
1 paten, the gift of Nath'l Kay in 1734.

Large Silver Waiter and Candelabra, about 150 years old, l. by Mrs. C. L. H. Chesbro'.

Sugar Bowl and Creamer, formerly owned by Deacon Jeremiah Diman, l. by Miss Lizzie B. Diman.

Tankard, "   "   "   "   "   "

Pap Spoon, 200 years old, formerly owned by Col. Job Almy, one of the original owners of the Pocasset purchase, l. by Mrs. C. F. Herreshoff, Jr.

Eight Table-Spoons, owned by Sion and Sally Martindale, 1756, l. by George J. Adams.

Sion Martindale was a successful ship master and merchant of Bristol at the beginning of the war of the Revolution. The commerce of the port had been destroyed by the restrictive acts of the British Parliament. When the Rhode Island General Assembly, immediately after the affair at Concord and Lexington, ordered the enlisting of troops into "the King's service," Captain Martindale promptly came forward and raised a company in Bristol and Warren for Colonel Thomas Church's regiment. He was commissioned as captain of the company, and with the regiment, early in June, reported for duty at Cambridge. Some members of his company were in the redoubt at the battle of Bunker Hill. When Washington arrived from the South, early in July, to take command of the troops around Boston, he took prompt steps to prevent supplies from reaching the British in Boston. This was easily done inland. To cut off their supplies by water three armed vessels were equipped, the first one put in commission being the brigantine Washington, of ten guns. Captain Martindale was commissioned as commander. As seamen were hard to be obtained, so many of them having enlisted in the army, the soldiers were called upon to volunteer, and Captain Martindale soon had a complement of men—numbers of his own company going with him. Their cruise was a short one, for they had been out only three days, when they were captured in Boston bay by the British Ship Foy, of twenty guns. They were soon transferred to the frigate Tartar, and carried as prisoners to England

Cream Pitcher, 167 years old, formerly belonging to Dr. John Coggeshall. Repoussé work. L. by Miss Sarah Coggeshall.

Silver Nutmeg-Grater, about 200 years old, in the shape of a shoe, l. by Mrs. M. J. Slade.

Pepper Box, in form of light-house, formerly belonging to the first Mark Antony DeWolf, l. by Mrs. M. DeW. Rogers.

Punch-Strainer, " " " " " "
Porringer, " " " " " "
Fish Spoon, " " " " " "
Tankard, " " " " " "
Sugar Tongs, " " " " " "
Cream Pitcher, " " " " " "

Tankard, l. by Mrs. N. Russell Middleton.

Tankard, formerly used by Capt. John DeWolf, l. by Byron D. DeWolf.

Sugar Bowl, l. by Miss Annie F. Munro.

This sugar bowl is an exceedingly interesting relic. It had stamped on the bottom of it, the letters S. P., and belonged to Capt. Simeon Potter, who captured it, with other plunder, in 1744, when in command of the ship *Prince Charles of Lorraine,* a Rhode Island privateer. War existed between England and France—the " Old French War"—and Capt. Potter was cruising along the " Spanish Main," near Cayenne, in quest of French merchantmen. Having occasion to land for water, they learned of *Fort d'Oyapoc,* a French Jesuit Missionary station, near by, and determined to capture it. There were but a few soldiers in the fort, and it was surprised and captured without loss of life. The only person wounded was Capt. Potter, who received a bullet wound in his left arm. Capt. Potter's vessel was armed with ten cannon, twelve swivel guns, and had a crew of sixty-two men. His clerk was Mark Antony DeWolf. A part of the crew only landed, and took part in the raid. An account of this affair was published in the *Overland Monthly* of San Francisco, in April, 1874. The late Gov. Arnold received advance sheets of the article, and read them before the Rhode Island Historical Society in Providence, in March of that year. It was a translation from the French, by Bishop Kip, of a letter from Father *Fauque,* the resident Priest at the mission captured, to a brother Priest, and is dated, "At Cayenne, the 22d of December, 1744." The *Overland Monthly,* in its preface to the letter, comments as follows : " It contains a chapter in the early history of the Rhode Island people, which has never before been published. Strange, that, after being buried so long, it should now be unearthed—that, after being locked up in the old French of the original writer for nearly 130 years, it should be brought to light for the benefit of a succeeding generation! Perhaps it may be a matter of interest to the descendants of Captain Simeon Potter, and of the others, who, in 'the Old French War,' were together in the good ship *Prince Charles of Lorraine*, 'as they sailed —as they sailed.'"

The spirit of the holy Father's letter is admirable. He begins as follows:

"MY REVEREND FATHER :—The peace of our Lord be with you! I will make you a partaker of the greatest happiness I have experienced in my life, by informing you of the opportunity I had of suffering something for the glory of God"

He concealed himself for a time outside the fort, for fear of being shot. When captured and taken into the fort, he says: "I saw every face expressing the greatest joy, each one congratulating himself that they had captured a priest." He describes Capt. Potter as follows: "The first one who approached me was the Captain himself. He was a man small in stature, and not in any respect differing from the others in dress. He had his left arm in a sling, a sabre in his right hand, and two pistols in his belt. As he was acquainted with some few words of French, he told me 'that I was very welcome; that I had nothing to fear, as no one would attempt my life.'" He speaks kindly of Capt. Potter, and of his Clerk, (DeWolf).

The capture of the fort was made on the 2d or 3d of November, and the interesting fact is brought out that Capt. Potter and his crew celebrated the "Gunpowder Treason Plot" on the fifth of November. Speaking of a conversation he had with the Captain, he says: "He made me, afterward, a disclosure which was sufficiently pleasant. 'Monsieur,' he said to me, 'do you know that to-morrow, being the fifth of November, the English have a great festival?'

'And what is the festival?' I asked him.

'We burn the Pope,' he answered, laughing.

'Explain to me,' I said; 'what is this ceremony?'

'They dress up in a burlesque style,' he said, 'a kind of ridiculous figure, which they call the Pope, and which they afterwards burn, while singing some ballads, and all this in conmemoration of the day when the Court of Rome separated England from its communion. To-morrow,' he continued, 'our people who are on shore will perform this ceremony at the fort.'"

The priest probably misunderstood the meaning of Capt. Potter as to the event to be commemorated. He describes their manner of celebration as follows:

"After a while, he caused his pennon and flag to be hoisted. The sailors manned the yard-arms, the drum was beaten, they fired the cannon, and all shouted, five times, 'Long live the King!' This having been done, he called one of the sailors, who, to the great delight of those who understood his language, chanted a very long ballad, which I judged to be the recital of all this unworthy story."

The ballad was, doubtless, the one so familiar to every Bristol boy thirty or forty years ago, beginning:

> "The fifth of November,
> Let us all remember
> The Gunpowder-Treason Plot"—

for, up to within twenty-five or thirty years, this singular festival was celebrated in Bristol annually, probably from the very settlement of the town. In fact, "Gunpowder-Treason Night" was as familiar to Bristol people as 'Lection Day at Newport, or the Fourth of July.

The *Prince Charles of Lorraine* hailed from Newport, and her cruise along the coast of Surinam was made the subject of inquiry before the Court of Vice Admiralty, at Newport, in May, 1746. Monsieur Hop, the Minister of the States General of the United Netherlands, made complaint "of several violences committed on the coasts of Surranam by an English Privateer called the *Prince Charles of Lorraine*, Simeon Potter, commander, in violation of the laws of nations, and desiring that the said commander, and those of the crew that were guilty of such outrages, might be punished." After a lengthy investigation, covering the examination of Captain Potter; Daniel Vaughn, of Newport, First Lieutenant; Reuben Shales, of Middletown, Conn., Second Lieutenant; Michael Phillips, of Bristol, Pilot; Mark Antony DeWolf, of Bristol, Clerk; Joseph Rodman, of Newport, Mariner, "being one of those people called Quakers;" and James Tucker, of Newport, Mariner—all members of the company of said *Prince Charles of Lorraine*—the Judge (William Strengthfield) exonerated Capt. Potter, and his officers and crew from all blame. His "Decree" closes as follows:

"It is undoubtedly true that Capt. Potter made a very extraordinary attack upon the French settlement to windward of Surranam, laying waste and destroying a whole country almost one hundred miles up the river Wyapoke, taking the fort, carrying away their cannon, and destroying the town as well as country—doing the same in his going down as far as Ceyane; so that, considering the smallness of his force, perhaps no one during the present war has weakened and distressed His Majesty's enemies to the like degree. And it appears that he was commissionated from said Colony of Rhode Island in the method there used in granting Commissions during the whole war, and herein acted according to instructions. But no act of hostilities appears to be done by him upon the territories of any of His Majesty's allies, or near 'em.

"And it being contrary to His Majesty's clemency and wise administration to admit of any his subjects being distressed without just cause appearing, the said Simeon Potter is released, as also the said Daniel Vaughn and Reuben Shales, for that nothing to me appeared worthy of punishment or bonds. But in further submission and obedience to their Lordships' commands, with this representation the examination and evidences taken are transmitted. The said persons paying costs each one should."

At the time of the bombardment of the town by a British fleet, in October, 1775, Col. Simeon Potter (he had been made Colonel of the Militia) was a member of the Town Council. The British commander, Wallace, made a demand for cattle and sheep, and threatened to bombard the town unless it was promptly complied with. This demand the townspeople, with more zeal than discretion, peremptorily refused. As soon as the vessels of war opened fire—there were five of them, and they took up positions along the entire water-front of the compact part of the town—a great fear and horror seized upon the inhabitants—rendered all the more terrible by the darkness of the evening. In the midst of the fire, Col. Potter went down upon Warehouse Point, which was a gravelly bluff point of land, now covered by Long Wharf, at the foot of Church street, and hailed one of the war vessels that lay a short distance off. After great effort, he succeeded in making himself heard, and beseeched them "for God's sake [to] stop firing!" They sent a boat ashore, and he was taken on board, and, after agreeing to deliver the sheep the next morning (they yielding the demand for the cattle), stopped the fire upon the town. The forty sheep were delivered on board the next morning, and the enemy, to the great relief of the inhabitants, sailed away out of the harbor.

CHINA, ETC.

The collection of china was large and interesting, some of it dating from the early settlement of the town, and having interesting local and historical associations connected with it. Some was imported many years ago from India and China, and is to-day as beautiful as any that reaches us from those countries, albeit the decorations and shapes are now more familiar since the opening of those countries to foreign trade. The different specimens were too numerous to be mentioned in detail, and we can only give those more interesting from association.

Pickle Dish, used by Gen. Washington at the house of Gen. James M. Varnum. Cream ware (Dolphins and Shells), l. by Mrs. J. DeWolf Perry.
Pair of Antique Majolica Pitchers, which formerly belonged to Deacon Nathaniel Diman, l. by Mrs. E. A. Diman.
Octagonal Plate, imitation of tortoise shell, about 125 years old, l. by Capt. C. H. Norris.
Japanese Drinking Cup, brought from Japan by Com. Perry at the signing of the first treaty with that country, l. by Mrs. J. DeW. Perry.
China Tea Caddy, used by Mrs. Gen. Varnum, l. by Mrs. J. DeW. Perry.
Barber's Basin, over 200 years old, l. by Mrs. Mary J. Slade.
Punch Bowl and Curious Old Pitcher, in the form of a man, l. by T. L. Fisher.

Punch Bowl, owned by Rev. John Usher, cream color, with floral decorations, l. by Miss Lizzie Simmons.

China Cup and Saucer, which belonged to the wife of Capt. John DeWolf, neé Reynolds, l. by Mrs. A. S. DeWolf.

Cup and Saucer, owned by Col. Benjamin Church 200 years ago, l. by Mrs. William Howe Church.

Large Blue and White Punch Bowl, or Standard, with large Salver, which belonged to Col. Benjamin Church, l. by Gilbert Norris.

Tea Pot, formerly used by Col. Simeon Potter, l. by Mrs. B. B. Coggeshall.

Shaving Basin, used by Mark Antony DeWolf, l. by Mrs. Maria D'W. Rogers.

China Figurine, female figure carrying fruit and flowers, l. by Mrs. H. W. Bache.

Pitcher, with figures of children in relief, l. by Miss M. G. DeWolf.

Square Platter, decorated with pictures of ship, l. by Capt. Isaac Liscomb.

Cup and Saucer, owned by Bishop Griswold, l. by Miss Maria G. DeWolf.

Punch Bowl, 120 years old, owned by Capt. Fletcher, l. by T. W. Easterbrooks.

Punch Bowl, with curious decorations inside, once owned by Rev. John Usher, 1720, l. by Mrs. M. Luther Simmons.

Blue and White Plate, conventional designs, brought to Bristol by Rev. Samuel Lee, the first minister settled in Bristol in 1686, l. by Mrs. Clara D. DeWolf.

Two Very Old Pitchers, floral decorations, l. by Mrs. B. B. Chadwick.

Very Old Cup and Saucer, rose colored and white decorations, l. by Miss Rebecca Turner.

Punch Bowl, with figures of ships, and curious tea set, deep cream color, with bright colored figures of animals, l. by Mrs. Gideon Sherman.

Sugar Bowl, owned by Rev. John Usher, 1720, white, with colored raised figures, very beautiful and rare, l. by Mrs. M. Luther Simmons.

Sugar Bowl, over 100 years old, raised ornaments, l. by Mrs. George W. Simmons.

Old China. Interesting selections of old china were also received from Mrs. Mary J. Slade, Mrs. Rebecca Simmons, Mrs. Viets G. Peck, Mrs. R. S. Andrews, George Smith, Miss Annie F. Munro, the Herreshoff family, Mrs. Clara D. DeWolf, Mrs. C. L. H. Chesbro', Mrs. James White, Mrs. Augustus Richmond, Mrs. Wm. Simmons, Miss A. Coy, and T. L. Fisher.

GLASS, ETC.

The first Glass Lamp in Bristol, l. by Mrs. B W. Darling.
Salt Cellar, in shape of hat, and **Night Lamp,** both over 100 years old, l. by Mrs. George W. Simmons.
Wine Glass, with fine gilt ornamentation, l. by Miss Lizzie Simmons.
Cruet, belonged to Sally Peck, wife of Sion Martindale, 1756, l. by Geo. J. Adams.
Large Wine Glass, 180 years old, l. by Mrs. Chas. Fales.
Jar Salts, 140 years old, l. by Miss M. E. Bourn.
Large Glass Sugar Bowl, (owned by Col. Benj. Church, who conquered King Philip, of Mount Hope), about 200 years old, l. by Mrs. Wm. Howe Church.
Tumbler, formerly owned by the great grandson of John Alden, now owned by the eighth in descent, l. by Mrs. Clara D. DeWolf.
Large Glass Tumbler, 106 years old, l. by Thomas Easterbrooks.
Wine Glass, more than 200 years old, buried for preservation at Greenwich during the Revolution, cut glass, with gilt ornaments, l. by Mrs. J. DeW. Perry.
Cut Glass Liquor Set and Tray, mounted with brass (sea set), l. by T. W. Easterbrooks.

FURNITURE.

Piano. The first one in New England, imported by John Brown for his daughter Sarah, afterwards Mrs. Herreshoff. Imported about 1785. It has a finely inlaid case, and is in every way in good order, every key sounding. It has been in the Herreshoff house at Point Pleasant during the present century. L. by the Misses Herreshoff.
Piano, one of the first made in America, for many years it was owned on the Island of Prudence, l. by Messrs. Cory Brothers, Providence.
Spinet, with maker's name, and dated, "London, 1520." A family relic brought to Bristol by Mrs. Henry Wight, l. by Mrs. Alex Perry.

The correspondent of the New York *Graphic*, in referring to this instrument, indulges in the following reflections: "This instrument bears the inscription, 'Johannes Hitchcock, *fecit*, London, 1520.' It is, you see, three hundred and sixty years old. What a web of romance might be woven out of its long history! Where now are the pliant fingers that awoke its sleeping harmonies when it was new? Where are the girls that sang alto, and those that sang air to the accompaniment of its chords when the plate with the maker's name on it flashed in brightness to the light of the parlor fires in 'ye olden time?' Gone, all gone—dust centuries ago, and forgotten. Heaven help us! and here is the ancient spinet, the forerunner of the piano of to-day—a wrecked musical ship whose music has vanished with the hearts that enjoyed it when the world was younger."

Large High Back Chair, with carved ornamentation, 160 years old, l. by Mrs. C. L. H. Chesbro'.

Mahogany "As You Like it" Chair, with claw feet, used by Gen. Washington, l. by Mrs. Chesbro'.

Small Bureau, made in Bristol in 1780, l. by Miss A. F. Munro.

Small Table, 170 years old, formerly owned by Mrs. Potter, the mother of Col. Simeon Potter, l by Miss A F. Munro.

Chair, made in 1755, l. by Wm. H. Mann.

Shoemaker's Bench, l. by Richard S. Pearse, who received it from his grandfather, Richard Smith, in 1821, it being the property of his father years before. Supposed to be about 140 years old.

First Communion Table used in the Episcopal Church in Bristol, mahogany, with silk damask cloth, l. by Wm. P. Munro.

Light Stand and Chair, formerly belonging to Rev. John Usher, l. by Wm P. Munro.

Chair, formerly owned by the *Walley* family, l. by William C. G. Cushman.

Fire Screen, worked in crewels, 100 years old, l. by Mrs. Jacob Babbitt.

Small Table, which belonged to Mark Antony and Abigail DeWolf, more than 130 years old, l. by Miss Abby L. DeWolf.

"As You Like It" Chair, once owned by Rev. John Burt, the Revolutionary Parson, l. by Mrs. E. A. Diman.

Card Table, made of Zebra wood, brought from the coast of Africa, by Capt. John DeWolf, l. by Mrs. Clara D. DeWolf.

Mahogany Brass Bound Celaret, l. by Mrs. W. B. DeWolf.

Straight Backed, Leather Covered Chair, once owned by *Nathaniel Byfield*, l. by the Misses Herreshoff.

Large Chest of Drawers on High Legs, inlaid, and with brass mountings, l. by Herbert H Bosworth.

Large Mirror, over 160 years old, from the old Sandford house; very heavy solid oak frame, with black and red ornamentation, l. by Miss Lizzie Simmons.

Chair, of set imported for the first Congress in Philadelphia, l. by Mrs. J. DeW. Perry.

Large Camp Chest, made of camphor wood, bound with brass, with four brass handles and three spring locks, about six feet long, and higher than an ordinary table. This was left behind, filled with clothing and other property, by Gen. Prescott, commander of the British troops on the island of Rhode Island, when he was captured by Col Barton; l. by Mrs. E. A. Diman.

Liquor Chest, " " "
Warming Pan, " " "

Desk, made by Rev. Henry Wight, and used by him for writing sermons on during his lifetime; l. by Mrs. E. A. Diman.

"**As you like it**" **Chair,** owned by Rev. John Burt, who died the night Bristol was bombarded by Wallace, in 1775; l. by Mrs. E. A. Diman.

Chair, 150 yrs. old, belonging to the Dimond family, l. by Mrs. Margaret Taylor.

Shaving Case of Col. Job Almy, now 200 years old, l. by Darwin Almy.

Chair formerly owned by Rev. John Burt, l. by Mrs. Sam'l White, Prov.

Chair 160 years old, high back, rush seat, l. by Mrs. C. L. H. Chesbro'.

Large Heavy Table, with eight legs, dating from the first settlement of Bristol. L. by Trinity Church.

Two very old high-backed Chairs, one with arms, l. by Trinity Church.

Brass Candlestick, 160 years old, once owned by Mrs. Hope (Power) Brown, great-great-grandmother of the Herreshoff family.

Table over 200 years old, l. by Mrs. Maria M Hazard.

Pair of Andirons in the shape of dogs, over 150 years old, l. by Miss Cordelia Chase.

Lignum Vitæ Sugar-Can and Cover, 180 years old, l. by William P. Munro

Pair of Andirons in the form of Scotch Highlanders, very old and curious, l. by Leonard Sandford.

Tall Brass Andirons, l by Veits G. Peck.

Pair very large and tall Andirons, made of Queen metal, l. by Mrs. C. L. H. Chesbro'.

Pair of Brass Camp Candlesticks, l. by Mrs. Gideon Sherman.

Pair of small old-fashioned Bellows, l. by Mrs. N. Coggeshall.

Inkstand belonging to John Throop, 134 years ago, l. by Mrs. H. W. Bache.

Lignum Vitæ Case or Casket, about 200 years old, l. by Miss A. F. Munro.

Pair of Andirons in the shape of negro boys, once the property of Mr. Hicks West, an old Revolutionary Pensioner; l. by Miss Emma E. Cary.

Brass Candlesticks and pair of Enamelled Curtain Knobs, 125 years old, l. by Thomas Easterbrooks.

Large Mahogany Arm Chair, formerly owned by the Bradford family of Mass. L. by Miss Annie F. Munro.

Large Covered Arm Chair, brought from England by Rev. John Usher in 1720, covered with different old-fashioned chintzes; l. by Miss Lizzie Simmons.

Three-Cornered Table, with leaf and hidden compartment, from the old Sandford house, l. by Miss Lizzie Simmons.

Bronze Candlesticks, 200 years old, l. by Mrs. Hope Blake.

Hard Wood Sugar Bowl, 200 years old, l. by Mrs. Asha Card.

Iron Candlestick, 135 years old, l. by Miss Abby F. Coy.

Foot Stove, used in the old Congregational Meeting House, l. by Mrs. Wm. B. Spooner.

Book Case, with drawers and glass doors, brass ornaments on top, formerly owned by Col. Simeon Potter, l. by Capt. John D. Dimond.

Stand, formerly owned by Col. S. Potter, l. by Capt. John D. Dimond.

Mahogany Chair, carved with claw feet, one of the prizes captured by a Bristol privateer 125 years ago, l. by Mrs Clara D. DeWolf.

Very old Looking Glass, l. by Miss A. F. Coy.

Sand Box, made from large African nut, dated D. W., 1744, l. by Herbert H. Bosworth.

Old-fashioned Mirror, l. by Herbert H. Bosworth.

Old-fashioned Brass Candlesticks, l. by C. F. Herreshoff.

Old Mirror, beveled edges, with mahogany and gilt frame, l. by George B. Diman.

Bull's-Eye Window Glasses, l. by George B. Diman.

Swift and two Spinning Wheels, for wool, l. by Mrs. Mary E. Slade.

Flax Wheel, l. by Mrs. Clara D. DeWolf.

Old-fashioned Rocker Chair, l. by T. L. Fisher.

Three-Legged Skillet, lined with bell metal. It belonged to William Cox, whose father brought it from England, and whose house was on the site of the Rogers Library. In May, 1777, the house was fired by British soldiers, and burned to the ground. The skillet was found in the cellar, where it had fallen. L. by Gilbert Norris.

Pewter Platter, Plate and Basin, dated 1730. **Keg**, 1745. **Little Bucket**, 1765. L. by Capt Peleg P. Rose.

Very Large Round Pewter Platter, over 150 years old, l. by Miss Sarah Coggeshall.

Collection of old Pewter Platters and Plates, l. by John DeWolf.

Tall Clock, that has been going over 100 years, l. by Samuel Coggeshall.

Handsome Molucca Wood Table, and very old **Round Top Table**, l. by Mrs. E. B. Coggeshall.

Finely Carved Wooden Spoon and Bellows, mahogany and ivory, l. by W. C. Manchester.

Mahogany Liquor Case, with gilt bottles, l. by Mrs. Clara D. DeWolf.

Linen Tablecloth, 180 years old, l. by Mrs. Mary Waldron Chase.

Large Chintz Curtains, over 100 years old, with quaint designs, covering the entire surface, l. by Mrs. C. L. H. Chesbro'.

Elegant Silk and Gold Tapestry, with gold bulion woven into the design, representing the waves of the sea, with dolphins and gold fish swimming through them, brought from China about 1770. L. by Mrs. C. L. H. Chesbro'.

Silk Bed-quilt, made by Alice B. Wight 60 years ago, from pieces of dresses then over 100 years old; l. by Miss A. F. Alden.

Napkin, brought from France to Rhode Island by a French Protestant about 190 years ago; l. by Mrs. Esther Powell Snow.

Sheet, spun and woven by Mrs. Rebecca Smith before her marriage in 1801, from flax raised and prepared in Bristol, R. I. L. by Geo. J. Smith. Mrs. Smith died a few months ago, in her 99th year.

Silk Brocade, for furniture covering, dark blue with large crimson and gold flowers. Imported from India over 100 years ago. L. by Mrs. C. L. H. Chesbro'.

Stand Cloth, 200 years old, l. by Mrs. Priscilla Allyn.

A Pew Door belonging to the "Parson's Pew" of the first meeting-house built in Bristol in 1684. It is made of oak wood cut on the Common, and when made was for the only pew in the church Each member of the church in those days built his pew at his own expense, and the first one was built by the society for the use of the minister's family. The "meeting-house" stood on the Common, near the site of the present Court House. L. by the Congregational Society.

The Window that was over the pulpit in the present Town Hall building when it was first built for a church nearly 100 years ago. L. by Geo. B Diman.

Large turned Arm Chair, over 150 years old, l. by Mrs. Clara D. DeWolf.

Bed-quilt, made of pink, green and blue silks, and with the following history:—In 1738, Esther Powell, a granddaughter of Gabriel Bernon, was married to James Helme. As America afforded but few luxuries then, the parents of the happy bride sent to London for the wedding trousseau. Those were the days of "short gowns and petticoats," and garments of finest textures and lustrous hue came from the mother country. In the course of years the clothes became worn, and were transformed into this bed-quilt. On the occasion of Gen. Washington's last visit to Newport, R. I., it was brought across the Ferry from Narragansett to cover the bed on which his august form was to repose. As yet it had never been finished; and when the granddaughter of Ester Powell Helme was married in 1795, a sempstress was hired to quilt it. The work occupied six months, and the woman received her board and twenty cents per week as her wages. The quilt has descended to an Ester Powell through each succeeding generation, and is now in possession of one of the name. L. by Mrs. Ester Powell Snow.

ARMS, CANES, ARMAMENTS, ETC.

Sword, formerly used by Capt. Benj. Church, one of the first settlers in Bristol, who defeated King Philip, and carried by Church during King Philip's war. Handsome silver handle. L. by Col. Peter Church.

"Benjamin Church is a prominent name in the early Colonial history. Born at Plymouth in 1639, he married Alice Southworth, granddaughter of the distinguished wife of Gov. Bradford. After the close of Philip's war, he removed to this town. He purchased largely of the original proprietors, and held for many years much landed estate. He built the house known as the "Old Talbee House," near the corner of Thames and Constitution streets. He was frequently elected to offices of trust, was public spirited, and contributed with great liberality for the support of institutions of religion and education. Died, January 17, 1717-18, in Little Compton, in the 78th year of his age."

Flag, presented to the town of Bristol by Nath'l Byfield, in 1723. Made of silk, with handsome staff, with silver pike and mountings, made in 1710. L. by the town of Bristol.

The lower end of the staff of this flag was thrust into the trunk of an old, decayed mazzard cherry tree, to keep it in a perpendicular position. There was a relevancy in this. This old tree is the last of a large number imported by Byfield from England soon after the settlement of the town. They stood on both sides of the Poppasquash road, leading south from the residence of Stephen T. Church. There are persons now living who remember when some of these trees bore fruit. In the great September gale of 1815, numbers of these trees were prostrated, and those that were left standing showed no signs of life afterward. The writer of this remembers when a boy, that numbers of these knarled and twisted trunks were standing spectres of a dead past, like so many mailed sentries, challenging the new generation. This old trunk, the last of all its companions, has been reverently kept by Mrs. Rogers and her sister, Miss Charlotte DeWolf, and was sent over from Poppasquash, with other interesting relics, for the exhibition.

Sword and Epaulets, worn by Benj. Wilcox during the war of the Revolution, l. by Benj. W. Davis.

Mr. Wilcox was a revolutionary patriot and soldier, but died at a good old age, a short time before Congress passed an act granting pensions.

British Musket, plowed up near Quaker Hill, Portsmouth, R. I., by Isaac Anthony, about 1779, l. by Edward Anthony, Jr.

Shot and Balls, lodged in the house of Hon. Benj. Bourne during the bombardment of Bristol by Wallace, 1775, l. by Mrs. J. DeW. Perry.

Iron Shot, four pounder, fired into the Walley house, on State street, during the bombardment of Bristol, by Wallace, in 1775, l. by William J. Miller.

Sextant, used by Capt. John DeWolf during his early voyages.

Compass, made in Lisbon, 1719, and used on board of the ship "San José," captured by "Tom Jones," in the brig "Yankee." L. by Mrs. E. A. Diman.

Handcuff and Shackles, used on board old Bristol slave ships.

Camp Broiler, used during the Revolution, l. by Mrs. R. S. Andrews.

Musket, (Queen Anne), 1745, l. by Capt. Peleg R. Rose.

Brass Pistol, 1745,   "   "   "   "   "   "

Brass Mounted Sword, 1789, l. by Capt. Peleg R. Rose.

Cannon Ball and Grape Shot, fired by British, and plowed up on the farm of Capt Wm. H. West, at Bristol Ferry, l. by Wm. H. West, Jr.
Two Flint-Lock Muskets, l by Jesse Gladding.
Cartridge and Grape Shot, " "   "   "
Wooden Lock,   " "   "   "
Chopping Knife, over 150 years old, l. by Mrs. Asha Card.
Boot Jack, 1715, l by J. A. C. Gladding.
China Till, from the old Lee house, l. by Mrs. Josephus Gooding.
Pewter Plate, about 200 years old, l. by Samuel Coggeshall.
Spinning Wheel, l. by Jesse Gladding
Sword, used by first Colonel (Samuel Wardwell) of Bristol Artillery, l. by M. A. DeW. Howe.
Gentleman's Dress Sword, of last century, l. by V. G. Peck.
Large Bombshell, fired by the British at the bombardment of Bristol by Wallace, 1775, and found in the garden of Jonathan Russell, on Hope street, l by J. R. Bullock.
Leg of Camp Bedstead, used in the Revolutionary war by Stephen Smith, l. by J. R. Bullock.
Bassoon and Drum, the latter used at Fort Dumpling in war of 1812, l. by George Alger.
Canteen, used by Preserved Abell during the war of the Revolution, l. by Miss E. Morse.
Double-barrelled Flint-lock Pistol, l. by Loring Coggeshall.
Pair of Flint-lock Duelling Pistols, l. by Lewis H. DeWolf.
Scales, with six weights, for weighing gold dust, used by Capt. Levi DeWolf on the west coast of Africa, 1790, l. by Cordelia L. Allen.
Grape Shot, found on the shore of Bristol Harbor imbedded in a stone, where it had worn a deep hole, probably by motion caused by the tide. From the shape and size supposed to have been fired by the British. L. by Dr. J. C. Gallup.
Brass Camp Candlesticks, l. by Mrs. G. Sherman.
Cup, made from part of man-o'-war Constitution, l by Mrs. J. DeW. Perry.
Flag, flown by Star of the West, when attempting to re inforce Fort Sumpter, April, 1860, and the first flag fired upon during the war of the rebellion. L. by C. Evans.
Whaleboat, made by W. C. Manchester, l. by W. C. Manchester, Jr.
Dressing Case, carried during the Revolutionary war, by Gen. James M. Varnum, l. by Mrs. James DeW. Perry.
Pin Case, of enamelled copper, belonging to the wife of Gen. Varnum, l. by Mrs. J. DeW. Perry.
Fans, of 100 years ago, l. by Mrs J. DeWolf Perry.
Fan, about 150 years old, formerly owned by the wife of Prof. Winthrop, of Harvard College, l. by Mrs. R. S. Andrews.
Fans, of the olden time, l. by John DeWolf.
Woven Silver Garters, with Knee Buckles set with Stones, worn by James Brown over 100 years ago, l. by the Misses Herreshoff.

Full Set Silver Buttons, worn over 100 years ago, l. by the Misses Herreshoff.

Silver Buttons, 150 years old, l. by Betsey H. Chadwick.

Buttons, made 120 years ago, from shells picked up on the shores of the Mediterranean, l. by the Herreshoffs.

Shoe Buckles, Brilliants and Sapphires, formerly worn by Levi DeWolf, l, by Mrs. T. DeW. Colt.

Silver Shoe Buckles, owned and worn by Benjamin Miller as early as 1750. He was the great-great grandfather of the present owner. L. by William J. Miller.

Old-fashioned Tortoise Shell Combs, l. by C. H. Norris.

Silver Knee Buckles and Shoe Buckles, l. by Mrs. Clara D. DeWolf.

Silver Knee Buckles, set with stones and curious old gold ring, l. by Mrs. Viets G. Peck.

Carved Snell Comb, l. by Miss Ida L. Munro.

Six Silver Buttons, 150 years old, l. by Benj. Davis.

Very Old Silver Watch, l. by Miss C. M. Shepard.

Interesting Collection of Rings and Jewelry, worn by old Bristol people, l. by Mrs. Clara D. DeWolf.

Spectacles, 206 years old, l. by Benj. Dawley.

Snuff Box, very old, formerly belonged to "Marm" May, l. by Mrs. Morgan.

Mourning Pin, over 100 years old, with gold setting, l. by Mrs. Charlotte Goode.

Gold Suspender Buckles, worn by Capt. Daniel Morice, l. by Mrs. E. S. Babbitt.

Ring, set with Stones, formerly worn by Col. Sim. Potter, l. by Mrs. M. J. Mason.

Two Gold Watches, enamelled and set with stones, l. by Messrs. J. and B. D. DeWolf.

Pocket Book, 1748, l. by Bennett J. Munro.

Cane, of the Hon. Benj. Bourne, l. by Mrs. J. DeW. Perry.

Cane, made from the flagship Lawrence, commanded by Com. O. H. Perry on Lake Erie, in 1813, l. by Mrs. J. DeW. Perry.

Cane, cut on the coast of Africa, by Com. M. C. Perry, when commanding the fleet to suppress the slave trade, l. by Mrs. J. DeW. Perry.

Cane, made from the keel of the "Gaspee," presented to the late John Brown Herreshoff, by Col. Ephraim Bowen, in 1825, then the only survivor of the Gaspee expedition. The gift to Mr. Herreshoff was in honor of his grandfather, John Brown, who planned and headed the expedition. L. by C. F. Herreshoff.

ARTICLES OF DRESS, ETC.

Piece of Wedding Dress, worn by Esther Powell, daughter of Gabriel Bernon, the French Huguenot, l. by Esther Powell Snow.

Silk Dress, embroidered in colors, over 100 years old, formerly worn by Mrs. Levi Lane, maternal grandmother of Mrs. C. F. Herreshoff

Piece of Wedding Dress, of figured silk, damask, of Prudence Miller, who was married to Ebenezer Cole, January 9th, 1737, l. by William J. Miller.

Satin Vest, elegantly embroidered in delicate patterns, with silk and spangles, formerly owned by James Brown, over 100 years old, l. by C. F. Herreshoff.

Piece of Silk Dress, formerly worn by Mrs. Simeon Potter, l. by Mrs. J. D. Mason.

Cotton Dress, a relic of 1765, l. by Mrs. John Collins.

Brocade Silk Dress, with large brilliant floral pattern, presented by Capt. James Gibbs to his daughter about 1730-40. l. by Mrs. Rogers.

Very Old Gold Pin, l. by Miss M. E Bourn.

Perfume Bag, brought from abroad, 1756, l. by George J Adams.

Pair of Curious Outside Stays, very finely stitched, worn over 150 years ago, l. by Mrs. James B. White.

Very old Stitched Needle Book, l. by Loring Coggeshall.

Wedding Vest, silk, with fine silk embroidery, 112 years old, l. by Viets G. Peck.

Old-fashioned Reticule, and two Pieces of Embroidery, 100 years old, done in Kensington stitch, l. by Mrs. J. DeW. Perry.

Two Figured Gauze Veils, one green, and one white, l. by Mrs. Morgan.

Two Samplers, one worked by Sarah Martindale, 1759, one by Nancy Martindale, 1761, l. by Mrs. Geo. J. Adams.

Piece of Embroidery, the work of Eliza Almy, great-granddaughter of Col. Job Almy, of the Pocasset Purchase, l. by Mrs. James Corthell.

Sampler, worked in 1785, by Hannah Drown, l. by Miss H. B. Luther.

Mortuary Piece, l. by Allen B Sandford.

Wedding Dress of Mrs. John Brown, great-great-grandmother of the Herreshoff family, heavy white watered silk, l. by the Misses Herreshoff.

Silk Dress, worn by Mrs. Brown, gorgeous brocaded bunches of flowers on light ground, l. by Mrs. C. L. H. Chesbro'.

Wedding Dress of Abby A. Diman, wife of Gov Byron Diman, with mantle, and thread lace veil, all elaborately embroidered by hand; satin shoes, lace, etc., l. by Mrs. C. D. DeWolf.

Part of Wedding Dress of Mrs. Z. Leonard, 1750, l. by Mrs. C. D. DeWolf.

Old Silk Dresses, l. by Miss C. DeWolf and Mrs. Rogers.

Traveling Bag and Child's Shoes, l. by Daniel Tanner.

Framed Needlework, l. by Mrs. Chas. F. Herreshoff. Jr.

DOCUMENTS AND OLD PAPERS.

History of the World, by Sir Walter Raleigh, published in 1614, l. by Miss E. B. Diman.

Letter written by Gen. Washington to his Wife, introducing James Brown, uncle of C. F. Herreshoff, l. by C. F. Herreshoff.

Bible, 200 years old, given by Mary Holmes to her daughter, Mrs. Benjamin Taylor, now owned and loaned by Mrs. Asha A. Card.

Bible, belonged to the grandmother of Bennet J. Munro, presented by her uncle on her 17th birthday, 1748, l. by Miss Sarah B. Munro.

Child's Picture Book of "Ye Olden Time," l. by Miss Sarah B. Munro.

Leaves, from the Pulpit Prayer Book used in St. Michael's Church before the Revolutionary war, and torn up by the Americans at that time, because of the prayers it contained for the King and Royal family, l. by Mrs. M. Luther Simmons, and Miss Lizzie Simmons.

Prayer Book, formerly used by Rev. John Usher, and containing several services not now used, l. by Mrs. M. Luther Simmons.

Subscription Paper, for starting the first Methodist Church in Bristol, l. by Augustus N. Miller.

Public Document, Proceedings of R. I. Legislature, 1763, l. by Mrs. John Gravlin.

Commission of Jonathan Russell, first Collector of the port of Bristol. This Commission is dated in 1804, and signed by Thomas Jefferson, President, and James Madison, Secretary of State. L. by J. Russell Bullock.

Book, The Fulfilling of the Scripture, published in 1671, once owned by Hopestill Potter. It has been in Bristol since the early history of the town. L. by Miss Annie F. Munro.

One Very Large Bible, l. by John P. Simmons.

New England Primer, l. by Miss Emily Morse.

Two Manuscript Sermons, by Rev. John Williams, l. by Miss Emily Morse.

Collection of Continental Money, l by Miss Emily Morse.

Life of Israel Potter, a Revolutionary soldier, l. by Geo. J. Adams.

Israel Potter enlisted a private in Col. Patterson's regiment, one of the first regiments raised in this State. He was severely wounded in the battle of Bunker Hill. In July, 1775, he volunteered as a seaman on board of the armed brigantine Washington, Capt. Sion Martindale, and was captured and sent over to England a prisoner, where he remained in exile more than fifty years. He finally returned to this country in his old age with an only son, the sole survivor of a large family.

Diary of Rev. Henry Wight, from 1721 until 1812, containing an account of the "dark day," May, 1780, the earthquake in New England, etc., etc., l. by Mrs. E. A. Diman.

Almanac, 1682, with notes, recipes, etc., in writing, l. by Mrs. E. A. Diman.
Eight Sermons, preached by Rev. John Burt before the Revolution, l. by Mrs. E. A. Diman.
Deed, signed by John Walley, 1685, l. by Mrs. E. A. Diman.
Book, containing a copy of the original constitution of the United States, l. by H. Herbert Bosworth.
Deed, signed by the four original proprietors of Bristol, Nath'l Byfield, John Walley, Nath'l Oliver, Stephen Burton, l. by S. Pomeroy Colt.
Copy of the Newport Mercury, March 11, 1760, l. by John DeWolf.
Copy of the N. Y. Gazette, November 15, 1773, l. by John DeWolf.
Copy of Newport Mercury, the type for printing of which was set by Benj. Franklin, l. by Miss C. DeWolf and Mrs. M. DeW. Rogers.
A number of old New York and Boston Papers, sent to Bristol subscribers, l. by George B. Diman.
Commission of William Munro, as Justice of the Peace, 1748, signed by ye Gov. Wm. Greene, l. by Miss Annie F. Munro.
Manuscript Letter of Gov. William Coddington, 1718, to William Munro, l. by Miss A. F. Munro.
Manuscript Letter of Nath'l Byfield, 1720, l. by Miss A. F. Munro.
Manuscript Bill from Dr. Tallman, 1721, l. by Miss A. F. Munro.
An Appeal to the Court at Cambridge, from a judgment by Nath'l Blagrove, Judge of Probate, by Nath'l Kay and William Munro, 1730, l. by Miss Annie F. Munro.
Contract, between Christo. Hopkins and Simeon Potter, for the delivery of a six-pounder carriage gun, 1759, l. by Miss Annie F. Munro.
Very Old Newspaper, l. by J. Gladding.
Old Deeds, l. by Mrs J. R. Gardner.
History of Demonology, l. by Miss M. G. DeWolf.
English Liberties, farewell Sermons, l. by Samuel B. Coggeshall.
Judge Bourne's Commission, signed by John Adams, l. by Mrs. J. DeW. Perry.
History of Britain, 1671, by John Milton, l. by Mrs. J. DeW. Perry.
Boston Gazette, 1749, " " " " " "
Boston Evening Post, 1749, " " " " " "
The Massachusetts Continental, 1788, " " " " " "
Funeral Sermon, on the death of Gov. William Bradford, by Rev. Alexander V. Griswold, Bristol, 1808, l. by William J. Miller.
Funeral Oration, delivered at R. I. College, 1775, l. by Mrs. J. DeW. Perry.
Funeral Sermons, on old Bristol people, by Rev. H. Wight, l. by Mrs. Clara D. DeWolf.

INDIAN RELICS.

The committee knowing that many specimens of Indian stone relics had been found at and near Bristol, desired to make a fine display of the same, and requested Mr. CHARLES GORTON, of Providence, to place on exhibition in the Town Hall, selections from his cabinet of Rhode Island Indian stone implements. He cheerfully complied with the request, also drawing attention to the following quotation he had made from Hutchinson's Massachusetts, from a copy in the John Carter Brown Library : " At the beginning of Philip's war it was generally agreed that the Narragansett tribe consisted of 2,000 fighting men. They were the most curious coiners of the Wampumpeag, and supplied the other nations with many pendants and bracelets, also with tobacco pipes of stone, some blue, and some white. They furnished the earthern vessels and pots for cookery, and other domestic uses." The following is a list of the specimens placed on exhibition by Mr. Charles Gorton :

1. Steatite Pot, from the Angell, Johnston, Indian Quarry.
2. Pipe, found in a grave near Silver Spring.
3. Sinker, found on the Hon. S. W. Church farm, Bristol.
4. Two specimens of Bracers, found in a grave near Silver Spring.
5. Spindle Whirl, from a grave near Apponaug.
6. Slickstone, found in East Providence, near Fort Hill.
7. Two frames of Arrow Points, found for the most part on Warwick plains, consisting of nearly all the varieties.
8. Lot of Borers, Awls and Drills, found at Wickford.
9. Amulet, found on the Armington farm, Kettle Point.
10. Four Pipes, found at Bristol, Quidnesset, Wickford and Potowomut.
11. Gouge, found in Coventry.
12. Skin Dresser, from Newport.
13. Chisel, from Pawtucket.
14. Roller, from Field's Point.
15. Pestle, found in an Indian grave at Swan Point.
16. Axe, found while excavating for the Rhode Island Hospital Trust Company building, South Main street, Providence.
17. Stone Mask, found in 1873, at Field's Point, one of only three specimens known in the United States.
18. Arrow Points, in process of formation, found near Old Maids' Cove.
19. Pipe, from Rumstick Point.
20. Hematite, or War Paint, found in a grave near Newport.
21. Two Copper Spoons, from a grave at Charlestown.
22. Spear Points, found on Point Judith.
23. Knife Blades, from different parts of the State.
24. Stone, used in Indian games, from Wickford.

25. Scraper, used with metal to produce fire, from Prudence Island.
26. Harrow Points, from Charlestown.
27. Hatchet, found near Apponaug.
28. Polished Celt, from Charlestown.
29. Hematite Paint Cup, from East Providence.
30. Sling Stone, from Warwick.
31. One foot of Bone Money, found in a grave in a sand hill, near Apponaug.
32. Seven feet of Wampumpeag, found on the farm of George W. Greene, Bristol.
33. Five feet of Wampum, found on the Poor Farm, Bristol.
34. Four feet of Wampum, found on the Dyer farm, near Devil's Foot Rock, Wickford.
35. Four feet of Wampum, found in a grave in a sand hill, on the Dyer farm, near Wickford.
36. Arrow, showing the manner of attaching the point.
37. Iron Hatchet, showing imprints of blanket, from an Indian grave, George W. Greene farm, Bristol.
38. Copper Cup, in which Wampumpeag was found in a grave on George W. Greene's farm.

Mr. Gorton exhibited many other Indian Stone Relics of equal interest, also a Deed of a Slave, dated at Newport, R. I., 1746; also an autographic letter of Samuell Gorton, dated Warwick, R. I., 1649; also a package of Colonial and Continental Currency.

Stone Tomahawk and Pestle, loaned by Mrs. Clara D. DeWolf.
Two large Stone Axes, l. by C. F. Herreshoff, Jr.
Two Stone Axes, l. by Jesse Gladding.
Indian Hammer, " " " "
String of Wampum, l. by. Jesse Gladding.
String of Wampum, l. by George W. Greene.
Indian Pestle, l. by " " "
Indian Pipes, " " " " "
Indian Stone Implements, l. by Mrs. J. DeW. Perry.
Kernels of Charred Corn, picked up on the site of the old Indian Fortress, in South Kingstown, the place of the Great Swamp fight, December 19, 1675, more than two hundred years ago—and yet they are well preserved, and some of the kernels quite perfect. Dug up August 19, 1873. L. by William J. Miller.

A fact worthy of mention, connected with this Loan Exhibition, is, that notwithstanding the large number of articles, and the freedom with which many of them were handled, not a single article was broken or missed in the entire collection.

CORRESPONDENCE.

NEWPORT, R. I., 8 September, 1880.

I am very grateful to the town of Bristol for doing me the honor of inviting me to join in celebrating the two hundredth anniversary of its existence; and I regret exceedingly that it will not be in my power to be its guest on that auspicious day. With the hope that its history for the next two hundred years may be as beautiful and patriotic and happy as for the last,

I am, most heartily,
Its greatly obliged well wisher,
GEO. BANCROFT.

CONSULATE OF THE UNITED STATES,
LISBON, Sept. 1st, 1880.

LeBaron B. Colt, Esq., President of the Bi-Centennial Committee of Bristol:

DEAR SIR:—I have much pleasure in acknowledging the receipt of the invitation of the Bi-Centennial Committee of the town of Bristol, to be present at the celebration of the two hundredth anniversary of the settlement of the town, on the 24th of September, 1880.

I regret very much that the long distance of my present residence from my native town, and my official duties here, render it impossible for me to be present, which would be to me a great pleasure.

I am proud to be a son of Bristol, and although I am separated from it by three thousand miles of space, and eighteen years of time, yet my interest in it is the same as ever.

During that time more than two thousand of the inhabitants of the town have died, and among them many of my old friends and acquaintances; yet as a proof of the conservative character of the town, I find on your committee of forty-five that all but *three* are old friends and acquaintances.

Descended, as I am, from the earliest settlers of the town, having cast my first vote as a landholder on land which had never been out of my family since the original charter was granted, having been made a representative of the town at a very early age in the legislature, and always having taken the greatest interest in the annals, local history, as well as the prosperity of the town, you can well imagine the sympathy I feel in the reünion you are about to celebrate.

With my best wishes for the good health and prosperity of you, and your fellow committeemen, as well as all our fellow townsmen in the good old town of Bristol,

I remain,
Yours very truly,
HENRY W. DIMAN.

BOULOGNE-SUR-MER, FRANCE, Aug. 13, 1880.

Mr. LeBaron Colt, President of Committee:

DEAR SIR:—I am in receipt of your invitation to attend, as a "Son of Bristol," the two hundredth anniversary of the settlement of that town. I regret that I shall be unable to accept, in person, but shall, in heart, be with you all. I should be very happy to clasp the hands of old-time schoolmates and friends, after an absence of thirty years, but the pleasure is denied me. On the "day we celebrate," I will drink to "Bristol, its sons and its daughters," hoping at some not far distant day, to meet and greet them all.

Very sincerely yours,
GEO. T. BOURNE.

CHICAGO, Sept. 17, 1880.

Messrs. LeBaron B. Colt, William J. Miller and Edward Babbitt, Committee, etc.:

GENTLEMEN:—Your highly valued communication of the first of September inst., inviting me to unite with the sons and daughters of Bristol on the 24th instant, in celebrating the two hundredth anniversary of the settlement of our venerated town, was duly received. Among the lasting regrets of my life will be that of not being able to have been with you in person on that interesting occasion But be assured I shall be there in spirit, and on that day shall at least in imagination listen to the eloquent words of Prof. Diman, as he calls up from the dim and misty past the many events of interest in our town's history; and to Bishop Howe, who will invest the stories of the past as only

"He best can paint them, who shall feel them most."

And now wishing you perfect success in your undertaking, hoping and fondly believing that the future of Bristol may be even more than the past, I look in imagination down the vista of Time to that day

"When other men our lands shall till,
When other men our streets will fill,
And other birds will sing as gay,
As bright the sunshine as to-day,
Two hundred years from now."

William J. Miller, Esq.:

MY DEAR SIR:—I duly received your Committee's note of invitation to the Bi-Centennial, and since then a similar one from your President, Mr. Colt. To-day I reply addressing myself to the Committee. I can assure you I am much grieved at the thought of not being with you on the 24th. I have had no time to prepare any proper expression of my thoughts fit for the occasion, and can only send my best wishes.

Yours with warm regard,
WILLIAM F. D'WOLF,
Chicago, Ill., 226 Dearborn avenue.

JERSEYVILLE, Ill., September 18, 1880.

LeBaron B. Colt, Esq., Bristol, R. I.:

MY DEAR SIR:—Mrs Warren and I each received from you as President of the Committee, your kind and cordial invitation to attend the Bi-Centennial Anniversary of the town of Bristol, and we desire to express to you our thanks for your kindly remembrance of us, and our unfeigned regrets on account of our inability to be present on that delightful occasion. Although nearly forty-five years have elapsed since I left the home of my boyhood, and many new and strong ties now bind me to the West, yet the very name of the dear old town of Bristol, awakens in my mind a host of pleasant memories, and I long to revisit the place where the sunny days of my childhood and youth were spent, clouded only by the sad bereavement I suffered in the death of my mother, whose dust now reposes in your cemetery. I can conceive of nothing temporal in its nature, that would afford my wife and myself so much pleasure as this contemplated reünion of the sons and daughters of Bristol, if we could be with you. It seems to me that it would be a foretaste of the blessed reünion of the redeemed in the bright home above the skies. There are living in Bristol many of our kindred whom we have never seen, and we should be most happy to meet them and exchange fraternal greetings, and together trace out our common lineage, and have our hearts bound with quicker pulsations as hand clasped hand in mutual recognition of the sacred ties of blood binding us together. Time has also spared a few whose faces we have seen and whose visages as they appeared in youth still sweetly linger in our memories. Oh! what joy it would give us to greet them once more on this side of the "river." I often think of your mother as I last saw her in Bristol, in the bloom and beauty of her girlhood, and her beautiful image is before me now as I write, and I grieve that I may not see her again. Circumstances beyond my control prevent my leaving here at this time, and I am compelled to forego the delight it would afford me to be with you. A kind Providence has favored me since my removal from Bristol. I came here a youth, and am now a *patriarch*. I have eight children, four sons, and four daughters, all married but one, and my grandchildren now number seventeen. I have lost by death one child, and one grandchild. My family are *all* pleasantly situated, and if I should bring them all with me to your Bi-Centennial, the *number* in attendance would be very materially increased; and I don't think Bristol would feel dishonored by the *twenty-five* lineal descendants of that son and daughter of hers who left her pleasant shores and her shady streets more than forty years ago, to seek a home in the "Prairie State."

With our kind regards to your mother, and our best wishes for the health and prosperity of all our old friends in the dear old town,

I am very truly yours,

GEO. E. WARREN.

NEW YORK, Sept. 10th, 1880.

Mr. Wm. J. Miller, Committee, etc.:

MY DEAR FELLOW TOWNSMAN:—The kind manner in which you have communicated to me the invitation of your committee to be present at the celebration of the two hundredth anniversary of the settlement of Bristol, the home of my ancestors; and the gratitude I feel for the honor conferred upon me, will constrain me, if possible, to comply with your invitation. If not, I shall endeavor to comply with the request to favor you "with a letter embodying such thoughts as the occasion may prompt"; which, of course, will contain the greater part of my intended speech.

Should our descendants inherit, and copy, the integrity, energy and piety of our forefathers, the sons of Bristol will already have made sure the prayer for her "*esto perpetua*," which is fervently breathed for her by the oldest of her surviving children,

BENJAMIN BOSWORTH SMITH.

REV. JOHN BURT WIGHT.

WAYLAND, Mass., Sept 21st, 1880.

To Mr. William J. Miller, Committee:

DEAR SIR:—My father's hand trembles so much that it is quite impossible for him to use it in writing, but at your request I will send you some of the recollections of his early boyhood.

He says: "I have never kept a diary, and must in my account be guided by definite impressions made on my mind by passing events. Bristol was purchased and settled by four English gentlemen. They probably were impressed by its commercial position and the remarkable beauty of its locality. In my boyhood I went frequently to a house near Mt. Hope, built by one of these gentlemen. It was then occupied by Governor Bradford. The walls of one room were hung with tapestry, representing the story of Jephtha and his daughter, the figures of life size. The streets were laid out with great regularity, and ornamented by hundreds of the mazzard cherry trees, brought from England; as these trees decayed from age, they were replaced by the Lombardy poplar.

"My mother was in delicate health, and some gentlemen of my father's society presented her with a chaise, which was the second covered wheel carriage in town; but in a few years chaises had become so numerous that a party of gentlemen and ladies rode out to meet my father on his return from his annual visit to Boston, and had a tea drinking at Warren.

"I went to school with other small children to Madam Burt, the widow of the former clergyman. Afterwards Mr. Joseph Rawson taught a private school in the Court House. He was a very able man, and a good teacher.

"Then a spacious academy building was erected. It contained a hall, used for occasional meetings of the Legislature, and other purposes; also a library room. This room was occupied by a Proprietors' Library.

"The town had been furnished with a few of the leading theological works, which were kept in the meeting-house for the perusal of the people who remained during the interval of religious services. The Proprietors' Library consisted of miscellaneous books, the popular tales, histories, travels. At an early date Col. Simeon Potter, of Scituate, gave several hundred dollars and a set of the Encyclopedia Britannica, in twenty volumes, two with plates. These books were all imported from London. The Library was called the Potter Library, in honor of Col. Potter.

"Bristol, at an early period, was engaged in the slave trade. I recollect seeing on the wharf long rows of hogsheads of New England rum, to be sent to Africa for the purchase of slaves. My father took me with him to see the last slave ship fitted out. It was owned by Philadelphians, and in derision of scruples which were beginning to be felt, was called the 'Merry Quaker.' There were handcuffs hanging in the blacksmith's shop. There were in town a number of Africans regarded as belonging to particular families. These had special seats provided for them in the upper gallery of the Congregational Church. They were headed by Scipio Burt, the servant of the former minister. Scipio was generally esteemed for his good nature and honesty, and was several years sexton of the church.

"The neighboring ministers, acquaintances and friends of my father, or, rather, some of them, were Drs. Hopkins and Patten, of Newport, Mr. Watson, of Barrington, Mr. Pipond, of Taunton, Dr. Fobes, of Raynham, Dr. Wilson, of Providence. My early years saw the discovery of electricity by Dr. Franklin. There was much interest on the subject, and my father gave fifty dollars for an electrical machine. The ladies came once a year to visit at their minister's, each of them bringing two skeins of linen as a present to his wife. There were two chimneys in the centre of the house, and the doors could be opened all around. The favorite amusement was to form a circle and receive an electric shock.

"The people of Bristol held funeral services on occasion of the death of Washington. A coffin was carried in procession, an oration pronounced, then the coffin was deposited in a tomb."

My father is not quite as well as usual, and what I send you is the best result I could obtain to-day. I do not know as it is at all what you want. At eighty years my father would have been able to be in Bristol on such an occasion, but at ninety, of course he has failed in body and mind.

Yours respectfully,
MARTHA B. WIGHT.

NEW YORK, Sept. 1, 1880.

LeBaron B. Colt, Esq., President:

DEAR SIR:—I have received the invitation to attend the celebration of the Bi-Centennial of the town of Bristol, and must thank the Committee for the attention, wondering that I should, at this distance of time, have been found out as one of her sons.

Believe me, I have not, without pleasure, written my birthplace as Bristol, that sturdy little town, well known in the war of 1812, which then, asserting her own, has not ceased to assert it to this hour.

The day for their first settlement at Bristol was chosen by our progenitors for good reasons doubtless; probably for the best of all reasons, necessity; but (what they could not be expected to foresee), its two hundredth anniversary happens on a day when one of her sons, at least, will be so engaged as to make it difficult, if not impossible, for him to be absent from the home to which he has wandered.

It would give me great pleasure to visit my birthplace again. A town two hundred years old may be proud of its antiquity in a country where cities come to maturity in a decade, having hardly known infancy, and quite ignorant of such an idea as childhood.

I trust the day may pass to the satisfaction and triumph of those present sons and daughters of their venerable parent, who have had the courage, as well as filial affection, to undertake to do her honor.

I would be glad, under such auspices, to look again on the places which seem very distinct to my recollection, albeit the long shadows of nearly sixty years intervene. I fear the remembered vastness of many of them would diminish greatly on actual sight. There was the Common, on which took place the general training, with the great cannon and the masterly manœuvres of the sham-fight, the journey across which was too great to be undertaken alone; the mighty harbor, the voyage over which to the opposite shore was only to be made in fair weather, and on a calm day; the lofty height of Mount Hope, reached with much climbing, rewarded by a fine lunch; the church, whose vast proportions were seldom quite filled by the congregation. Ah, sir, I fear the pleasure of the pictures would be destroyed by too great familiarity now. It is well, perhaps, that I cannot come.

Wishing every success to the effort to make the day worthy of the occasion, I am respectfully,

And cordially yours,
MARLBOROUGH CHURCHILL.

CALVARY CHURCH, RECTORY, MANHEIM STREET,
GERMANTOWN, Philadelphia, Pa., Sept. 22, 1880.

Messrs. LeBaron B. Colt, Wm. J. Miller, Edward S. Babbitt, Committee:

DEAR SIRS:—Pardon my delay in replying to your gratifying invitation bearing date of September 1. My apology is absence from home, enforced by an inflamed knee joint, which disabled me and prevented my return until yesterday. I am still unable to walk, and accordingly am compelled to decline the invitation which you kindly extend to me.

I sincerely regret that I cannot participate in this anniversary of my native town, to renew early compansionship, and to recall pleasant memories. Of these many cluster around the old Academy, which is now supplanted by the Byfield School, and from which I passed to our Rhode Island college, having been prepared by him who is now in Paradise, exchanging the knowledge which is in part for that which is perfect. His diversified acquirements, and his marked abilities as a teacher, being joined with retiring, studious habits and great humility, never received that public recognition which they deserved. But those of his pupils who knew him intimately and affectionately, will, I am confident, feel that the name of the Rev. N. B. Cooke should have a grateful mention at this anniversary, and that his years of faithful and wise instruction made an enduring impression upon those Bristol youth, who were so fortunate as to come under the influence of his honest scholarship and of his manly meekness.

Other features of the town now erased recur to me as I write, such as the two old wind mills, standing like two sentinels at each end of the town, challenging the Quixotic exploits of us boys, who, disposed "to run amuck and tilt at all we meet," with the vandal spirit of youth, hastened their overthrow and gradual removal.

Amid these pleasant paths of memory one might wander on to the point of weariness. I will halt here, wishing God's blessing upon dear old Bristol, and a complete success for its Bi-Centennial Celebration.

Were I so fortunate as to form one of your goodly company, I would be disposed to offer some such sentiment as this: If Cowper said truly that "God made the country and man made the town," then should the moral architects and artizans of our community build in harmony with the design and beginning made by the Divine Originator, building up its morality pure and undefiled as the unpolluted waters which encircle the town for its protection and purification,—fostering manners gentle and graceful as the curving lines of her shores—maintaining the straight paths of virtue as her streets stand four square to all the winds that blow; and as her shores are ever ringing with the echoes and ripplings of the boundless sea beyond, so may the blending of thought and action, of earnest tongue and honest toil be telling of a near and larger future, and form a chime to

> "Ring out false pride in place and blood,
> The civic slander and the spite;
> Ring in the love of truth and right,
> Ring in the common love of good."

Yours very truly, JAS. D'WOLF PERRY.

AKRON, O., Sept. 15, 1880.

LeBaron B. Colt:

DEAR SIR:—I received the kind invitation of your Committee to attend the Reünion of the Sons and Daughters of Bristol, and I sincerely regret that I cannot be present to celebrate with you that happy occasion.

Years have passed since I walked the shady streets of dear old Bristol. In fancy I stand once more beneath the waving branches of the elms that shadow my childhood's play-ground, the grassy Common; again I linger by the shore, looking out upon the sparkling waves of old Narragansett, and take one long, delicious draught of that cool, invigorating air. I breathe again—alas, the vision has vanished, and the smoke and fumes of bituminous coal are wafted to me on the evening air, reminding me that I am far away from those delightful ocean breezes, in the neighborhood of a busy, bustling inland town.

How gladly would I meet (were it possible) with the many dear friends and old acquaintances who will, on the twenty-fourth day of September, throng the streets of our ancient town.

Hoping that the occasion may indeed be a joyous one to all present, I remain,

Yours respectfully,

MRS. O. S. WARNER.

SYLVANIA, Bradford Co., Pa., May 7th, 1880.

To B. J. Munro, Esq.:

DEAR SIR:—Yours of 1st inst. traveled slow, for some reason or other, only reaching me last evening, 6th. In reply, shall be pleased to give you any information that I can. I am always pleased to hear from any one in our "Father land." You said in your letter that you were going to have a Centennial Celebration to celebrate the two hundredth anniversary of its settlement (Bristol), and that you were going to invite all her sons and daughters to "come home" and join you in that celebration. Certainly it must be a pleasure beyond expression to those who have been long absent in other lands to visit the home of their childhood again on such a day, devoted to the recollections of the past. Will it not be one of the grandest days in her history, for many a gray-haired old man, as he returns to the home of his childhood to stand again upon his native soil, to look again upon the waters of the beautiful Narragansett, and seek out his playgrounds of fifty years ago, though long absent, not forgotten? It will renew their attachment to old Bristol again, if anything were necessary to do it; but I do not know as there is, for her children, wherever they may wander or seek homes in far-off lands, will remember her with the same affectionate regard as the captive Hebrew remembered his much-loved Jerusalem. I send to you such names as occur to me now; perhaps

I shall think of some more, and will send them to you. Shall be pleased to answer any inquiries, and hoping to be able to join you in the reünion on the 24th of September next, I remain,

Very respectfully yours,
HENRY B. CARD.

NEW HAVEN, Sept. 13, 1880.

Messrs. Colt, Miller and Babbitt, Committee:

GENTLEMEN:—I thank you for the invitation to me to be present at the Centennial Celebration of the settlement of the town of Bristol. It would give me great pleasure on many accounts to be present on that interesting occasion. I hope that if my health, which has been and still is quite imperfect, permit, I will comply with your kind invitation. Fifty-four years have passed since I resigned my pastorate in that agreeable place of residence. Yet I have not lost my attachment to that town, and to its highly favored people.

It was through the kind ordering of a wise Providence that I was associated with the venerable, kind-hearted senior pastor, Dr. Wight, as colleague with him for eleven years. This pastoral relation was very agreeable and uniformly harmonious. He was willing to assist me in any of the ministerial labors incumbent on us. For many years he had been the sole pastor, and was capable of giving advice to his junior associate. We were together as mutual laborers in the same field of spiritual culture.

With him and his family we enjoyed that pleasant intercourse which becomes the household of faith. The memory of it has given me pleasure to this day.

The year 1820 was signalized by a precious and powerful revival of religion. It was a truly pentecostal season. It commenced in our congregation, and soon spread into the other congregations of the place. The whole population was aroused and deeply interested, and converts by the power of the Holy Spirit were multiplied. A deep solemnity and religious joyfulness pervaded the whole community. Worldly business was for a time laid aside as far as practicable. Stores and shops were closed, and attention to ordinary affairs was suspended. Attending religious meetings from day to day became the most important occupation. An aged wealthy man met me in the street, and said with surprise, "What does all this mean? It seems as if the people did not want to do much else than to attend religious meetings." It was even so.

May the God of all grace soon give you such another copious effusion of the Spirit which shall occasion great joy in fair old Bristol, and also joy among the holy beings in heaven.

I hope to be with you on the day previous to the celebration.

Yours respectfully,
J. MANN.

CHICAGO, Sept. 16, 1880.

GENTLEMEN:—I have received your kind invitation to attend the two hundredth anniversary of the settlement of Bristol. I regret very much my inability to attend. The name of the town, something of its history, and legends, were made familiar to me in childhood by the conversation of my father and mother, who were born in its neighborhood.

Certainly one of the most heroic and interesting characters in all our Indian annals was the great Chief of the Wampanoags. I hope to see the rocky heights of Mt. Hope crowned with a monument to King Philip.

The day you celebrate will be full of the memories of the past, and hopes for the future; not only for your town and State, but for the great Republic, which has grown so rapidly and become so great. You will join with me in the prayer that our country may continue to advance through other centuries, and that the principles of liberty, *regulated by law*, and based on virtue and intelligence, of which your State furnishes so bright an example, may extend over the whole continent of America.

With many thanks, I am, gentlemen,
Very truly yours,
ISAAC N. ARNOLD.

Messrs. Colt, Miller and Babbitt, Committee.

PROVIDENCE, September 20th, 1880.

William J. Miller, Esquire, Bristol:

DEAR SIR:—Your communication, accompanied by an invitation to be present at the celebration of the two hundredth anniversary of the town of Bristol on the 24th instant, has been received.

I have waited thus long before replying, in order that I might be able to determine whether I could accept the invitation. My time, as I am now situated, is not my own.

It would give me great pleasure to be present on that occasion and revive some pleasant memories of men and things in Bristol forty years ago; but my official duties will require my presence in this city on that day.

Yours respectfully,
JAMES C. HIDDEN.

BROWN UNIVERSITY, PROVIDENCE, Sept. 21, 1880.

Messrs. LeBaron B. Colt, Wm. J. Miller, and Edward S. Babbitt, Committee:

GENTLEMEN:—I have delayed replying to your polite invitation, in the hope that I might find myself able to accept it; but I regret to say at this late hour, that my college engagements for the 24th inst. compel me to forego the great pleasure of being present at the celebration of the two hundredth anniversary of the town of Bristol. I thank you for the invitation to be present on an occasion of so great interest and importance, and I pray you to accept my hearty wish, that the heavens may smile upon you on that day, and that all fortunate influences may conspire to make it a great and a good day in the history of your town.

I have the honor to be,
Yours very truly,
J. L. LINCOLN.

PROVIDENCE, Sept. 18, 1880.

GENTLEMEN :—I am greatly obliged to you for your polite invitation to take part in the forthcoming celebration of the two hundredth anniversary of the settlement of Bristol. It would give me great pleasure to be present on the interesting occasion, but the state of my health compels me, very reluctantly, to decline. I have deferred replying sooner to your invitation in the hope that I might give a favorable reply.

Yours very respectfully,
JOHN R. BARTLETT.

Wm. J. Miller, Esq., for Committee.

PROVIDENCE, Sept. 24, 1880.

Messrs. Colt, Miller and Babbitt, Bi-Centennial Committee:

GENTLEMEN :—It is with deep regret that I find myself precluded the enjoyment of participating in your festivities to-day; but a form of disease which has kept me within doors for several days, is not so far mastered as to render it prudent for me to risk the fatigue and excitement incident to the occasion. While, therefore, I cannot participate with the throng in the pleasures of the Bi-Centennial of your town, I feel prompted to congratulate you on propitious skies, the zeal with which the inhabitants of Bristol have entered into the work of preparation, and the skill, taste, and good judgment exhibited by the Committee of Arrangements in executing their plans. Bristol has an honorable history, and can justly boast a long line of noble representative men. In the Revolutionary struggle—a successful struggle for national life—no town in the Colony was more patriotic, or resisted the assaults of the enemy with more firmness; and from the day that the late venerable President of our Historical Society, John Howland—then a mere stripling—joined the Company of Capt. Pearce, at the Battery, for the defence of the town against the apprehended attack of Wallace, until the present day, the patriotism and public spirit of its people have never been questioned. That the inspirations of to-day will energize that spirit for time to come, I cannot doubt, and that the Bristol inhabitants of 1980 will prove worthy descendants of worthy sires, the commemoration of the third century of the town's life will unquestionably make clear.

Very truly yours,
EDWIN M. STONE.

Messrs. LeBaron B. Colt, William J. Miller, Edward S. Babbitt, Committee:

GENTLEMEN:—Your Bi-Centennial Celebration will take place during the first week of the session of the Supreme Court in this county, which precludes my accepting the very kind invitation with which you have honored me.

I have long been interested in the history of Bristol, and it would afford me great pleasure to receive instruction in its facts from its students, who in its study have had the aid and inspiration which locality always affords, and I very sincerely regret that this pleasure will be denied me.

Very respectfully and truly yours,

W. P. SHEFFIELD.

NEWPORT, Sept. 3, 1880.

PROVIDENCE, R. I., Sept. 14, 1880

Messrs. LeBaron B. Colt, Wm. J. Miller, and Edward S. Babbitt:

GENTLEMEN:—I am very sorry that previous engagements will prevent the acceptance of your invitation to be present at your Bi-Centennial. I cannot make arrangements to change them. I trust that it will be a glad and glorious day to the people of Bristol, and that from it may spring an inspiration to a grand and noble future for the old town. It has passed the period of adolescence; may its maturity be marked by perpetual freshness and vigor, and by steady advancement in intelligence, morality, religion, enterprise, and all those elements of prosperity and excellence so tersely summed up in the motto of the town—virtue and industry.

Very truly yours,

D. A. WHEDON.

---

24 WEST ST., BOSTON, 18th Sept., 1880.

Messrs. LeBaron B. Colt, W. J. Miller, Edward S. Babbitt:

DEAR SIRS:—I regret that engagements beyond my control will prevent my acceptance of your very kind invitation to be present at the celebration of the two hundredth anniversary of the settlement of Bristol, and to show my sympathy in an event so deeply felt by your community.

Hoping that the recollection and example of the good old times will not fade from the memories of the descendants of the fathers of New England, I remain, gentlemen,

Your obedient servant,

WM. W. GREENOUGH.

BOSTON, 14 September, 1880.

MY DEAR SIR:—I have delayed answering your note, hoping I might be able to attend your most interesting anniversary. But I find the severe illness in my family renders this impossible, and I am very reluctantly obliged to decline the part you honor me with.

Let me remind you that Mr. Henshaw B. Walley, of this city, (45 Kilby street, and Chestnut street), is the representative of the family, and will, in all probability, be able to attend.

Cordially yours,
WENDELL PHILLIPS.

Mr. E. S. Babbitt.

TAMWORTH IRON WORKS, N. H., Sept. 21, 1880.

E. S. Babbitt, Esq., Committee:

DEAR SIR:—Your letter of 15th inst., enclosing invitation, was forwarded to me at this place.

I thank you most cordially for both, and regret exceedingly that ill health must prevent me from being with you on Friday next.

I have delayed answering your letter till I could hear from my brother, W. P. Walley, as I greatly hoped that he might be able to represent the family, but he writes me that he will be unable to go.

I have written my cousin, Wendell Phillips, requesting him to convey the invitation to Mr. J. C. Phillips. If he cannot be present, I don't know of any descendant who will be able to dedicate the Walley tree, which I deeply regret. I hope, however, the tree will bear the name of Walley, and that it may live and flourish for centuries, and I shall take great pleasure in visiting your town as soon as possible, and becoming acquainted with the place where my ancestor lived. I have long desired to do so.

There is an oil painting of General Walley taken when he was quite young, in the possession of a relative in California. I have a large photograph of this picture, which I shall be happy to loan you for your exhibition.

Very truly yours,
HENSHAW B. WALLEY.

Letters acknowledging receipt of invitation, and expressing regret at inability to be present, were received from Judges Potter, Burges and Knowles; Hon. W. B. Lawrence, Bishop Hendricken; Wm. H. Nelson, Esq., Chairman Board of Selectmen, Plymouth, Mass.; F. Walley Perkins, a descendant of John Walley; Profs. Bancroft, Appleton, Davis, Packard and Blake, of Brown University, and others.

FIRST LIGHT INFANTRY VETERAN ASSOCIATION.
PROVIDENCE, R. I., Sept. 8th, 1880.

Col. L. B. B. Colt, Chairman:

DEAR SIR:—At a meeting of the First Light Infantry Veteran Association held last evening, it was unanimously voted to visit Bristol, September 24th inst., and participate in the celebration of the two hundredth anniversary of the settlement of the town, and the Association would be pleased to accept such position in the column as may be assigned them by your Committee.

The Veterans have received and accepted an invitation from Col. A. C. Eddy, to make his house their headquarters during their stay in Bristol.

Respectfully,

CHAS. C. ARMSTRONG, *Clerk.*

The following is the Roster of the F. L. I. V. Association, as furnished by Col. Staples. In the procession they were preceded by their own band in the costume of the year 1800—B. P. Robinson, leader; also by the National Band, of Providence, R. I , W. E. White, leader.

ROSTER OF F. L. I. V. A.

Colonel—Major-General William W. Brown.
Lt.-Colonel—Colonel Henry Staples.
Major—Major-General A. E. Burnside.
Adjutant—Captain D. S. Remington.
Clerk—Lieutenant C. C. Armstrong.
Treasurer—Col. Henry Staples.
Quartermaster—Captain J. T. Pitman,
Commissary—Lieutenant H. J. Steere.
Paymaster—Captain Samuel H. Thomas.
Surgeon—F. L. Wheaton, M. D.
Chaplain—Rt. Rev. T. M. Clark, D. D.
In two Companies of about one hundred men, as follows:

FIRST COMPANY.

Captain—Colonel A. C. Eddy.
First Lieutenant—Colonel A. Crawford Greene.
Second Lieutenant—Lieutenant W. E. Barrett.

SECOND COMPANY.

Captain—Major I. M. Potter.
First Lieutenant—Lieutenant H C. Bradford.
Second Lieutenant—Lieutenant D. B. Anthony.

SONS AND DAUGHTERS.

The following is a list of the Sons and Daughters of Bristol, to whom invitations were sent. Those marked with an asterisk were present at the celebration: —

A

A. W. Archer, Richmond, Va.
Hon. G. W. Allen, Grand Rapids, Mich.
Samuel J. Allyn, Taunton, Mass.
*Mrs. J. A. Angell, Providence, R. I.
" Kate L. Anthony, Fordham, N. Y.
Miss A. Fanny Alden, Marietta, Ga.
*Mrs. F. E. Abbott, Worcester, Mass.
Mark A. DeW. Allen, Elizabeth, N. J.
Charles H. Alger, Chelsea, Mass.
*George J. Adams, Providence, R. I.
George Ackerman, New Rochelle, N. Y.
Frank Ackerman, " " "
*Mrs. Lloyd Aspinwall, New York.
Dr. Charles H. Alden, Hingham, Mass.
Mrs. Charles M. Adams, Ashland, Mass.
" Helen Arnold, Grand Rapids, Mich.
*Mrs. Sarah Allen, Fall River, Mass.
Mrs. Kate M. Allen, Flushing, L. I.
Samuel N. Allen, Newark Valley, N. Y.
Mrs. B. T. Allen, Worcester, Mass.
*Charles Allen, Pawtucket, R. I.
Miss Julia Allyn, Taunton, Mass.
Miss Sarah Albro, Fall River, Mass.
*Miss Jennie Allen, Stonington, Conn.
* " Minnie Allen, " "
Mrs. Perry Asken, Baylis, Pike Co., Ill.
* " Smith Albertson, Providence, R. I.
* " Bridget Andem, " "
Isaac J. Austin, Jr., " "
*Mrs. Samuel Allen, Warren, R. I.
James Allen, Berkshire, N. Y.
Mrs. James Allen, " "
Charles E. Albro, Fall River, Mass.
Henry L. Arnold, Colorado.
*Mrs. Mary A. Andrews, Warren, R. I.
* " Enoch Adams, Pawtucket, R. I.
William Anthony, Fall River, Mass.
*Mrs. Irene E. Alexander, Prov., R. I.

B

*Earl P. Bowen, Fall River, Mass.
Wm. J. Bowen, New Bedford, "
Mrs. Frank Blood, East Prov., R. I.
*Miss Anne E. Baker, Providence, R. I.
Mrs. Elliot W. Brainard, S. Glastonbury, Conn.
Loring Brown, Brooklyn, N. Y.
*Martha Bowen, Barrington, R. I.
*Percy Brown, Providence, R. I.
Mrs. Susan A. Barlow, Fall River, Mass.
" William Bennett, Warren, R. I.
*Mrs. Susan E. Bailey, Fall River, Mass.
*Miss Anne T. Baars, Grand Rapids, Mh.
J. Fred. Baars, " " "
Mrs. Jane Bassit, Peoria, Ill.
*Samuel B. Bullock, Providence, R. I.
Daniel Bradford, Courtland, N. Y.
Gershom Bradford, " "
Miss Eliza Babcock, Providence, R. I.
Increase Bosworth, Elgin, Ill.
Henry Bryant, Olneyville, R. I.
*Mrs. Hattie Bliss, New Bedford, Mass.
Sydney Burker, Warren, R. I.
*Charles F. Barker, " "
Clarence E. Barker, Orange, Mass.
*George B. Barker, Warren, R. I.
*Francis P. Barker, " "
Ellen B. Barker, " "
*Anne T. Barker, ' "
Ida A. Barker, " "
Mrs. Abby Barker, " "
Richard Blake, Baylis, Ill.
William Blake, " "
Mrs. Sarah Bullock, Brockton, Mass.
Henry T. Bullock, " "
William H. Bullock, " "
*Mrs. Anne Burt, Taunton, Mass.
*Mrs. J. H. Blanchard, Boston, Mass.

*Mrs. Mary T. Bunt, Warren, R. I.
Mrs. Mary R. Butterfield, Bakersfield, Cal.
*Jonathan Bosworth, Little Neck, L. I.
Nelson Bosworth,   "   "   "
Wm. G. Bradford, Sylvania, Pa.
Mrs. Harriet Bliss, Springfield, Pa.
*Horatio H. Bedell, Providence, R. I.
*Harriet P. Bedell,   "   "
*William H. Bedell,   "   "
Wm. J. Blake, Boyton. Ill.
Richard A. Bagg, West Springfield, Mass.
*J. Crawford Brown, South Boston,   "
Charles A. Bourne, Chicago, Ill.
*Mrs. Henry G. Ballou, Woonsocket, R. I.
Lemuel A. Bishop, Attleboro', Mass.
*Mrs. L. A. Bishop,   "   "
Durfee T. Bradford, Grand Rapids, Mich.
Mrs. Durfee T. Bradford, "   "   "
*L. C. Bunn, East Providence, R. I.
Leonard J. Bradford, Grand Rapids, Mh.
Robert N. Bradford,   "   "   "
Charles H. Bradford,   "   "   "
Clarence Bradford,   "   "   "
*Mrs. W. H. Bourne, Detroit, Mich.
Kate DeW. Budd, New York.
Daniel Bradford, 2d., Sylvania, Pa.
*James M. C. Barker, Warren, R. I.
Mrs. Gustavus Burbanks, Chicago, Ill.
Frank N. Bush, Ithica, N. Y.
Charles Blake, Providence, R. I.
*Mary J. Babcock, Richmond, R. I.
Mrs. Tulley D. Bowen, Providence, R. I.
Wm. C. Breed, Worcester, Mass.
*Charles Barker, Warren, R. I.
Alfred G. Barker, Philadelphia, Pa.
*Mrs. S. P. Burdick,   "
Mrs. Mary E. Barker, Newport, R. I.
Mrs. Frances P. Barker,   "   "
George T. Bourne, Paris, France.
*Nathaniel Bosworth, Norwood, R. I.
Mrs. Susan P. Bell, Liberty, Va.
*James W. Briggs, Boston, Mass.
Mrs. John R. Babcock, Providence, R. I.
*Rev. Edward Brown, Troy, Pa.
*Ambrose De Lois. Quincy Point, Mass.
Sylvanus S. Bowen, Natick, Mass.
*John H. Barney, Providence, R. I.
Charles E. Barney, New Bedford, Mass.
James Barney, Virginia.
*Miss Sarah T. Birene, Providence, R. I.
Frank P. Barney, Attleboro', Mass.
Benj. M. Bosworth, Warren, R. I.
*Susan F. Boyd, Portsmouth, R. I.
*Minnie E. Boyd,   "   "
*Julia E. Boyd,   "   "

Mrs. Mary B. Barker. Grand Rapids, Mh.
Mrs. Georgianna Baxter, "   "   "
*George B. Brown, Warren, R. I.
Wm. S. Brown, New Bedford, Mass.
*Cyrus Brown, Providence, R. I.
*William Breck, Providence, R. I.
Charles Breck,   "   "
Mrs. Jemima Bradford, Providence, R. I.
*Wm. J. Bradford,   "   "
*Mrs. Wm. J. Barker, Warren, R. I.
*James C. Blake,   "   "
*Mrs. Fred. A. Burgess, "   "
Mrs. Geo. Blackman, Scio, N. Y.
*Mrs. C. F. Brown, Warren, R. I.
*Mrs. Lydia Brumond, Brockton, Mass.
*Eben F. Bullock, Central Falls, R. I.
*Wm. H. Bullock,   "   "   "
*Hattie L. Bullock,   "   "   "
George Barrett, Brookline, Mass.
Theo. Barrett, Boston, Mass.
Gerzelle Barrett,   "   "
Mrs. Olive Barrett, "   "
*Mrs. Joseph R. Burgess, Prov., R. I.
*Robert B. Buchanan,   "   "
*Margaret C. Buchanan,   "   "
Mrs. Frank Bagnell, Stockton, Cal.
Wm. Bradford, Jr., New York.
*Nelson Bosworth, Glen Cove, L. I.
*Miss Henrietta Bofine, S. Boston, Mass.
Charles S. Beane, Lansingburgh, N. Y.
*Sullivan Ballou, Woonsocket, R. I.
Mrs Ann E. Bacon, Providence, R. I
*Wm. B. Bosworth, Glen Cove, L. I.
*James Bosworth,   "   "   "
*Miss Anne Bosworth, Great Neck, L. I.
*Wm. J. Bosworth, Little Neck, L. I.
*Royal Bosworth, Fall River, Mass.
Mrs. Isaac Braley,   "   "   "
Isaac L. Braley,   "   "   "
Samuel G. Braley, Swansea, Mass.
Miss Ida M. Braley, Fall River, Mass.
*Hez. M. Bunn, East Providence, R. I.
Selie Burr, Denver City, Col.
*Miss Mary L. Booth, Providence, R. I.
Wm. J. Booth, Providence, R. I.
Charles E. Barrus, Westport, New Zealand.
Jerome Barrus, Warren, R. I.
*Daniel A. Barrus,   "   "
Arthur A. Bosworth, "   "
*Arthur M. Burr, Melrose, Mass.
*Mrs. Thom. Burlingham, Newport, R. I.
*Frank A. Barnard, Lynn, Mass.
*Mrs. F. A. Barnard,   "   "
*Mrs. Mary A. Barnard, "   "
Mrs. Jos. Buffington, Providence, R. I.

*Harriet Battey, Providence, R. I.
*Josephine D. Bowler, Stoughton, Mass.
Peleg Brown, Providence, R. I.
Mrs. Saml. Briggs, Independence, N. Y.
*Mrs. John Brown, New Bedford, Mass.
Mrs. C. T. Brown, Warren, R. I.
Susan A. Barlow, Fall River, Mass.
Jonathan Browning, "   "   "
Miss Genevieve Brown, Warren, R. I.
*Rev. Benj. B Babbitt, Columbia, S. C.
Miss Rebecca Bosworth, Little Neck, L.I.
Hunt Blake, New York.
*Geo. T. Bowler, Brooklyn, N. Y.
James E. Baker, Providence, R. I.
*Mrs. Charlotte Barney, Warren, R. I.
*Rev. Shearjashub Bourne, Patterson, N. J.
Mrs. Mary E. Brownell, Newport, R. I.
Benjamin Boarn, Providence, R. I.
M. Toscan Bennett, Hoboken, N. Y.
Geo. F. Barnard, Lynn, Mass.
Wm. H. Bennett, Topeka, Kansas.
*Benj. P. Bennett, Newport, R. I.
Henry Bishop, North Andover, Mass.
*Nathan Bishop, Lawrence,   "
Russel Bishop,   "   "
*Mrs. Sarah A. Burt, East Taunton, Mass.
Mrs. Samuel W. Brown, Fall River,   "
Samuel E. Bunn, Otter River,   "
*Nath'l F. Bunn, Warren, R I.
*Lina Bush,   Providence, R. I.
*George A. Bush,   "   "
*Mrs. Geo. A. Bush,   "   "
*Miss Julia A. Bush,   "   "
*Miss Minnie H. Bush, "   "
Charles Burgess,   Warren, R. I.
Miss Hattie Burgess,   "   "
Erwin J. Baker, Jr ,   Providence, R. I.
*Mrs. Erwin J. Baker, Jr.,   "   "
Mrs. Laura Buffington, Pawtucket,   "
*George Babcock, Barrington,   "
Wm. H. Baker, Crompton,   "
Mrs. Susan M. Baxter, Providence,   "
Mrs. Anne R. Burrows,   "   "
Samuel Butts,   "   "
Mrs. Samuel Butts,   "   "

C

*Henry B. Card, Sylvania, Pa.
Mrs. Charlotte Corbett, Jerseyville, Ill.
Mrs. Capt. Henry T. Cobb, Dighton. Ms.
Stephen W. Church, Chicago, Ill.
*Le Baron B. Church, Taunton, Mass.
*Hezekiah W. Church,   "   "
*Mrs. Wm. B. Church,   "   "
*Mrs. Hannah W. Chase, Fall River, Ms.
*Wm. B. Church, Taunton, Mass.

*John H. Church, Taunton, Mass.
Sylvester M. Copeland, Fall River, Mass.
*Mrs. Dr. Augustus Clarke, Cambridgeport, Mass.
Mrs. Eliza Covell, New Bedford, Mass.
Mrs. B. M. Cleaveland, Marietta, Ga.
*Stephen B. Chafee, Middletown, Conn.
Wm. A. Church,   Warren, R. I.
*Miss Emily Church, "   "
*Mrs. Henry Church, Annawan, Ill.
*Mrs. Anne L. C. Chase, Newport, R. I.
*George Chubbucks, Valley Falls,   "
*Mrs. Ruby Cole, Warren,   "
*Rowland T. Chase, Portsmouth,   "
*John Cane, Newport,   "
*Lulu Cox, Providence,   "
*Anne Capwell, Providence,   "
*Charles M. Chase, Portsmouth,   "
*Marion W. Clarke, New Bedford, Mass.
*James T. Card, Providence, R. I.
*Stephen Chafee, Jr., Middletown, Conn.
*George A. Chafee,   "   "
*Mrs. George A. Chafee,   "   "
*Samuel R. Chafee,   "   "
*Mrs. Samuel R. Chafee,   "   "
*Wm. Clarke Chafee,   "   "
*Mrs. N. B. Cooke, Pawtucket, R. I.
Mrs. Amos B. Corwin, New Rochelle, N. Y.
*Mrs. Henry T. Colwell, Cambridgeport, Mass.
Freeborn C. Coggeshall, Philadelphia, Pa.
*Mrs. Wm. B. Cheney, Fall River, Mass.
*Luther Cole.   Warren, R. I.
*Nathan P. Cole,   "   "
*Mrs. Nathan P. Cole.   "   "
*John G. Cole,   "   "
*Mrs John G. Cole.   "   "
George C. Coomer,   "   "
Mrs. Charlotte Coomer, "   "
Henry R. Coggeshall, Boston, Mass.
*Edward L. Chase, Portsmouth, R. I.
*James E. Conley, Warren,   "
*Miss Hannah M. Cooke, Prov.,   "
*Thomas D. Chafee, Taunton, Mass.
*Mrs. Anna C. Chafee,   "   "
*Mrs. Kate L. Chase, Fall River, Mass.
*Mrs. Sarah M. Cole, Warren, R. I.
Geo. M. Coit, North Sterling, Conn.
*Mrs. Alice Curtis. Warren, R. I.
Mrs. Henry F. Cobb, Dighton, Mass.
Mrs. Josiah Caldwell, England.
*Mrs. J. T. Cooper, Brooklyn, New York.
*Mrs. Eliza Coit,   Providence, R. I.
*John Coggeshall,   "   "
*Mrs. John Coggeshall,   "   "

Dyer C. Coomer, Warren, R. I.
Lewis Carr, " "
Thomas Coomer, " "
George T. C. Church, " "
*Shubael B. Cole, " "
*Charles Cole, " "
*Mrs. Elizabeth Cole, " "
Mrs. Alfred B. Cornell, " "
*Wm. Henry Church, " "
Mrs. Chas. C. Clarke, Selo, N. Y.
*Mrs. Alice Calvoort, New London, Ct.
Mrs. Martha Copeland, Brockton, Mass.
*Mrs. Mary L. Collins, Providence, R. I.
*Joseph Carnes, " "
Mrs. Virginia Chester, Springfield, Ill.
Mrs. Catharine Chester, " "
Mrs. Charlotte Corbett, Jerseyville, "
John Corbett, " "
*Henry Corbett, Tecumseh, Neb.
*Mrs. Laura A. Chase, Erie, Pa.
Mrs. Betsey Chase,
Mrs. Mary A. Condor, South Boston, Ms.
*John Connerton, Lowell, Mass.
John F. Cooke, Fall River, "
Mrs. Eliza Crowell, New Bedford, Mass.
*Mrs. Eliza B. Cole, Stonington, Conn.
*Almira Curren, Valley Falls, R. I.
*Mrs. Anne G. Cole, Providence, R. I.
Marlborough Churchill, New York.
Ellen F. Cole, Warren, R. I.
*George D. Cole, " "
*Mrs. Mary Chase, " "
Frederick M. Chadwick, Prov., R. I.
*Mrs. Bridget Carter, " "
*James F. Christee, Boston, Mass.
*Dan Callahan, New Bedford, "
*Mary J. Callahan, " "
*John G. Connerton, Lowell, Mass.
*John F. Costigan, Lawrence, "
*Mrs. Lizzie W. Connery, Pawtucket, R. I.
Frank L. Cumm, Brooklyn, N. Y.
*Joseph N. Collins, Warren, R. I.
*Mrs. Emily Corey, Portsmouth, R. I.
" Maria Cooke, " "
Edwin Church, Quincy, Mich.
Henry P. Church, Annawan, Ill.
*Mrs. Wm. T. Chase, Auburn, R. I.
* " Sarah Cunliff, Providence, R. I.
* " Mary A. Curtis, " "
Miss Eliz. G. Coit, Batavia, N. Y.
* " H. E. Coggeshall, Fall River, Mass.
Wm. T. Coggeshall, Lowell, "
*Mrs. Robinson Chace, Fall River, "
" Almira Curry, Providence, R. I.
" Sarah J. Chase, " "
*Miss Martha Cole, Warren, "

*Miss Anne E. Cole, Warren, R. I.
Mrs. Martha Carr, Newport, "
" Charles S. Cross, Providence, R. I.
* " Joseph Cole, Woonsocket, "
*Thomas Cole, Warren, "
*George Coggeshall, " "
*Wm. N. Coggeshall, " "
*Mrs. Benj. Clarke, New Bedford, Mass.
Edward P. Clarke, Providence, R. I.
*Marion W. Clarke, New Bedford, Mass.
George L. Chase, New Mexico.
Samuel Cables, Jamaica Plains, Mass.
*Mrs. Nathaniel Chadwick, Hornelsville, N. Y.
Mrs. J. C. Calvert, New London, Conn.
" Laura Cooly, Providence, R. I.
* " Georgiana Chubbuck, Valley Falls, R. I.

D

Henry W. Diman, Lisbon, Portugal.
*James Darling, Fall River, Mass.
Mrs. Alexander Dyer, Plainsbery, Cal.
* " Saml. W. Drown, Drownsville, R. I.
* " Joshua C. Drown, Warren, "
*John W. Diman, Fall River, Mass.
Wm. F. DeWolf, Chicago, Ill.
Charles H. Dunbar, Newport, R. I.
*Byron D. DeWolf, New York.
Mrs. Mary T. Dean, Galveston, Texas.
Wm. B. DeWolf, New York.
*Wm. H. Doty, Providence, R. I.
*Dr. John J. DeWolf, " "
*J. Halsey DeWolf, " "
*Prof. J. Lewis Diman, " "
Dr. James A. DeWolf, Port of Spain, Trinidad.
*Mary M. Donahue, Warren, R. I.
*Nellie F. Donahue, " "
Wm. Donahue, " "
*Johanna Donahue, " "
*Robert Dunbar, Providence, "
*Mrs. Mary Day, " "
*Henry B. Dearth, Waterbury, Conn.
Charles Dearth, " "
Mrs. Elizabeth Drown, Warren, R. I.
Mrs. Emily Devol, East Providence, R. I.
Miss Ellen Devol, " "
Charles Devol, " "
*Miss Ella F. Dorman, New London, Ct.
Francis M. Dimond, Providence, R. I.
John N. Dimond, " "
Wm. F. Dimond, " "
*Miss Bridget Dougherty, Warren, R. I.
* " Sarah Abby Davis, East Smithfield, Pa.

Miss Eliz. B. Dearth, Waterbury, Conn.
Mrs. Thad. Davis, Rochelle, N. Y.
Charles C. Dimond, Boston, Mass.
*Miss Mary Douglass, Newport, R. I.
* " Mattie Douglass, " "
*Mrs. Lyman D. Deane, Fall River, Mass.
Frank L. Diman, Providence, R. I.
Jonathan Drown, Killingly, Ct.
*Chas. W. Dunbar, Providence, R. I.
*Mrs. Chas W. Dunbar, " "
Thomas Durfee, Rockville, Conn.
*Henry B. Diman, Providence, R. I.
*Mary T. Dougherty, East Prov., R. I.
Winthrop DeWolf, Boston, Mass
*John M. Doty, Newport, R. I.
*Peleg Dunbar, Warren, R. I.
*Mrs. Charlotte Davenport, Newport, R. I.
*Mrs. Eunice Dyer, Portsmouth, R. I.
" Wm. Dunham, New Bedford, Ms.
Nellie Davis, Providence, R. I.
*Mrs. Joshua C. Drown. Jr., Prov., R. I.
*Frank Dunbar, Newport. "
*Mrs. L. T. Dodge, Providence, "
*Phebe M. Devol, Fall River, Mass.
*Susan R. Dennis, Pawtucket, R. I.
*Alfred Devol, Warwick, "
*Imogene Dunbar, Providence,"
*William Dyer, Warren, "
*Mrs. Ann Drown, " "

E

Geo. R. Easterbrooks, East Prov., R. I.
Clara Easterbrooks, Warren, "
T. R. Easterbrooks, Providence, "
*Abby M. Ellis, " "
Sarah S. Easterbrooks, " "
Giles Easterbrooks, Warren, "
Mrs. J. A. P. Eppinger, Georgia.
S. B. Eldridge, New Bedford, Mass.
*Benj. T. Easterbrooks, Newport, R. I.
*James A. Easterbrooks, " "
Capt. Geo. T. Easterbrooks, Oysterville, Wash. Ter.
Dr. George T. Easterbrooks, Oysterville, Wash. Ter.
Mrs. George T. Easterbrooks, Oysterville, Wash. Ter.
*Allen Easterbrooks, Providence, R. I.
*Mrs. Allen Easterbrooks, " "
*James H. Easterbrooks, " "
*Alfred Evans, " "
Theodore R. Easterbrooks, " "
*Wm. H. Easterbrooks, " "
*Stephen G. Easterbrooks, " "
Mrs. John C. Ellis, Newport, R. I.

Frank A. Easterbrooks, Boston, Mass.
*Mrs. Hannah Ellis, Providence, R. I.
Charles A. Edwards, " "
*Wm. Easterbrooks, " "
*Mrs. Myra Eaton, Pawtucket, R. I.
" Thomas H. Eddy, Fall River, Ms.
*Moses P. Easterbrooks, Cambridgeport, Mass.
Simeon A. Easterbrooks, Eagleville, Ct.
Daniel Easterbrooks, Fall River, Mass.
*Abby M. Ellis, Providence, R. I.
Mrs. Julia A. Eddy, " "
*Wm. Y. Easterbrooks, Warren, R. I.
Mrs. Wm. Y. Easterbrooks, " "

F

*Edward A. Fish, Wellsborough, Pa.
Francis R. Fish, Troy, Pa.
*Mrs. Hattie A. Fish, Millford, Mass.
*Mary A. Fish, Fall River, "
Adelbert Frisbrie, Grafton, Cal.
Mrs. Adelbert Frisbrie, " "
Miss Martha Foster, Newburg, N. Y.
Mrs. John N. Furnham, West Chester, N. Y.
*Smith B Fales, Warren, R. I.
*Horace R. Fenner, Harmony, R. I.
Charles H. Fenner, Southbury, Conn.
*James H. Furgeson, Millbury, Conn.
Peter Furgeson, " "
*John L. D. Furgeson, " "
Wm. C. F. Furgeson, " "
*Mrs. Mary S. Fletcher, New Bedford, Mass.
Mrs. Nellie Fox, Southbridge, Mass.
*Mrs. E. J. Fairbanks, New Britain, Ct.
Samuel Fales, Philadelphia, Pa.
*Jeremiah Fenner, Lisle, N. Y.
Mrs. Eliz. F. Freeman, Wakefield, R. I.
*Joseph H. Fish, Providence, "
*Mrs. Julia Frances, " "
Mrs. George Fraprie, New York.
Mrs. Addie J. Ferril, Boston, Mass.
*Lewis B Fish, Brockton, Mass.
Mrs. George F. Foster, Brooklyn, N. Y.
*Miss Ruth A. Fish, Providence, R. I.
Mrs. Ellen F. Field, Danville, Conn.
Chas. C. Fisher, San Francisco, Cal.
Mrs. Alice G. Fisher, Oakland, Cal.
Lucian Fitts, Providence, R. I.
*Mrs. Mary M. Freelove, Fall River, Ms.
Martha B. Fenner, Providence, R. I.
*Mrs. Mary E. Fletcher, New Bedford, Mass.
Wm. C. Fales, Providence, R. I.
*Mrs. Wm. H. Fenner, " "

*Patience L. Fish. Warren, R. J.
Henry F. Fish, Milton Centre, Mass.
Wm. A. Fish, Philadelphia, Pa.
*Isaac L. Fish, Portsmouth, R. I.
Lewis Felix, Boston, Mass.
James Franklin, Portsmouth, R. I.
Emily E. Fairbrother, Providence, R. I.
*J. M. Fales, Warren, R. I.
*Miss Hattie L. Fisk, Millford, Mass.
*Susan C. Fish, Portsmouth, R. I.

G

Emily F. Greene, Warren. "
*Stephen D. Grey, Providence, R. I.
*Wm. H. Getty, Warren, "
*Mrs. Sophia F. Greene, Leominster, Ms.
*George E. N. Gladding, Brooklyn, N. Y.
*Mrs. Maria Greene, Warren, R. I.
Allen J. Gladding, Oakland, Cal.
*Sarah DeW. Gardiner, New York.
Amos T. Gorham, Cincinnati, O.
*Charles A. Gladding, Baltimore, Md.
*Mrs. Abby M. Gooding, S. Vineland, N. J.
Mrs. S. Dana Greene, Annapolis, Md.
*Susan Gifford, Fall River, Mass.
*Irenus Gooding, Malden, "
Miss Gertrude Gooding, " "
Mrs. D. C. Grheme, New York.
*George P. Gifford, " "
*Mrs. Abby A. Greenman, Newport, R. I.
Thomas S. Gladding, Leavenworth, Kan.
John W. Gladding, Philadelphia, Pa.
Mrs. Etta N. Gifford, Fernandina, Fa
*Albert C. Greene, Newport, R. I.
Henry C. Gifford. " "
*Henry W. Gladding, Warren, R. I.
*Mrs Henry W. Gladding, " "
*George T. Greene, " "
*Mrs. George T. Greene, " "
*Jeremiah I. Greene, Warren, R. I.
*Mrs. Dr. J. B Greene, Providence, R. I.
*J. B Greene, Jr., " "
*Joseph W. H. Gayton, " "
*Gustavus T. Grey, " "
*Stephen D. Grey, " "
*George E. Grey, " "
Charles Grey, " "
Ellery W. Greene, Manitou Springs, Col.
*Mrs. John C. Greene, Leominster. Mass.
*Mary G. Gardiner, Attleboro', "
Mrs. E. S. Gove, Monmouth, Me.
*Mrs. Geo. H. Glidden. Springfield, Mass.
*Mabel D. Goff, Warren, R. I.
*Miss Martha J. Goff, Pawtucket, R. I.
* " Mary I. Goff, Warren, "

Miss Nancy Goff, Springfield, Mass.
" Susan Goff, Pawtucket, R. I.
* " Elizabeth Goff, Warren, "
Dr. Grafton W. Gardner, Atlanta, Ga.
*John A. Godloff, Boston, Mass.
Mrs. Abby W. Gutman, Lewiston, Me.
Charles B. Gladding, Franklin, Mass.
Mrs. Mary Grant, Warren, R. I.
*Benj M. Greene, Providence, R. I.
*Mrs. Benj. M. Greene, " "
*Benj. M. Greene, Jr., " "
John Gladding, East Smithfield, Pa.
Stephen Gladding, " " "
*Thomas C. Grant. Rehoboth, Mass.
*Mrs. Thomas C. Grant, " "
*Miss Rosa W. Grant, " "
*Henry P. Grant, " "
*Mrs. Eliz. McGoval. Providence, R. I.
John H. Gifford, Boston, Mass.
*Mrs. Ann H. Grey, New Bedford, Mass.
Rev. John Grey, Denver City, Col.
Mrs. Ann Gifford, Providence, R. I.
*Miss Rebecca Gorham. Wakefield, R. I.
*Miss Nettie Gorham, " "
James Goff, Jr., Locust Valley, L. I.
Mrs. Emma Goddard, Wallingford, Ct.
*John A. Godloff, Boston. Mass.
Mary H. Gifford, Newport, R. I.
Frederick Gladding, Providence, R. I.
Mrs. Wm. B. Gordon. Burlington, Iowa.
*Charles W. Greene, Warren. R. I.
Emma B. Goddard, Wauhegan, Conn.
Joseph W. Greene, Manitou Springs, Col.
Mrs. Joseph W. Greene, " " "
J. F. Gooding, Lowell Mass.
*Joseph L. Gardner, Calumet, Mich.
*Charles T. Gladding. Providence, R. I.
*Mrs. David W. Graffam, " "
*Lilian A. Grey, " "
Mrs. Sarah M. Gladding, " "
Walter N. Gifford, " "
*Job Grey, Somerset, Mass.
*Wm. O. Gladding, Newport, R. I.
*Stephen Grego, Providence, "
*Frank I. Gladding, Warren, R. I.
*Lewis Gladding, " "
*Mrs. A. M. Grunard, Fall River, Mass.
*Miss Henrietta Gladding, Warren, R. I.
*James H. Gladding, New Bedford, Ms.
*Joseph A. Gladding, Woonsocket, R. I.
*Mrs. Stephen Grego, Providence, "
*George T. Greene, Jr., Warren, "
*Mrs. Andrew Gale, Providence, "

H

*Thomas Henderson, Providence, R. I.

*Thomas O. Holmes, Providence, R. I.
*Patience C. Hilburn, " "
*Mary A. Hixon, Woonsocket, "
*Sarah M. Harideen, Woodstock, Conn.
*Mary B. Hale, Swansea, Mass.
*John W. Hart, Taunton, "
*John B. Hatch, Providence, R. I.
*Caroline R. Hyde, " "
*Eliza M. Hubbard, " "
Minor Hedges, Lamont, Mich.
Mrs. Henry Hall, Bloomfield, Cal.
*Mrs. Martha T. Hathaway, New Bedford, Mass.
John B. F. Herreshoff, Brooklyn, N. Y.
James B. Herreshoff, Nice, France.
*John G. Harding, New Bedford, Mass.
*James H. Harding, " " "
Mrs. James H. Harding, " " "
Wm. N. Hall, New Bedford, Mass.
Mrs. Hannah Hall, " " "
*Nathan S. Hoard, Taunton, Mass.
*Cyrus Hoard, " "
*Mrs. C. M. Hoard, " "
Mrs. Lydia P. Houghton, Boston, Mass.
Rosalie DeW. Hopper, New York.
Silas Holmes, Diamond Hill, R. I.
Jabez S. Holmes, Boston, Mass.
*Miss Ruth G. Hall, Warren, R. I.
*Rt. Rev. M. A. DeW. Howe, Reading, Pa.
H. B. Hubbard, New Haven, Conn.
*Patrick Hurney, Jamesville, Wis.
*Nathan B. Heath, Charlestown, Mass.
Arnold B. Heath, Boston, "
Alanson Heath, Rockville, Conn.
Mrs. Edwin M. Hill, Haverhill, Mass.
Mrs. Dr. Wm. H. Hutton, Detroit, Mich.
*Mrs. Jemima Hathaway, Fall River, Ms.
N. E. Harvey, East Providence, R. I.
George C. Hatch, Warren, R. I.
Mrs. George C. Hatch, " "
Mrs. E. N. Hartley, Fall River, Mass.
Mrs. Caroline Hedges, Lamont, Mich.
Mrs. Jane Hewlitt, Haverhill, Mass.
*John W. Hoard, Providence, R. I.
*Mrs. Benj. Hall, Warren, "
*Luther Handy, " "
*Mrs. Clara P. Humphreys, Cedar Grove, R. I.
Mrs. Henry Hall, Bloomfield, Cal.
Wm. P. Hall, " "
*Mrs. Wm. B. Hubbard, Providence, R. I.
*Isaac R. Hadwin, Somerville, Mass.
Mrs. Louisa S. Hodges, West Maryland, Conn.
*Mrs. Wm. H. Horton, Providence, R. I.
*John F. Husso, Fall River, Mass.
*John J. Holmes, Brockton, "

*Mrs. Mary E. Hayes, Hagerstown, Md.
Mrs. Eliz. Harvey, Thomaston, Me.
*George H. Harding, Providence, R. I.
Freeman C. Hincks, Pawtucket, "
*Mrs. Julia Hixon, Millford, Mass.
Charles W. Hurst, Boston, "
*Wm. R. Handy, Providence, R. I.
Charles Handy, " "
*Mrs. Joseph Handy, Barrington, R. I.
*Joseph Handy, " "
*Mrs Emily Hoar, Warren, R. I.
Mrs. Mary Henshaw, Providence, R. I.
Edward Handy, Warren, "
*Manton E. Hoard, Providence, "
Mrs. Manton E. Hoard, " "
*Mark A. Heath, " "
Rev. Leonard B. Hatch, Warren, "
*Seth L. Horton, Providence, "
*Mrs. Ann B. Hamm, " "
Mrs. Anne G. Holmes, " "
*Mrs. Dr. Hemple, Grand Rapids, Mich.
Mrs. Octavia A. Hustis, Auburndale, Ms.
Mrs. Lewis T. Hoar, Warren, R. I.
Mrs. Wilfred B. Hodgkin, Tunbridge, England.
Winfield G. Hubbard, South Lyndeboro', Conn.
*Mrs. Alice G. Hancock, Providence, R. I.
Minerva H. Hopkins, Providence, R. I.

I

Mrs. David Ingerson, Groton, Conn.
*Mrs. Eliz. Ingraham, Wellsville, N. Y.
*Miss Eliz. Ingraham, " "
*Thomas U. Ingraham, " "
Wm. H. Interman, Cincinnati, Ohio.
*Smith M. Ide, New Bedford, Mass.
*Mrs. John Ingraham, Swansey, " .
*Alex. G. Ingraham, Providence, R. I.
*John H. Ingraham, Baker City, Oregon,
*Miss Lily R. Ide, Providence, R. I.
*Mrs. Anne R. Ide, " "
*Mrs. D. H. Ingerson, Meriden, Conn.
Mrs. H. M. Ingerson, " "

J

*Mrs. Ann E. Jackson, Fall River, Mass.
Charles W. Jones, N. La Crosse, Wis.
Mrs. Zora E. Jameson, Frosburgh, Ver.
Mrs. Henry B. Jackson, Boston, Mass.
Thomas W. Joy, Bordentown, N. J.
Jedidiah W. Johnson, San Francisco, Cal.
Henry L. Johnson, Utica, N. Y.

Henry A. J. Johnson, Baltimore, Md.
*Mrs. Julia Jennings, New Bedford, Ms.
Mrs. Fanny M. Jones, Warren, R. I.
Mrs. Nancy S. Johnson, Nar. Pier, R. I.
Mrs. Wm. H. Jennings, Providence, R. I.
Mrs. Henry B. Jackson, Roxbury, Mass.
Mrs Capt. Sandford Jones, Pasadina, Cal.
*Mrs. Hannah Johnson, Staten Island, N. Y.

K

Frederick W. Kingman, Pascoag, N. Y.
Mrs. Frederick W. Kingman, "   "
Mrs. Dr. H. B. Kenyon, Towns Head, Ver.
Miss Louisa Kingman, Pascoag, N. Y.
Miss Florence C. Kella, River Side, Cal.
*William Kingsley, Providence, R. I.
George Kingsley,   "   "
Walter Kingsley,   "   "
Sandford A. Kingsley,   "   "
*Mrs. Hiram B Kelly, Ayer, Mass.
*Mrs. J. Eliz. Keys, New York.
*Mrs. Debra Kelly, Providence, R. I.
*John Keith, Valley Falls,   "
*Mrs. Ida Kent, Providence, R. I.
*Chas. W. Kingman,   "   "

L

*Mrs. Ann Loomes, Providence, R. I.
Miss Ellen M. Luce, New Bedford, Mass.
William Lincoln, Warren, R. I.
Gustave G. Lansing, New York.
*Mrs. Abby C. Liscomb, Fall River, Ms.
*Miss Julia Lake, East Providence, R. I.
*Miss Anne E. Leonard,   "   "
Henry Lowry, Fall River, Mass.
*Thomas Lowry, "   "   "
Mrs. Sarah A. Ling, Grand Rapids, Mich.
*Edward Lanigan, Warren, R. I.
*Welcome Lawton, Fair Haven, Mass.
*Mrs. Welcome Lawton, Fair Haven, Ms.
Nathan Lawton,   "   "
Lorenzo Ludewissey, Waldoboro', Me.
*Mrs. Edward Lewis, Boston, Mass.
Mary K. Livesey, Warren, R. I.
Mrs. Edward Lancaster, Hartford, Conn.
Edward Lancaster,   "   "
Lorenzo Ludwig, Danville, Mich.
*Mrs. Abby Liscomb, Fall River, Mass.
Charles F. Liscomb, Poughkeepsie, N. Y.
Mrs. Lydia P. Luther, Lamont, Mich.
*Gilbert R. Lawless, N. Swansey, Mass.
*William Lindsey, Fall River,   "
*Nathaniel Lindsey, "   "   "

Abby F. Lucas, Hazelwood, N. Bedford.
Mrs. C. DeW. Lovett, Springfield, Mass.
Mrs. John N. Lansing, New York.
Mrs. E. F. Lucas,   "   "
*Mrs. Abby Leonard, Providence, R. I.
Mrs. E. P. Lette, Southburgh, Va.
Mrs Capt. John Y. Lawless, Galveston, Texas.
Wm. B. Lawless, Galveston, Texas.
James A. Leet, Jr., Ipswich, Mass.
Mrs. Ida Little,   "   "
Miss Mary L. Leet, "   "
Wm. S. Luther, South Boston, Mass.
*Joseph S. Luther, "   "   "
Benj. Luther, Lamont, Mich.
*Miss Susan C. Lacy, Attleboro', Mass.
John Luther, Lamont, Mich.
Sylvester Luther, Grand Rapids, Mich.
*Nathan Lawton, Fair Haven, Mass.
*Isaac F. Liscomb, Providence, R. I.
*Wm. Littlefield,   "   "
Benj. F. Lindsey, Attleboro', Mass.
*John Lindsey, Fort Nevarra, Nebraska.
James Lewis, New Haven, Conn.
John Luther,   Grand Rapids, Mich.
Mrs. Mary A. Luther, "   "   "
*John Ludewissey, Wakefield, R. I.
Charles H. Luther, New York.
*Manton H. Luther, Providence, R. I.
*Alfred E. Luther,   "   "
*Winfield V. Luther, "   "
Mrs. E. A. Loomis,   "   "
*Capt. John I. Liscomb, Boston, Mass.
Mrs. Lizzie Lyman, Philadelphia, Pa.
Horace Lawton, New Bedford, Mass.
Charles Lawton,   "   "   "

M

George F. Manchester, Harpville, N. Y.
G. W. Markham, Atchinson, Kansas.
Peter Munro, Sylvania, Pa.
Bateman Munro, New York.
*Lewis S. Munro, Boston, Mass.
*Mrs. Lewis S. Munro, "   "
Charles H. Mosher Grand Rapids, Mich.
Mrs. Jonas Minturn, Plainsburg, Cal.
Thomas C. Minturn.   "   "
James W. Minturn,   "   "
Mrs. Frank Mollen, Boston, Mass.
Thomas F. Mason, New York.
*David Eddy Munro, Portsmouth, R. I.
Hezekiah U. Munro, West Philadelphia, Pa.
Frank A. Munro, Worcester, Mass.
Nathaniel Maxfield, Whiteside, Ill.
A. J. Maxfield, Lyons, Iowa.

William H. Maxfield, Whiteside, Ill.
Mrs. Wm. B. Morrison, " "
*Miss Susan J. Maxfield, " "
Albert J. Maxfield, Tampico, Ill.
Mrs. Dr. Luther A. Martin, Ill.
Willie B. Martin, Atlantic City, Ill.
Miss Abby B. Martin, Roebuck Junction, Ill.
Mrs. Philip C. Macomber, Fall River, Ms.
Wm. H. Munro, Yankton, Arkansas.
*Wm. H. Martin, Warren, R. I.
Mrs. Wm. H. Martin, " "
Frank Manchester, Providence, R. I.
Mrs. Frank Manchester, " "
*George H. Munro, " "
*George Munro, Warren, R. I.
*James Munro, " "
*Mrs. John Maxfield, Warren, R. I.
*R. Elliot McCartney, Providence, R. I.
*Mrs. R. Elliot McCartney, " "
Mrs. James H. Maxwell, Warren, R. I.
Wyatt Manchester, Attleboro', Mass.
Seabury Manchester, " "
Henry R. Manchester, " "
Mrs. Eliza Marble, " "
John W. Mutton, Toronto, Can. West.
Mrs. Edward Markham, Atchinson, Kansas.
Robert Manchester, Prov., R. I.
*Eliz. E. Miller, S. Swansey, Mass.
*Mary E. Martin, Warren, R. I.
*Chas. Mason, " "
J. Flaviel Manchester, Newport, R. I.
Mrs. Julia E. Manchester, " "
Wm. J. Munro, Boston, Mass.
*Mrs. Wm. H. Macomber, Prov., R. I.
*Miss Katy Malone, New Bedford, Mass.
*Wm. H. Munro, Edgartown, Mass.
*Jonathan Munro, " "
Dr. George Munro, Mercer, Pa.
Mrs. Stephen W. Morgan, Philadelphia, Pa.
Mrs. Mary A. Munro, Pottsville, Pa.
Mrs. Caroline Matthews, New Bedford, Mass.
Mrs. Lydia D. Mason, Providence, R. I.
*Mrs. Anne McDougal, Hebronville, Ms.
*Benj. S. McDougal, " "
Herbert Manchester, Locust Valley, L. I.
Jeremiah Munro, Boston, Mass.
*Miss Jennie W. Munro, Prov., R. I.
*Wm. H. Munro, " "
*Hugh Mulligan, Providence, R. I.
*Mary R. Morse, " "
Mrs. Horace E. Medbury, Barrington, R. I.
Thomas P. Myers, New York.

Mrs. Ada B. Morton, Providence, R. I.
Ringold Mott, Locust Valley, L. I.
Miss J. Sophia Muenscher, Taunton, Ms.
Miss Laura Martin, Providence, R. I.
*Miss Martha Martin, " "
*Miss Gertrude Martin, " "
Wm. Martin, " "
*Mrs. Russell Middleton, Charleston, S. C.
Miss Alicia Middleton, Charleston, S. C.
*Mrs. James Madison, Newport, R. I.
Mrs. Har. F. Morton, Louisville, Ky.
H. F. Marchant, Providence, R. I.
*Mrs. Horace Miller, Pawtucket, R. I.
*Stephen C. Munro, Portsmouth, "
*Mrs. Geo. W. Millard, Providence, R. I.
*Miss Abby D. Munro, West Pleasant, S. C.
Samuel N. G. Munro, Providence, R. I.
Mrs. Samuel N. G. Munro, " "
Samuel N. G. Munro, Jr., " "
*Miss Amy Munro, " "
*Nath'l H. Munro, " "
*Charles Munro, " "
*George T. Munro, " "
Fred. A. Manchester, " "
Mrs. Fred. A. Manchester, " "
Mrs. Jas. S. McO. Very, Portland, Me.
*Eliz. Munro, Providence, R. I.
*Wm. A. Munro, " "
*Mrs. Wm. A. Munro, " "
Bridget McDonald, Lawrence, Mass.
*Mrs. Rosa McKenna, Boston, "
Joseph A. Monks, Norfolk, Va.
*George A. Munro, Ogdensburg, N. Y.
*Frank A. Munro, " "
*Mrs. Frank A. Munro, " "
*Mrs. Walter P. Munro, Providence, R. I.
Fred. H. Manchester, Warren, "
*Daniel G. Manchester, Providence, "
*Mrs. Mary F. Milliken, " "
Joseph H. Manchester, Pawtucket, "
*James C. Manchester, " "
Mrs. Sarah Martin, Providence, "
*Mrs. Alice R. Munro, Portsmouth, "
*Martin McNeal, Warren, "
John McSherry, " "
*Ellen Muldoon, Providence, "
Mrs. Eleanor Manchester, Prov., "
*Mrs. Ambrose B. Mason, Warren, "
*Miss Eliz. Mason, " "
*Martha E. Mason, " "
*Ellen McSherry, East Providence, "
*Mary E. Murphy, Fall River, Mass.
Chauncey E. Martin, Warren, R. I.
Wm. Martin, Chester, Vt.
Jas. Martin, Londonderry, Vt.

Nath'l L. F. Munro, Decatur, Ill.
Jas. W. Munro, Providence, R. I.
*Dr. Wm. McCaw, Warren, "
Mrs. Wm. McCaw, "
James McCaw, Leadville City, Col.
Jas. Munro,   Warren, R. I.
Mrs. Betsey Mason, " "
*Sarah H. Maxfield, " "
Alex. G. Manchester, Providence, R. I.
*Mrs. Mary A. Munro, Fall River, Mass.
Mrs. Chas. B. Mosher, Grand Rapids, Mh.
Russell Manchester, Newport, R. I.
Philip Manchester, Locust Valley, L. I.
Mrs. Randall H. Mole, Baltimore, Md.
James McCanny, Providence, R. I.
*Mary Ellen Murphy, Fall River, Mass.
Sarah E. Munro, Warren, R. I.
*Mrs. Susan E. Mitchell, N. Bedford, Ms.
Wm. H. Mitchell, New Bedford, Mass.
Samuel Mitchell, " " "
*Edward Munro,   Providence, R I.
*Dennis Mahoney, " "
Willard N. Munro, " "
Mrs. John Mulcahey, Newburyport, Ms.
*James Murphy, East Providence, R. I.
*Katie A. McLean, Fall River, Mass.
William W. Munro, Warren, R. I.

N

Mrs. Wm. H. Newman, Batavia, N. Y.
Alex. G. Noyes,   Detroit, Mich.
Mrs. Alex. G. Noyes, " "
Thomas J. Noyes, " "
Mrs. Thomas J. Noyes, " "
Miss Saraphina Noyes, " "
Wm. C. Norris, New York.
Henry L. Norris,   Providence, R. I.
*Miss Kate Norris, " "
Louisa Noyes, " "
*Simeon Newman, " "
*David E. Munro, Portsmouth, R. I.
*Martha A. Munro, " "
*Mrs. Rebecca Mason, Providence, R. I.
*Susie Macomber, Fall River, Mass.
*Abby M. Munro, Hebronville, R. I.
*Frank A. Manchester, Locust Valley, L. I.
*Reliance Meiggs, Warren, R. I.
*Abby Manchester, Fall River, Mass.
*Miss Ann A. Munro, Providence, R. I.
*Mrs. Lloyd Marble, Attleboro', Mass.
*Mrs. Betsey Mason, Warren, R. I.

O

*Miss Maggie O'Brien, Pawtucket, R. I.

Samuel P. Otterson, Davenport, Iowa.
Mrs. Hannah N. Otterson, Brockton, Ms.
Mrs. Mary E. Owen, New Haven, Conn.
John D. O. Mara, Boston, Mass.
Christian Oldenfieldt, Chicago, Ill.
Mrs. Mary C. Osler, New Haven, Conn.
*Kate O'Hurney, Norwalk, "
Mary O'Hurney, " "
*Mrs. Bridget O'Leary, Pawtucket, R. I.
Mrs. Nellie O'Hara, Springfield, Mass.
Mrs. Mar. O'Mara, Lowell, Mass.
*Michael O'Brien, Fall River, Mass.
Mrs. Mary E. Owen, New London, Conn.
*George Oxx, Providence, R. I.
Miss Mary Ann O'Donell, Warren, R. I.
Mrs. Nellie O'Brien, Fall River, Mass.
*Wm. O'Brien, Warren, R. I.
Wm. H. O'Rourke, Westerly, R. I.

P

*Mrs. Clinton Puffer, Woonsocket, R. I.
*Miss Hannah Peck, Providence, "
*Andrew Pitman, Brooklyn, N. Y.
Mrs. Wm. D. Powell, Rochester, N. Y.
Mrs. Robert D. Pinckney, Charleston, S. C.
*Wm. S. Perry, New York.
*Wm. G. Peabodie, Providence, R. I.
Rev. B. B. Peck, Auburn, R. I.
Geo. B. Peterson, Portsmouth, R. I.
*Mrs. Hon. W. Parkhurst, Plattsmouth, Neb.
J. B. Pearse, New Mexico.
Joseph C. Pearse, New York,
*Wm. G. Pearse, Warren, R. I.
Rev. Henry C. Potter, New York.
Wm. Peck, Troy, Pa.
Mrs. Jonathan Peck, Troy, N. Y.
Wm. D. W. Peck, Gonzales, Texas.
Mrs. Wm. H. Powers, Grand Rapids, Mh.
*Mrs. Hiram Perry, Barrington, R. I.
*Josiah K. Pitman, Newport, "
*Fitz H. Peabodie, Providence, R. I.
*Mason W. Peirce, " "
Mrs. Anne Poole, Buffalo, N. Y.
Mrs. Henry S. Parker, Worcester, Mass.
Mrs. Chas. Potter, Newport, R. I.
Frank H. Peck, Boston, Mass.
*Charles H. Phelps, New York.
Charles B. Pearse, " "
Fred. Pepper, S. Boston, Mass.
Fritz H. Pepper, " "
Mrs. Theodore Phinney, Newport, R. I.
*Mrs. Hannah C. Perry, Providence, R. I.
*Rev. Francis Peck, Brooklyn, N. Y.
Mrs. Rev. Francis Peck, " "

*George T. Pearse, Worcester, Mass.
*George C. Pearse, Providence, R. I.
Cornelius Pearse, " "
Edward T. Pearse, " "
*Henry C. Pearse, " "
Ezra B. Pearse, Phenix, R. I.
*Howard B. Pearse, Providence, R. I.
*George G. Pearse, Wakefield, "
Mrs. Josiah K. Pitman, Newport, "
*Josiah K. Pitman, Jr., " "
Charles L. H. Peirce, Baylis, Ill.
Mrs. Eliz Pitman, Grand Rapids, Mich.
Miss Jos. Pitman, " " "
*Charles C. Pitman, " "
*Wm. H. Peirce, Swansey, Mass.
Mrs. Abby M. Palmer, Providence, R. I.
*Mrs. Mason W. Peirce, " "
*Mrs. Jeremiah Pidge, " "
Mrs. James Pidge, " "
Mrs. Jane Pond, Franklin, Mass.
Mrs. Emily Pond, " "
Wm. Pearse, Jersey City, N J.
Rev. Jas DW. Perry, Germantown, Pa.
*Rev. Calbraith B. Perry, Baltimore, Md.
*Raymond Peirce, Providence, R. I.
*Mrs. M. M. Pratt, Brooklyn, N. Y.
*George W. Peck, Boston, Mass.
Wm. Ellsworth Peck, Block Island.
*Miss Hannah Peck, Providence, R. I.
Mrs. Ashton Pillings, Baylis, Ill.
*Henry P. Peirce, New Bedford, Mass.
*Mrs. Jennie T. Peck, Barrington, R. I.
Mrs. Ruth B. Perry, Locust Valley, L. I.
Isaac A. Pearse, East Smithfield, Pa.
George T. Peck, Galesborough, Ill.
Mrs. George T. Peck, " "
Isaac G. Peck, Brooklyn, N. Y.
*Walter Palmer, East Greenwich, R. I.
J. M. Pelton, New York.
*Samuel S. Paine, New Bedford, Mass.
*Geo. W. Paine, " " "
Mrs. Lucy Pease, Edgartown, Mass.
Paul Pilkey, Ogdensburg, N. Y.
Flora Pilkey, " "
George Pitman, Newport, R. I.
Miss Sarah Pitman, " "
*Miss Lizzie Pitman, " "
*Alfred Peabodie, Providence, R. I.
Mrs. Wm. Peck, Barrington, "
*Mrs. Anne F. Pratt, Brooklyn, N. Y.
Nelson Palmer, Providence, R. I.
*Mrs. Amelia Pearse, Fall River, Mass.
*Wm. S. Perry, New York.
Mrs. Geo. F. Peterson, Washington, D. C.
Mrs. Phinney, Warren, R. I.
Mrs. Louisa B. T. Perry, Locust Valley, L. I.

*Mrs. W. H. Phelps, Putnam, Conn.
*Ruth Ellen Pearse, Warren, R. I.
*Betsey P. Paine, Providence, "
Josiah H. Pitman, Fall River, Mass.
Mrs. Josiah H. Pitman, " " "
Samuel Pitman, " " "
*Mrs. Abby W. Palmer, Central Falls, R. I.
*Mrs. Nancy Presbey, Taunton, Mass.
Reginald Heber Palmer, Prov., R. I.
Walter Pearse, Hartford, Conn.
Mrs. Walter Pearse, " "

Q

*Thomas M. Quirk, Fall River, Mass.
Patrick M. Quinn, " " "
*Dennis Quirk, Tiverton, R. I.
*Miss Ellen M. Quirk, Newport, R. I.
Miss Mary A. Quirk, Warren, "

R

*Samuel Reynolds, Boston, Mass.
*George T. Reynolds, Providence, R. I.
*Francis B. Reynolds, " "
Betsey Reynolds, East Greenwich, R. I.
*Mrs. Clara L. Rowland, Chicago, Ill.
Mrs. Geo. Richmond, New York.
Joseph Reynolds, Providence, R. I.
*Theodore Rutherford, " "
Mrs. John Roberts, " "
James Robbins, Nebraska.
*Miss Hattie R. Robbins, New Bedford, Mass.
*Mrs. Abby A. Rogers, New Bedford, Ms.
Mrs. Alone Robinson, Philadelphia, Pa.
*Maude Richmond, Providence, R. I.
*James O. Reid, Fall River, Mass.
*Miss Sarah E. Reid, " " "
Miss Sarah T. Russell, Providence, R. I.
Mrs. Eliz. Rich, East Smithfield, Pa.
*Mrs. John L. Ross, Pawtucket, R. I.
John Riley, Frankport, Me.
Mar. Riley, Manchester, Mass.
Mrs. Evylyn Rathburn, Albany, N. Y.
*Lydia G. Reynolds, Providence, R. I.
William Allen Reed, San Francisco, Cal.
*Charles H. Richards, Providence, R. I.
*George L. Richards, Providence, "
Mrs. Joanna M. Rogers, Chicago, Ill.
Mrs. Joel F. Rainsford, Meriden, N. H.
Mrs. Prudence Randall, Wiscasset, Me.
Wm. A. Rowland, Rockford Ill.
Ellery W. Rich, Warren, R. I.
Isaiah S. Rich, Providence, R. I.
Frank H. Rich, " "

Joseph J. Ralph, Colchester, Conn.
Mrs. Susan G. Ralph, " "
John Robbins, Woonsocket, R. I.
Mrs. Frank Reynolds, Providence, R. I.
*Miss Ambrosia A. Rovelts, " "

S

George A. Starkey, Galveston, Texas.
Mrs. Eliz. Spencer, Providence, R. I.
George T. Smith, Newport, "
*Mrs. William H. Stebbins, Swansey, Ms.
*Miss Susan A. G. Sherman, Prov., R. I.
*Walter M. B. Sherman, " "
*Henry M. Slocum, " "
Charles A. Slocum, " "
Miss S. Seymour, Warren, R. I.
*Mrs. C. F. Stephens, Worcester, Mass.
*Bertha E. Slade, Newport, R. I.
*Cato Slocum, East Providence, R. I.
*Lizzie J. Sherman, Providence, "
*Mrs. Henry Smith, " "
Mary J. Sweet, " "
*Abby Salisbury, Providence, R. I.
*Julia Simmons, Warren, R. I.
Wm. A. Swan, Taunton, Mass.
*Hattie G. Sheldon, Providence, R. I.
*Miss Emma Snively, " "
Mrs. Hannah Shepard, Mansville, N. Y.
William R. Reynolds, Providence, R. I.
*Benj. S. Simmons, East Providence, R. I.
*Belle Simmons, Pawtucket, R. I.
Etta May Simmons, " "
Miss C. Seymour, Warren, "
*Frank Simmons, Pawtucket, "
*Edgar Simmons, " "
*Erwin Simmons, " "
*William H. H. Swan, Providence, R. I.
*Charles H. Springer, Fall River, Mass.
*William S. Springer, " " "
*Joseph T. Springer, " " "
*Benj. F. Smith, Warren, R. I.
*Charles H. Swan, Providence, R. I.
*Edward M. Springer, Pawtucket, R. I.
George B. Sandford, Camp Halleck, Nevada.
*Solon F. Smith, Grafton, Mass.
Josiah Simmons, Fair Haven, Mass.
*Wm. H. Springer, New Bedford, "
John Springer, " " "
*Isaiah R. Simmons, Boston, Mass.
John F. Speeater, New London, Conn.
*Samuel R. Swan, Providence, R. I.
*Samuel B. Swan, " "
Madaline D'W. Smith, New York.
*Mary B. Smith, Sylvania, Pa.

Mrs. Rev. Wm. Stowe, Clyde, N. Y.
Davenport S. Simmons, Plainfield, Ct.
*Mrs. Allen Simmons, New Bedford, Ms.
*Robert Simmons, Fair Haven, "
*Allen Simmons, New Bedford, "
Mrs. Dr. Job Sweet, " " "
*Right Rev. Benj. B. Smith, New York.
*George P. Smith, Cleveland, Ohio.
*Mary Signfoo, North Vineland, N. J.
*Edward B. Southworth, Patterson, N. J.
*R. Simmons, Warren, R. I.
*Wm. M. Springer, New Bedford, Mass.
Mrs. Ansel J. Sears, Coventry, Vt.
*Jonathan Simmons, Warren, R. I.
*Mrs. Jonathan Simmons, " "
*Gilbert R. Simmons, " "
*Alex. G. Sandford, " "
*Mrs. Alex. G. Sandford, " "
*George Smith, " "
*Mrs. George Smith, " "
Mrs. Mary Sumner, Lamont, Mich.
*Edward M. Springer, Pawtucket, R. I.
*W. S. Simmons, Warren, R. I.
Wing Spooner, New Bedford, Mass.
Josiah Simmons, Fair Haven, "
*Samuel B. Swan, Providence, R. I.
*Thomas Swan, " "
*Mrs. Thomas Swan, " "
*Joel M. Spencer, " "
*Orrin S. Spencer, " "
*Harvey Spencer, Coventry, "
Miss Eliza B. Swan, Providence, "
Sheffield A. Swan, " "
John Swan, Bloomfield, Cal.
*Henry F. Smith, Providence, "
Mrs. Sydney Smith, Hornelsville, N. Y.
*Samuel C. Smith, Jamestown, N. Y.
*Mrs. Allen C. Slade, Stonington, Conn.
Mrs. Rebecca J. Shannon, Toronto, W. Canada.
*Mrs. Eliz. Seeling, Darien, Conn.
*Samuel J. Smith, Salem, Mass.
*William H. Smith, " "
Mrs. Anne Stocking, Waterbury, Conn.
*John T. Smith, Fall River, Mass.
James L. Smith, New York.
William J. Smith, Brooklyn, N. Y.
*George M. Smith, New York.
*Harriet Simmons, Dighton, Mass.
Ellery Sandford, Tecumseh, Neb.
*Arthur B. Spink, Providence, R. I.
Mrs. Arthur B. Spink, " "
Mrs. Samuel Spink " "
*Christopher C. Simmons, East Providence, R. I.
*Lewis H. Snakenborger, New York.
*John H. Shay, Fall River, Mass.

Mrs. Celia A. Santeana, N. Bedford, Mass.
Mrs Mary A. Smith, " "
Andrew Salisbury, Providence, R. I.
Mrs. Mary J. Smith, Worcester, Mass.
*Mrs. Margaret Studley, Providence, R I.
*Mrs. Wm. Sayer, Hyde Park, Mass.
Wm. Sayer, " "
*Mrs. Mary A. Stetson, Providence, R I.
*Miss Ella Stetson, " "
P. J. Sullivan, Boston, Mass.
John S. Shurtz, New York.
Jason T. Simmons, Chicago, Ill.
Jason T. Simmons, Jr., " "
Mrs. Jason T. Simmons, Quincy, Ill.
Elnora Simmons, " "
Abby Simmons, " "
Mrs. Julia M. Sherman, Providence, R.I.
John H. Shay, Fall River, Mass.
*Miss Minnie Seymour, Warren, R. I.
*Mrs. Joseph Seymour, " "
*Mrs. Abraham B. Stillwell, Providence, R. I.
Mrs. Joseph Simmons, Walnut Hill, Mass.
*Mrs. George R. Shaw, Providence, R. I.
Osborn Swan, " "
*Thomas Swan, Jr. " "
*Mary J. Sparks, East Providence, "
Mrs. James E. Swan, Providence, "
*Mrs. Emily Smith, Vergennes, Vt.
*Miss Ella Shaw, Providence, R. I.
Mrs. Hannah Smith, " "

T

*Edwin H. Tilley, Newport, R. I.
James Thompson, Williamsburg, Pa.
*Edward M. Tilley, Norfolk, Va.
Prof. Wm. E. Thompson, Sinia, N. Y.
Mrs. Dr. Sam'l Theobold, Baltimore, Md.
Mark A. DeW. Tanner, Bangor, Cal.
Mrs. Nelson B. Tanner, South Abington, Mass.
*Henry H. Tilley, Washington, D. C.
*Benj. Tilley, Norfolk, Va.
William P. Tilley, Portsmouth, Va.
Thomas C. Tilley, Norfolk, Va.
Lydia Eva Tilley, Williamsburg, Va.
Mrs. Lucy B. Tilley, Norfolk, Va.
Lewis W. Taft, Providence, R. I.
*Mrs. Chas. Talbot, Martha's Vineyard, Mass.
*Sam'l P. Thornton, Elizabeth, N. J.
*Charles H. Tilley, Newport, R. I.
*Mrs. Henry H. Tilley, Washington, D.C.
*Rev. William J. Tilley, Middlebury, Vt.
Benj. F. Tilley, Annapolis, Md.

*J. B. Tallman, Syracuse, N. Y.
Mrs. Olive Twaddle, New York.
Timothy I. Tanner, Grand Rapids, Mich.
Wm. H. Tanner, " "
John B. Tanner, " "
Benj. B. Tanner, " "
Michael Thomas, Boston, Mass.
*Mrs. John Tweedale, Washington, D.C.
*Samuel Trenn, East Providence, R. I.
Peter Trenn, East Smithfield, Pa.
Frank W. Tanner, North Abington, Mass.
*William R. Taylor, jr., Providence, R.I.
*Frank L. B. Taylor, " "
*Mrs. Wm. H. Teele, " "
Russell H. Teele, " "
*Henry Tanner, Buffalo, N. Y.
Cornelius E. Tanner, Grand Rapids, Mich.
*Miss Ida C. Taft, Meriden, Mass.
B. C. Tillinghast, Philadelphia, Pa.
H. G. Tillinghast, " "
Mrs. Marion Townsend, Wareham, Mass.
Mrs. Mary C. Taylor, N. Bedford, Mass.
*Mrs. Charles Tallman, Portsmouth, R. I.
Benj. Tripp, Providence, R. I.
Mrs. Sarah Thomas, Jersey City, N. J.
*Mrs. Wm. Tallman, New Bedford, Mass.
Mrs. Francis W. Tanner, Swansey, "
William Toye, jr., Providence, R. I.

U

Emily F. Usher, New Bedford, "
*Benj. B. Usher, Warren, R. I.
*Aaron F. Usher, Goodell, Pa.
*Miss Anne Usher, East Smithfield, Pa.
George Usher, " " "
*John Usher, " " "
William Usher, East Smithfield, Pa.
Frank B. Upham, Boston, Mass.
*Nathaniel W. Usher, Scio, N. Y.
*John Usher, Fall River, Mass.
*Eliz. B. Usher, Warren, R. I.

V

*Mrs. Sam'l J. Vickery, Pawtucket, R. I.
*Mrs. Giles F. Vernier, South Creek, Pa.
John W. Vernon, Providence, R. I.
*Thomas S. Vickery, Fall River, Mass.
*Samuel J. Vickery, Warwick, R. I.
Mrs. Lydia Van Zandt, Newport, R. I.
*Henry Van Doorn, Providence, R. I.
*Mrs. C. D. Vosburgh, Grand Rapids, Mich.
*Giles F. Vernier, South Creek, Pa.
*Joseph R. Van Doorn, Quincy, Ill.
William H. Van Doorn, " "

*F. Vaughn, Providence, R. I.
Lydia Van Doorn, Quincy, Ill.
Mary C. Van Doorn, " "
John H. Vansburgh, New York.
*Mrs. Mary Verry, Woonsocket, R. I.
*Edward P. Van Doorn, Providence, R.I.
Mary P. Van Doorn, " "
*Lewis Vaughn, " "
Fred N. Viall, East Providence, "

W

*Mrs. H. B. White, Providence, R. I.
*William H. White, " "
*H. S. Williamson, " "
*Mildred L. Williams, New York.
*Margaret E. Woodman, Fall River, Mass.
*William J. Wilcox, Providence, R. I.
*Mrs Lydia F. Williams, Taunton. Mass.
*Alfred Wright, Warren, R. I.
*Miss Jane H. Walker, Somerset, Mass.
*Mrs. Elisha Watson, Wakefield, R. I.
*Wm. H. Waldron, Cambridgeport, Mass.
Mrs. Benj. T. Wilbur, Long Plains, "
Marion W. Wheeler, New York.
*James R. White, Newport, R. I.
Lewis F. Waldron, East Saginaw, Mich.
*Nathan G. West, Hartford, Conn.
Miss Martha G. White, Marietta, Ga.
Capt. Wm. Williston, San Francisco, Cal.
Mrs. P. L. Wells, Staten Island, N. Y.
D. West, " " "
Frank D. Waldron, Grand Rapids, Mich.
Nelson Waldron, Queechy, Vt.
*John H. Waldron, " "
Mrs. Mary A. Whitehead, Whiteside, Ill.
Rev. John B. Wight, Wayland, Mass.
Joseph Waldron, Butterville, Ill.
Allen Wood, Angelica, N. Y.
Algernon Wood, " "
*David A. Waldron, Barrington, R. I.
*William H. West, " "
Mrs. Wm. G. Wilcox, Fall River, Mass.
Mrs. Sarah J. Wright, Providence, R. I.
*Nathaniel Wilson, Newport. "
*John West, " "
*James R. White, " "
George E. Warren, Jerseyville, Ill.
Mrs. Mary Wheaton, Providence, R. I.
*Benjamin Wardwell, " "
*William Wilmarth, Warren, "
Miss Annie Wilmarth, " "
Mrs. Susan Warner, Ackron, Ohio.
Charles Wilkinson, New York.
Mrs. Isaac Washburn, Taunton, Mass.
*Mrs. Mary M. West, Attleboro, "

Mrs. Annie E. Weeks, Mystic Bridge, Ct.
Mrs. Caleb Williams, Elizabeth, N. J.
John Waldron, Fair Haven, Mass.
Joseph M. Wardwell, Warren, N. Y.
Miss Martha Weaver, Norton, Mass.
*John S. Weeden, Providence, R. I.
Miss Maria Waldron, Barrington, R. I.
Mrs. Louisa Walton, Providence, "
*Edmond M. Waldron, " "
Benjamin B. Waldron, Newport, "
Alfred Waldron, Providence, "
Mrs. Adelaide Wordell, Fall River, Mass.
*Emeline Wordell, Valley Falls, R. I.
Mrs. Hattie Williams, Providence. "
*Mrs. Emily Webster, " "
Miss Susan White, Warren, "
Mary M. Wesson, Fair Haven, Ct.
Charles Wesson, " "
*William M. Wardwell, Monsville, N. Y.
Miss Abbie M. Wardwell, " "
*James H. Wright, Newport, R. I.
James M. Winslow, Warren, "
*Miss Jennie Winslow, " "
William P. Williams, Fall River, Mass.
James West, Plymouth, "
*Peter M. Williams, Fall River, "
Samuel R. Warren, Montreal, Canada.
*Benjamin White, Providence, R. I.
*Ellen P. White, " "
Mrs. Ann E. Warning, Burlington, Ct.
*William A. Wardwell, Providence, R. I.
*John H. White, " "
*Davis Wilson, " "
Amos C. Weeden, Rye Beach, N. H.
William B. Weeden, Providence, R. I.
*Alimon T. White, " "
Miss Hannah Wardwell, Watertown, N. Y.
*Benjamin Wilson, Barrington, R. I.
Rev. Timothy F. Wardwell, Watertown, N. Y.
Jonathan Wardwell, Watertown, N. Y.
William B. West, Newport, R. I.
Mrs. J. M. Wheaton, Lawrence, Mass.
*Mrs. Augustus Winship, Providence, R. I.
Mrs. Frank D. Woodmancy, Fall River, Mass.
*Mrs. Manuel Wilcox, Fall River, Mass.
Mrs. Samuel Wilcox, " "
Mrs. Samuel B. Wilcox, " "
Miss Ardelia Wordell, " "
Miss Emeline Wood, Valley Falls, R. I.
Mrs. Anne Wilkie, Jersey City, N. J.
Henry Wight, Cairo, Ga.
Mrs. Abby Wight, Cairo, Ga.
Samuel B. Wight, Albany, Ga.

BI-CENTENNIAL OF BRISTOL. 183

Jeremiah M. Wardwell, Corpus Christie, Texas.
Allen Wood, Friendship, N. Y.
Algernon S. Wood, Friendship, N. Y.
Miss Sarah Wood, "   "
Mrs. Rebecca W. Wood, "   "
*Mrs. Lydia M. Warren, Boston, Mass.
'Charles D. White, Warren, R. I.
*Annie R. Willis, "   "
*Charles M. P. White, "   "
William H. White, "   "
Mrs. Almira B. Williston, New Bedford, Mass.
*Mrs. Benjamin Warren, Fall River, Ms.
*Mrs. Susan L. Wood, Providence, R. I.
Mrs. Sarah M. West, "   "
*Mrs. Lydia Worsley, "   "
Mrs. Clara H. Whittemore, Charlestown, Mass.
Mrs. Charlotte M. Williams, Taunton, Mass.
*Mrs. Mary A. Waite, Middletown, R. I.
Miss Annie P. Waldron, Salem, N. J.
Mrs. Emma J. Weaver, Fair Haven, Ct.
Mrs. Chas. Williams, East Smithfield, Pa.
Mrs. Jane Waldron, "   "   "
*John B. Wilson, Providence, R. I.
William West, "   "
Mrs. Henry Wilkins, "   "
*Frank B. Whi e, "   "
*Ida E. Wright, Warren, "
*Wm. J. Wright, "   "

Mary E. Whittemore, E. Providence, R.I.
*Louisa Walton, Providence, R. I.
*Mary Y. Whiting, "   "
Joseph Winslow, Fall River, Mass.
Julia I. Weeden, Newport, R. I.
*Andrew J. White, Providence, R. I.
*Mrs. Elizabeth White, "   "
*Miss Emma White, "   "
*Willie G. White, "   "
*Miss Sarah Warner, "   "
William Waldron, East Smithfield, Pa.
*Harriet T. Willis, Providence, R. I.
William Whitaker, Seekonk, Mass.
*James Whitaker, "   "
*Alfred B. Waldron, Troy, Pa.
*Horatio Waldron, Providence, R. I.
Theodore Waldron, Troy, Pa.
'William T. Wardwell, Stanford, Ct.
'Samuel Wardwell, Monsville, N. Y.
*Charles H. Wardwell, "   "
*Margaret E. Woodmancy, Fall River, Mass.
*William J. Wilcox, Providence, R. I.
'Mrs. Lydia F. Williams, Taunton, Mass.
*Alfred Wright, Warren, R. I.
*Jane H. Walker, Somerset, Mass.
Mrs. F. L. Williams, New York.
*Mildred L. Williams, New York.
'Henry S. Williamson, Providence, R. I.
*William Henry White, "   "
*Mrs. Henry B. White, "   "

MEMORANDUM OF RECEIPTS AND EXPENSES, BI-CENTENNIAL COMMITTEE.

RECEIPTS.

Received from the town of Bristol,				$1500 00
" " sundry entertainments furnished by the Committee:				
" " Pinafore exhibition,		$130 14		
" " lecture by Isaac N. Arnold,		12 55		
" " ladies' sale,		91 72		
" " concert,		23 00		
" " readings by Mrs. Charles Smith, (Fanny Morant),		23 60		
" " minstrels' concert,		1 55		
				282 56
" for interest,				11 23
" from members of the Committee,				35 03
				$1,828 82

EXPENSES.

Expenses for bands of music,	$420 54
" " tents and putting up,	279 93
" " platforms, seats, and dinner tables,	171 31
" " carriages used in the procession,	166 00
" " exhibition of relics,	128 61
" " decorating public buildings,	100 00
" " dinners to invited guests,	100 00
" " " " band and police,	39 75
" " badges of all kinds,	78 74
" " printing circulars, programmes, etc.,	61 50
" " procession,	53 65
" " electric light,	46 35
" " postage, etc.,	47 21
" " advertising,	34 56
" " salutes and bell ringing,	33 85
" " fencing memorial trees,	31 82
" " children's choir,	25 00
" " town seal,	10 00
	$1,828 82
There was an additional expenditure of	334 50

for the dinners given to the returning Sons and Daughters of Bristol, made under the direction of the Committee, which amount was furnished by members of the same, and other citizens of the town.

The following lines, from the pen of a "daughter of Bristol," Miss ANNE E. COLE, of Warren, blend in sweet harmony with the grand refrain of our Bi-Centennial, and most appropriately close the record of the festal day. They originally appeared in the *Providence Journal* a few days after the celebration. They are now published with a slight addition, having been revised by the fair author. We give them—sweet echoes of a grand chorus:—

BI-CENTENNIAL ECHOES.

We heard from afar a sweet refrain;—
"Children, my children, come home again.
Come home, come home, a welcome will meet you,
 Come to your birthplace, wherever you roam,
In festal adornments I wait now to greet you,
 From the east and the west, my children, come home."

 As Mercury fleet,
 On swift-flying feet,
 With white pinions neat,
  The missives were sent;
 And hundreds were polled
 In the soft satin fold,
 With the quaint letters old,
  Past centuries lent.

 In the councils of State,—
 In the halls of the great,—
 Where the humble ones wait,
  The summons was laid.
 And the message conned o'er,
 They sped homeward once more,
 As they never before
  Their parent obeyed.

Steed, steam and wind, their powers combined
 With favoring sun and air;
The inbound trains bore martial strains,
 And cannon hailed them there.

Badges displayed,—the grand parade,—
    Th' adorned and bannered way,—
The joyful word of greeting heard,
    Gladdened the centuries' day.

But abler pens than mine have traced
    The festive hours along,
And loftier chords more sweetly swelled
    The bi-centennial song.

The breath of devotion, and childhood's pure strain,
Blent o'er the thousands, home-gathered again;
Through the rifts of the tent the soft breezes strayed,
And glints of warm sunlight in ambush there laid.

The grave historic muse was there,
Scanning each word with jealous care,
    The massive pages musing o'er,
Lest Romance tinge the sober lore.

Legend and tale of Viking old,
Though traced in annals clear and bold,
    Alike, the plain statistics shock,—
They antedated Plymouth rock.

No earlier footprints here were found,
The red man held the primal ground,
    And Plymouth next the treasure wins,
Rolled up in seven beaver skins.

Nor yea, nor nay, we said amen,
When listening to the Diamond pen
    Which bore no tribute, gave no meed,
To hero of the mythic deed.

Good Massasoit, Philip too,
Some words of calm approval drew;
    Some pen-marks few were made to trace
The history of the conquered race.

The story of the ancient town,—
The honored four of old renown,—
    The wealth and commerce o'er the seas,—
The home-bound, freighted argosies—

The grand historic altar graced,
With many records I've not traced;
His moral then the Historian drew,
And o'er the rest Time's mantle threw.

Then Poesy awoke her sweetest lays,
And a full tone rolled forth in tuneful praise.
Not broken was *that* shell, nor still *that* lyre,
The " force of will " woke all the olden fire;
It streamed afar o'er the wild Norsemen's way,
And shed on Metacom a pitying ray.
We saw well nigh a thousand years of time,
By light electric of historic rhyme.
Those " chords unstrung," re-echoed through the wild,
Fair Gudrid's Norse-notes to her Vinland child.
In Montaup's shades we heard a nation's wail,
And saw the white man o'er the red prevail.
We met to-day with gleeful notes attune,
Fair as the May, and sweet as flowers of June.
And classic ground awhile we wandered o'er,
Then turned once more to bless our native shore.

The pain of sweetness, and the sweet regret
This poem chaste awoke, is lingering yet.

To this mind-feast we fain would tarry late,
But dinner calls us to its stern debate.

  Sons and daughters come,
   The moments are fleeting,
   Receive the warm greeting,—
  The fond welcome home.

  Sons and daughters haste
   While the garlands are bright,
   Feast now in our sight,
  Of the banquet now taste.

And there was spread a royal feast;
From north to south, from west and east,
 Was gathered a vast store.
The sea, the land, the realms of air,
The fattening stall, the fowler's snare,
 Their varied tributes bore.

The fruits of many a distant clime,—
The products of our harvest time,—
    The luxury of *cold*,—
In viands rare, and richly wrought,
With golden words of welcome fraught,
    Revealed their wealth untold.

We feasted at the gracious board,
Where Plenty its libations poured ; —
    The flying hours sped on.
We listened to the parting word,
The parting melody we heard,
    'Twas finished all too soon.

With music sounding to the breeze,
Were planted four memorial trees,
    Just at the sun's last ray.
O'er hill and stream, through wood and dell,
The cannon thundered its farewell ; —
    Two centuries rolled away.

I pause beside the festal board once more
To hear those gracious words repeated o'er
By bard and scholar, statesman and the sage,
As each traced out the progress of the age.
Bright scintillations flashed from mind to mind,
And grace and feeling answered back in kind.
Each laid his tribute on the household shrine,
And sought some flowery wreath of love to twine.
There, too, upon home's olden altar-stone,
The light of thanks and filial homage shone.
At twilight hour we went with reverent tread,
To view the portraits of the honored dead.
We saw the worthies of the olden town,
Who reared this commonwealth of fair renown.
With busy care they wrought out far to-day,
Which in the coming centuries dimly lay.
We spanned these centuries,—saw the years along,
Telling their stories to the passing throng.
Each pictured face, in framework quaint and dark,
Held its lone post,—Time's silent finger mark.
Founder and preacher, ruler, statesmen too,
And far-famed beauties met the admiring view.
The wondering light of every moveless eye,
Thus mutely seemed to ask the passers-by ; —

"By whose rude right have we obeyed the calls
Which tore us from our own familiar halls?
Yours is our heritage,—a fair bequest,—
Leave us our past, its silence and its rest."
And thus across two centuries green and fair,
Those vanished generations met us there.

From hallowed scenes, dim with the far away,
We turn again to our own bright to-day.
The evening time speeds on in light and song,
And joyous hearts the festive hours prolong.
Fair as its day, on History's page, appears
The Bi-Centennial of the Bristol years.

APPENDIX.

The following account of the "High School Reünion," held on Saturday evening, September 25th, was furnished by HENRY H. TILLEY, Esq., of Washington, D. C. : —

THE HIGH SCHOOL RE-UNION.

The reünion of the Bristol High School, in Byfield Hall, on Saturday evening, was a most successful and enjoyable affair, and formed a pleasing conclusion to the bi-centennial festivities of the week. The hall was tastefully decorated, the walls showing appropriate mottoes, chiefly in Latin, and the front of the platform being covered with plants in bloom. When the meeting was called to order, at 8 P. M., an audience of over two hundred were assembled, comprising the present pupils of the school, with former ones from the time of its inauguration, in 1848. Henry H. Tilley, of the Navy Department, Washington, D. C., presided, and called upon Rev. J. P. Lane, for many years, and until his recent removal from the town, a member of the School Committee, to open the meeting with prayer. Mr. Tilley then made the following introductory address:

Ladies and Gentlemen, Teachers and Pupils, of the High School:

As one of the original members of the High School, I have been selected to preside on this occasion, and in the name of the present school, to welcome the returning members. Although I have not the honor and satisfaction of being a graduate, and at the time of my connection with the institution it was yet in its infancy, I yield to none in my appreciation of its importance and advantages, and have ever esteemed the influence of the comparatively limited period which I was permitted to pass within its walls, as among the most important upon my subsequent career in life. And in this connection I cannot omit paying a passing tribute to the memory of our first principal, the lamented Prof. Wm. E. Jillson, whose firm and dignified, yet gentle and persuasive manner—so happily combining the *suaviter in modo* with the *fortiter in re*—was of more value to us, by inspiring a love of learning for his, as well as its own sake, than the actual instruction which he so lucidly imparted. Of my other teacher, the genial and polished Lafayette Burr—whose name is a decided misnomer, since if he ever had any such rough outside covering, he must have shed it very early in life—I need not make further mention, as we still have the pleasure of reckoning him, as well as Mrs. B., our former schoolmate and the daughter of Dr. Shepard, the earliest and firmest friend of the school, among our living friends, and only regret that circumstances did not allow of their being present with us this evening.

Those early days, together with the venerable old Academy in which they were passed and, alas! with some of the old companions then so dear to us, are gone. And many of those still living, scattered throughout the world, are unable to be with us to-night. To them we send a hearty greeting, with the hope that we may, ere long, have the pleasure of once more grasping them by the hand. But to us who look back with regret to those happy days, and who only get a glimpse of the scenes amid which they were passed once a year or less, it is a source of much gratification that the High School, after all the vicissitudes through which it has passed, not only still lives, but is located in such pleasant and commodious quarters as the Byfield building, in which we are now assembled, and that our places are occupied by such promising pupils—the sons and daughters of our old schoolmates - as I saw there the other day, and most of whom are with us this evening, prepared to cordially welcome their predecessors of all the former years. In the light of my experience since I left the school, I cannot forbear to impress upon them the importance of improving to the utmost the advantages which old Bristol so generously offers them, and which, in some respects, far exceed those that the National Capital, where I now reside, is yet able to afford its school children. With its population of over 150,000, and all its fine school edifices, Washington has no high school where, as here, pupils can be fitted for college; nor, I may add, with all its literary advantages for scholars and men of leisure, has it any free circulating library like the Rogers. Remember, then, my young friends, " of him to whom much is given, much shall be required," and do not neglect the opportunities now offered you, or it will prove a source of unceasing regret in after life.

And to my schoolmates and other former pupils of the school who, having entered on the active duties of life, remain here at the old homestead, and have taken the places of the fathers, who, in my boyhood, had the direction of affairs, I would simply say, " Freely ye have received, freely give"; and I urge you to see that the reputation which, as the orator of the day and others informed us yesterday, the town has enjoyed even from its foundation, for liberality on the subject of education, be not diminished or obscured; and especially that the High School which, as President Robinson claimed, formed so important a link in our State educational system, and whose advantages you can appreciate, is not allowed to decline or perish. But, as our time is limited, I am reminded that I was not put here to make a speech, but merely to serve as a portico to the temple.

The chair announced that the committee had been disappointed in the absence of Mr. Burr, the second principal of the school, to whom he had already referred, and read a letter from him regretting his inability to be present, on account of other engagements, and also the following extract from a private letter to himself:

"I have no doubt that my 'boys,' most of whom are occupying positions of trust and responsibility, will give a good account of themselves, while the girls' 'carae alumnae' will also be present, if the claims upon them as wives, mothers, or teachers permit. They may not speak of what they have accomplished in life, but their good deeds and true lives are known, and their happy influence is felt wherever they may live. May God bless them all, and long spare them to be good and useful men and women, and when they all have crossed the flood, may our reünion in the spirit-land be happy and complete."

Another disappointment was caused by the absence of Hon. T. W. Bicknell, a former principal, who had given the committee encouragement to expect him, but telegraphed at the last moment that he was unable to cancel a prior engagement in Boston.

Robert S. Andrews, for many years Superintendent of Public Schools, being called upon, made a brief address, and *en passant* related an anecdote communicated to him by the poet of the bi-centennial (Bishop Howe), of his early school-days in the old Academy.

Rev. Calbraith B. Perry, of Baltimore, Md., a comparatively young graduate of the school, made a most amusing extempore speech, commencing with an allusion to an item in a Baltimore paper, to the effect that he had "gone to his native place to celebrate *his* bi-centennial, and would stop in the house in which he was born, *which was still standing.*" He adverted to the work in which he is now engaged among the colored population of Baltimore, describing one of his original pupils, styled the "India Rubber Boy," and ended with some telling allusions to his early school days, which brought down the house.

He was followed by Rev. Joseph Trapnell, rector of St. Michael's twenty-five years ago, when his children were pupils of the school, who gave some excellent advice as to the true end of education.

Prof. Wilfred H. Munro, the historian of Bristol, and Chandler H. Coggeshall, Secretary of the High School Association, gave entertaining reminiscences of their school days, and Rev. W. J. Tilley, of Middlebury, Vt., a former pupil, made a brief but spicy speech.

Hon. Wm. H. Spooner, one of the first pupils, late President of the Town Council, and member of the Legislature, being called upon, expressed his gratification at the reünion, but excused himself from a speech, and offered as a substitute Hon. Wm. J. Miller, he being a member of the School Committee, and married to a High School girl. Mr. Miller responded with some interesting reminiscences of the Bristol schools fifty years ago, paying a high tribute to Otis Storrs, one of the most efficient teachers of that day, who, he said, had first taught him the true end of school education, which was not so much the acquisition of facts, as *how* to learn, which should be a life pursuit.

The literary exercises, which were agreeably diversified by vocal music admirably rendered by the Zerrahn Quartette, Messrs. Burgess, Spinning, Young and Liscomb, being brought to a close, a portion of the seats were removed, refreshments, provided in part by the ladies, were distributed, and the true reünion commenced, a season of social intercourse between the present and past pupils, many of whom now greeted each other for the first time for many years. Many regrets were heard for those who had passed away, particularly on the part of the pupils of Rev. N. B. Cooke and Mr. Morley, two of the most highly-esteemed and successful among the former principals. After the refreshments were disposed of, Prof. John Tweedale, of the War Department, Washington, D. C., the husband of a former pupil, read, by request, "Centennial Bells," and in response to persistent encores, gave several humorous selections in capital style.

The company separated about 11 P. M., with a general expression of satisfaction with the happy occasion, and a hope that it might soon be repeated. In conclusion, we may remark that it is a great source of gratification to its friends, that the school, which had rather languished for several years, is fast regaining its former prestige under its present efficient Principal, J. E. Estee, who entered heartily into the project of the reünion, and to whom, with Miss A. B. Manchester, his assistant, its success is largely due.

www.ingramcontent.com/pod-product-compliance
Lightning Source LLC
Chambersburg PA
CBHW020918230426

43666CB00008B/1490